Creativity, Culture and Commerce:
Producing Australian Children's Television with Public Value

Creativity, Culture and Commerce:
Producing Australian Children's Television with Public Value

Anna Potter

intellect Bristol, UK / Chicago, USA

First published in the UK in 2015 by
Intellect, The Mill, Parnall Road, Fishponds, Bristol, BS16 3JG, UK

First published in the USA in 2015 by
Intellect, The University of Chicago Press, 1427 E. 60th Street,
Chicago, IL 60637, USA

A catalogue record for this book is available from the British Library.

Cover designer: Shin-E Chuah
Copy-editor: MPS Technologies
Production manager: Heather Gibson
Typesetting: Contentra Technologies

Print ISBN: 978-1-78320-441-0
ePDF ISBN: 978-1-78320-442-7
ePUB ISBN: 978-1-78320-443-4

Printed and bound by Hobbs, UK

Contents

Acknowledgements

This book would not have been possible without the contributions and support of many individuals and several institutions. I owe a particular debt to Tom O'Regan, for his guidance, intellectual generosity and the valuable insights shared during the many conversations we had as this book took shape. Thanks are due also to Jason Jacobs for providing the initial impetus to write this book and practical advice on how to undertake the project. I am also indebted to Graeme Turner for his feedback and ideas and for giving me access to a peaceful research space in the Centre for Critical and Cultural Studies at the University of Queensland. Colleagues and friends including Laurent Borgmann (who read and commented on each chapter), Rachel Davis, Ben Goldsmith, Jill McGuire and Sue Ward each offered assistance and encouragement at various stages of this project, and all contributed to its eventual completion.

I am very grateful to the members of the children's television production and broadcasting communities who despite being incredibly busy people generously shared their industry knowledge and creative practices with me. While some participants have chosen to remain anonymous, my thanks must go to Donna Andrews, Hugh Baldwin, Cherrie Bottger, Michael Bourchier, Jenny Brigg, Tim Brooke Hunt, Ewan Burnett, Kylie Du Fresne, Kim Dalton, Patrick Egerton, Monica O'Brien, Bernadette O'Mahony, Stuart Paul, Noel Price, Jonathan Shiff, David Webster and Joanna Werner. Their willingness to share their expertise and passion for Australian children's television with me is very much appreciated.

The staff of the Australian Children's Television Foundation, particularly its chief executive officer Jenny Buckland and her assistant Glenda Wilson, were unfailingly helpful in providing me with access to their archives and sharing their encyclopaedic knowledge of the sector, as well making me feel very welcome at the organisation's renowned morning teas. I would also like to acknowledge the contribution made by Joanne Scott and Rod McCulloch of the University of the Sunshine Coast in allowing me the time and space to complete this book. Thanks are due also to Heather Gibson at Intellect, for its meticulous production.

For the use of photographs that appear here I would like to acknowledge:

Fremantle Media
Goalpost Pictures
Werner Film Productions
Jonathan Shiff Productions
Matchbox Pictures
Sticky Pictures
The Australian Children's Television Foundation
ZooSky Media

And finally to Wally, Josh, Tom and Georgia, thank you, as always, for your support, good humour and tolerance.

Introduction

This book is the story of the dissolution of long-standing settlements in Australian children's television that occurred from 2001 to 2014 during Australian broadcasting's transition from an analogue to a digital regime. It is an account of how changes in the creative, economic, technological and regulatory circumstances in which children's television is produced and distributed gradually undermined the ability of much contemporary Australian children's television to speak directly to Australian children. It explains why Australian children's television, particularly live action drama, has a global reputation for excellence, while the circumstances of contemporary production have rendered children's live action drama one of television's most vulnerable genres.

A set of public value principles that underwrite and authorize the Australian policy settings designed to ensure supplies of children's television is also identified here. These principles recognize that much of the worth of the Australian children's television made with state support lies in its ability to situate Australian children within their own culture (in contrast to any monetary returns generated through its programme sales and merchandising activities). The complexities of creating identifiably Australian children's television, with both state subsidy and significant international investment, for fiercely competitive local and global markets in digital regimes are described here as well.

As the following chapters make clear, the production of Australian children's television is at a critical juncture. In the 1960s and 1970s, public concern about the lack of well-produced, locally made television available to Australian children led to the establishment of important policy instruments including, in 1979, the Children's Television Standards (CTS). The CTS are intended to ensure that age-specific drama, animation, reality, quiz and game shows, and entertainment and documentaries are offered to children by Australia's commercial networks. The benefits for the child audience of having access to a variety of television programmes, including locally made live action drama, justify the levels of state subvention required for their production. When Australian children's best interests are met through the provision of television that situates them within their own social and cultural context, this valuable form of cultural production meets its policy objectives.

Unfortunately, there is a growing disconnect between the achievement of long-standing policy objectives for Australian children's television and the production of much of the children's television that is made in contemporary Australia. Many of the causes of this disconnect lie in the fragmentation created by digital television regimes that caused a shifting of the sands under commercial television. From 2001 onwards, as Australia embarked on its digital transition, free-to-air channels proliferated, pan-global pay-TV networks matured and multi-platform delivery became the norm. Audiences, including the child audience, fragmented across multiple platforms. So did advertising revenue and programme budgets.

Fragmentation challenged long-standing business models for television and exerted downwards pressures on the licence fees networks were prepared to pay for programme rights. Reduced licence fees further increased the need for the international investment that Australian producers have always required to finance their children's programmes. New policy instruments that came into effect during the digital transition created additional incentives for the independent screen production sector to internationalize, despite a significant screen policy emphasis on the achievement of the goals of national cultural representation. The combination of fragmentation and increased internationalization led to new production norms in Australian children's television that reduced quality standards and cultural specificity in many programmes. The new production norms often undermined the ability of these programmes to speak directly to Australian children.

This book is not, however, a narrative of decay and demise. Many of the changes that accompanied the digital transition were of enormous benefit to children's television, with the potential to substantially increase its production and cultural visibility. Abundant spectrum and multi-channelling created niche television markets and enabled Australia's commercial networks to provide dedicated destinations for their children's television offerings for the first time, on their newly established multi-channels. The public service broadcaster the Australian Broadcasting Corporation (ABC) was able to launch Australia's first free-to-air dedicated children's channel, which quickly became the most popular children's channel in Australia. Fragmentation meant, too, that the child audience became highly sought after, by pan-global subscription networks and public service broadcasters alike.

During the digital transition Internet-based television services such as Netflix confirmed the international popularity of high-quality Australian children's drama. These new mechanisms of distribution have the potential to remove broadcaster involvement from distribution arrangements that can see a children's drama premiere in 51 countries on the same day. Australia remains a safe, sunny, stable environment in which to film, where a canvas can be created that the rest of the world wants to see. Australian screen producers are still passionate, resilient and highly accomplished storytellers, while Australian children's television retains a global reputation for excellence first established in the 1980s. A range of state subsidies designed to encourage screen production in Australia continues to be offered. Clearly digital regimes create exciting new possibilities for the production and distribution of children's television.

The Australian children's programmes that secured distribution on the pan-global networks, or Internet-based services that developed during the digital transition, enjoyed international sales and increased cultural visibility. But while some culturally specific Australian drama continues to circulate in global markets, international distribution and co-production arrangements frequently entail a loss of cultural specificity and with it a capacity to speak directly to Australian children. As a result, many contemporary children's programmes made in Australia neither look nor sound Australian. Frequently these programmes are not even based on Australian stories. Their ability to situate Australian children within their own culture is therefore diminished. The effects of internationalization on Australian children's television were amplified during the digital transition, when a combination of market forces and new policy settings encouraged international investment in both Australian programmes and in the production companies creating them.

The market conditions that accompanied the digital transition not only increased the need for international investment in Australian children's television, they also favoured the production of animation over live action drama. Animation is often cheaper to make, and much more easily distributed, largely because it tends to be a less culturally specific form of storytelling than live action drama (and in any case is much simpler to revoice). Many governments are prepared to subsidize its production in order to establish or retain animation production industries. Animation is a perfectly legitimate and enormously popular genre, long considered as children's drama by Australian policy-makers. It can be used to fill content quotas in exactly the same way as live action drama. But the skewing of the ratios between animation and live action drama from the mid-2000s exacerbated the loss of cultural specificity and contributed to the downturn in production values in much contemporary Australian children's television.

Public activism in the 1970s persuaded the Australian government to introduce policy settings, screen organizations and funding mechanisms that would support the production of Australian children's television by an Australian independent production sector. Generally these instruments of state support are financed by Australian taxpayers; thus the Australian public has always been a key stakeholder in the production of children's television. In this environment, producers, networks, regulators and screen bodies ignore the public, notions of public value and their responsibilities to the Australian taxpayer, at their peril.

State support for children's television brings its own set of obligations to the Australian public, which campaigned for those vital measures and continues to fund them through taxation. But since 2001 producers, networks and regulators have been engaged in intramural conversations about the funding of children's television that have largely failed to include the public. A sense of a reciprocal obligation to the Australian public in return for regular access to various taxpayer-funded supports for their children's production slate can, at times, be difficult to detect. The supports that are available to those who produce children's television in Australia are predicated, however, on the understanding that children are a special and distinctive audience. When the children's television produced with state support fails to situate Australian children within their own culture, justifications for public subsidies of the genre are undermined.

When the Australian public is recognized as the key stakeholder in children's television, the risk that various policy instruments including the CTS become seen as mere measures of industry protectionism is reduced. If the public and the importance of the achievement of long-standing policy objectives for Australian children are forgotten, however, the screen production industry is in danger of becoming hostage to its own sense of entitlement. When the special status of the Australian child audience is ignored, the industry behind it becomes just another industry. Creative industries may well be deserving of some form of state subsidy, but the state subsidies that underpin children's television in Australia were never intended to be mere industry protectionist measures.

Ten years ago confident predictions were made that the Internet would lead to television's demise, while the lack of regulation surrounding the new medium caused public concern to shift to the need to protect children from the dangers of the online environment. It became increasingly obvious during the digital transition, however, that the Internet rejuvenated television, including children's television. Free-to-air television remains the most popular television in Australia, with 'second screen' activities often accompanying viewing, particularly children's television viewing. While legitimate concerns about children's use of the Internet remain, it is time for public focus to return to the continued provision of high-quality, locally made television for Australian children. The public should be encouraged to engage in debate about how best to secure value for its investment in the genre, and in turn for the Australian child television audience.

In order to have that debate, the increasingly complex settlements in children's television that emerged during the digital transition require scrutiny, so the changes in production, distribution and consumption can be understood. It is entirely possible that after a period of reconsideration and reimagining of Australian children's television a new and dynamic set of production and distribution norms could develop. Australia's international reputation for excellence in children's programming would be maintained and indeed, enhanced. Such developments would require a significant rethinking and refashioning of existing policy settings and, particularly, the means of securing supplies of locally made, high-quality, age-specific television for the child audience. Australia's commercial networks continue to sit at the heart of Australian television production. They remain central to the achievement of these policy objectives, despite their long-standing reluctance to invest in television deliberately made for Australian children.

From 2001 to 2014 the transition to a digital regime in Australia led to the emergence of new settlements in Australian children's television. It is essential that all those committed to the creation of high-quality, culturally specific television for the child audience acknowledge the transformations that occurred during this period. While contemporary Australian children's television experienced renewal, as old patterns of production and distribution dissolved, this renewal was accompanied by a gradual reduction in television's ability to situate Australian children within their culture and hence its public value. Australian children's television can still ride the digital wave that has reinvigorated contemporary television but the rethinking of the institutional, economic and regulatory arrangements that underpin its creation and distribution is a matter of urgency now.

Chapter 1

Understanding Children’s Television During the Digital Transition

The child audience in Australia has always been considered a special television audience. Children, it is commonly accepted, must be protected from the worst aspects of television while being provided with access to certain desirable types of television made especially for them. The various roles ascribed to children's television—the education and socialization of children, the protection of children from unsuitable content and the allaying of adult fears about television's possible ill effects on children—mean it has a distinctive set of functions that are different from television made for adults.

The complexity of expectations around Australian children's television places its production under unusual regulatory, cultural and economic pressures, which include an inherent vulnerability to market failure for live action drama. Special taxpayer-funded supports, administered by national screen bodies such as Screen Australia, are designed to ensure supplies of high-quality, local children's television that the market would not normally provide. Since the late 1960s state support for children's television has included content quotas on Australia's free-to-air commercial networks. These quotas were introduced following public outcry about the poor quality of the television on offer to Australian children; they include specific requirements for minimum amounts of locally made children's drama, which can be filled with either animation or live action drama.

The circumstances within which children's television is produced and distributed in Australia were transformed from 2001 to 2014, as Australian television underwent its transition to a digital regime. Technological and industrial changes in broadcasting began as early as 1995 with the introduction of pay-TV in Australia. The pace of change accelerated in 2001 with digital transmission. Between 2001 and 2014 in Australia free-to-air channels proliferated, well-resourced pan-global pay-TV networks increased their presence, online television catch up services developed, and smart phones and tablets became ubiquitous.

Technological developments meant that for the first time viewers, including children, could access television on multiple devices, on the move and outside the home. Free-to-air advertiser-funded television struggled to adjust to the altered circumstances of broadcasting, as audiences and advertising revenues fragmented across the new platforms on offer. One effect of fragmentation was a downward pressure on the licence fees networks were prepared to pay for children's television during this period, which added further challenges to the already difficult task of raising the finance required for its production.

Australia's digital transition saw the gradual development of specialized niche services for audiences, including children, who are recognized drivers of pay-TV subscription uptake.

The television landscape changed again for the child viewer with the arrival of dedicated free-to-air children's channels ABC3 in 2009.[1] Provided by public service broadcaster the Australian Broadcasting Corporation (ABC), the new children's service quickly became the most watched free-to-air channel in Australia among children aged 5–12. The proliferation in children's television services that occurred during the digital transition saw the child audience transformed from an unwanted obligation for free-to-air commercial operators in Australia to a sought after audience for specialist providers such as The Disney Channel, Nickelodeon and ABC3. The changed status of the child audience in Australia reflected international trends in television, including the rise of pan-global channels providing themed content for niche audiences.

As all audiences, including the child audience, fragmented into niche markets and licence fees fell in Australia and internationally, the need increased for what quickly became very complex international funding and co-production arrangements. One effect of the increased internationalization in the financing and production of Australian children's television was a requirement to minimize the cultural specificity that might inhibit its circulation in world television markets.

Not all of the effects of these altered circumstances of television were felt simultaneously nor did they necessarily bring about immediate, measurable changes; many production practices and industrial norms altered gradually and without fanfare. Cumulatively however the transition to a digital regime led to the creation of new settlements in Australian children's television. These new settlements are characterized by abundant supply, pan-platform distribution, internationalization, budget pressures, and a reduced ability of much of the Australian children's television produced with direct and indirect state support to situate Australian children within their own culture.

The analysis undertaken here explains how the digital transition led to new industrial, creative, regulatory and economic circumstances for the production of Australian children's television. This account is important and timely because of the special status of the child audience, the regulatory and financial supports that underpin the production of children's television in Australia and the worldwide reputation for excellence that Australian children's television has enjoyed since the 1980s. The new settlements in Australian children's television must be understood if future supplies of locally made, culturally specific, high-quality children's television are to be safeguarded.

Children and Television

Television was first introduced to Australia in 1956. Even before its introduction, concerns were expressed about television's possible ill effects on Australian children and family life. By the mid-1960s these concerns about the relationship between children and television had crystallized into public dissatisfaction with the poor quality of the television on offer to Australian children. Since that time various forms of state intervention have been justified in order to secure the presence in the schedule of the age-specific, quality children's programming that the market would not normally support. These include the important legislative instrument the Children's Television Standards (CTS) that has, since 1979, mandated minimum amounts of good quality children's programmes including drama on Australia's free-to-air commercial networks.

A long-standing tradition of state intervention and funding supports for the provision of Australian screen content, including children's content, from the 1960s onwards helped to support the emergence of a resourceful and creative Australian independent production sector. Australian children's television is an important part of that independently produced local content. It has won numerous international awards and is shown in over 100 countries. Indeed programmes such as *Skippy* (1968–69), *Round the Twist* (1999–2001), *H2O: Just Add Water* (2006–08) and *Dance Academy* (2010–13) have led to Australian children's television becoming some of the most successful children's television ever made.

These original and unique live action drama series, which, with the exception of *Skippy*, were partly state-funded, managed to maintain high production standards and situate Australian children within their own culture, while circulating in international markets. Live action drama of this sort became increasingly difficult to fund during the digital transition however, with its production levels declining sharply on Australia's free-to-air commercial networks. Live action drama requires substantially higher budgets than most forms of animation and is generally more difficult to distribute in international markets, because of its cultural specificity and cost.

Considerable societal and technological changes have occurred since the 1950s. Nonetheless children's television and media consumption continues to be the subject of discussion, regulatory attention, optimism and concern. Children are considered both vulnerable and corruptible television viewers who deserve protection from the wrong kind of content and access to the right type (Keys 1999; Simpson 2004). Witness the furore surrounding the ABC's decision to feature a child with lesbian parents on *Play School* on May 31 2004, which led to condemnation from both sides of politics. Indeed the then minister for children Larry Anthony accused the producers of the programme of failing in their responsibility to parents.

The right type of television, with high production values, pro-social values and local cultural relevance, is considered beneficial for children. Featuring children with Australian accents and dealing with recognizable Australian situations, such television enables children to be better situated within, and have a grasp of, their own national space and its history and traditions. The public value provided through the provision of programmes that speak directly to the Australian child audience and in doing so situate Australian children within their own culture helps justify the taxpayer-funded supports these programmes, particularly drama, require. Such television does not come cheaply, with an hour of children's drama costing on average $550,400 to make in 2013, compared with $14,000 on average for an hour of news and current affairs (ABS 2013a).

The abundant supply of children's television available to contemporary Australian children is made up of the specialized programming and multi-platform content provided by free-to-air advertiser-funded networks, by public service media ABC (including dedicated children's channel ABC3) and by eight children's pay-TV channels. (Australia's second public service broadcaster, the multi-cultural Special Broadcasting Services (SBS), does not usually transmit children's content.) So unlike their 1950s counterparts, contemporary Australian children are overwhelmed with choice, of both content and viewing platforms.

In Australia's digital regime, children consume their media across a wide array of electronic devices, only one of which is a television set. As a result, many have drifted away from free-to-air commercial channels to the Internet, pay-TV services and mobile devices. Nonetheless free-to-air commercial channels remain the prime site for the regulation of Australian children's television, the enforcement of its content quotas and the quality requirements of the CTS. Considerable taxpayer funding is invested in the children's programmes these networks transmit, although the networks themselves are under no obligation to pay any sort of minimum licence fee to producers for their children's programmes.

Cultural and social concerns about the well-being and special status of the child viewer in Australia exist within the context of a television system that is largely, although not entirely, governed by business principles. The majority of the children's television made in contemporary Australia, particularly drama, is produced by independent production companies, although some networks also produce children's television in-house. The survival of privately owned production companies depends on their ability to generate profits from the children's programmes they produce with public subsidy, in contrast to any public value created by these programmes.

The production of children's television is complicated then by the tensions that have always existed between television's free market operations, shaped by consumer demand and the pursuit of profit, and television as an instrument for social, cultural and civic improvement, deserving of state subsidy. These long-standing tensions were exacerbated by their intersection with the creative, industrial, economic and regulatory changes that occurred in television from 2001 to 2014 as Australia made its transition to a fragmented digital regime.

Public Value and Australian Children's Television

At this point it is useful to clarify the terms that will be used throughout this book, crucially what the terms 'children', 'children's television' and 'public value' can be understood to mean. Various differences in legal status are ascribed to a number of developmental stages of the child (in Australia, for example, a young person is considered to be criminally responsible at 10, is allowed to have sex at 16 but cannot vote until they are 18). This book will rely however on government regulatory body The Australian Communications and

Media Authority (ACMA's) definition of a child as being aged under 14 years, which is the definition used in the CTS.

Policy-makers chose this age range because the CTS are designed to create programming for pre-school and primary school children who may be aged up to 13 due to state by state differences in the ages at which Australian children start high school (ABT 1991). While pre-school television provides a rich area of investigation, its production circumstances are not the subject of analysis here. Pre-school television is underpinned by a different business model (see for example the global success of *Bananas in Pyjamas*, *The Wiggles* and *Hi-5*), and has a differently conceived audience and different aesthetics from other forms of children's television (Steemers 2010).

The multi-platformed nature of contemporary television distribution suggests television can no longer be thought of in its analogue-era sense as a mass medium that broadcasts simultaneously to a collective audience. Indeed it is not unusual to hear Australian children (and their parents) claim that they do not watch television at all. Nonetheless these same children will often demonstrate a familiarity with many children's series, a familiarity probably explained by the popularity of the new platforms of delivery available for children's television. These include the mobile devices, online catch-up services, tablets and computers that enable children to watch television on demand and away from home. The first episode of Series Two of ABC3's live action drama series *Dance Academy* attracted 1.8 million programme plays on the ABC's online catch-up service iView and its *Watch Now* website (Screen Australia 2013a). So while children's television viewing may often be asynchronous, self-scheduled and platform-agnostic, Australian children are still watching television programmes with enthusiasm.

Children's television will be understood then as programmes that are made specifically for a child audience (as opposed to G-rated material, which is not deliberately made for children). This sort of television can range from the high budget live action drama screened to satisfy sub-quotas in the CTS to the animated series distributed by pan-global pay-TV children's services in order to attract subscribers and revenue. The term will include but not be limited to: live action drama, animation, reality, quiz and game shows, entertainment and documentaries. While children's television can be understood as programmes made specifically for children, they are not of course the only programmes that children watch. *Masterchef*, *Australia's Got Talent* and *Dancing with the Stars*, all of which were Australian content airing on commercial free-to-air networks, were the most popular programmes with children in 2011 (Screen Australia 2011a: 69).

Although some fluidity surrounds the term 'children's television', Australia's media policy-makers, since 1979, have expressed clear beliefs about children's television through policy instruments such as the CTS. The current standards state that a children's programme is one which is made specifically for children or groups of children and:

(a) is entertaining;
(b) is well produced using sufficient resources to ensure a high standard of script, cast, direction, editing, shooting, sound and other production elements;

(c) enhances a child's understanding and experience; and
(d) is appropriate for Australian children.

(ACMA 2009: 4)

while C drama, of which commercial free-to-air networks must transmit 32 hours of first-run content annually, is required to meet the following criteria:

(a) the programme must be classified by the ACMA as a C programme;
(b) the programme must, in the opinion of the ACMA, be a fully scripted screenplay or teleplay in which the dramatic elements of character, theme and plot are introduced and developed so as to form a narrative structure;
(c) the programme may include sketch comedy programmes, animated drama and dramatized documentary, but may not include sketches within variety programmes, or characterizations within documentary programmes, or any other form of programme or segment within a programme that involves only the incidental use of actors; and
(d) the programme must, in the opinion of the ACMA, meet the requirements for an Australian programme in the Australian Content Standard.

(ACMA 2009: 9)

The inclusion of an Australian drama quota is implicit acknowledgement that while children should have access to age-specific, quality television, programmes sourced from countries other than Australia can be expected to make up a significant proportion of this television. These programmes take into account children's particular developmental stages and social needs, while one of Australian drama's key purposes is to situate Australian children within their own culture. Drama is also a genre most vulnerable to market failure and least likely to be provided without special support.

The term 'public value' as applied to this analysis of Australian children's television relies on Mark Moore's work (1995, 2013). Moore defines public value as the public enterprise equivalent of the shareholder value that private companies are obliged to create for their private investors (1995). The public value of Australian children's television is understood here as a quality that exists over and above any private value realized in its consumption through programme sales, merchandising, advertising or pay-TV revenues. Public value is created instead when national cultural and political agendas are served through the presence of minimum amounts of identifiably Australian, age-specific television in Australian television schedules. The CTS are themselves an expression of public value in children's television, intended to secure television, including drama that is made in the best interests of the child, rather than in the best interests of producers, broadcasters and regulators.

The market would not normally support the production of desirable levels of local content including children's drama on Australian commercial television. Instead the ACMA and various publically funded screen industry support organizations would typically generate public value for the Australian tax payer. They would do this by mandating or supporting the production of identifiably Australian stories that situate children within their own culture, and other forms of age appropriate content. Broad and sustained community support for the investment of public money in the provision of locally made, quality children's television exists because this kind of television is considered to have a higher purpose than the mere generation of financial profits. Television that speaks directly to Australian children realizes the larger goals of child socialization, citizenship and identity. Australian children's television secures public value then when it meets the objectives of policy settings underpinned by societal and political agreement that children are a special television audience. On the other hand, television that serves the interests of broadcasters, producers and screen bodies but not of the child audience lacks public value.

The public funding that is required to underpin the production and distribution of Australian children's television is derived 'through the coercive power of taxation' (Moore 1995: 30). This coercion entails a diminution of consumer sovereignty, as citizens have little opportunity to exert control over what is produced, as they would have in the private sector through their individual purchasing decisions. Nonetheless democratic systems of government allow individual citizens to exert some degree of control over public enterprises through their support, or lack of, for certain political mandates (Moore 1995).

The democratic will to provide certain forms of cultural content for Australian children prevails, despite broadcasting transformations, because the public continues to believe that locally made children's television has social and cultural worth. The public, whose contributions through taxation fund state support for Australian children's television, remains its key stakeholder. This study of the Australian children's television reveals the myriad ways in which the creation of public value is facilitated, and threatened, by the contemporary circumstances of its production.

Australian Children's Television as Part of a Production Ecology

In order to make sense of the technological, economic, creative and regulatory circumstances in which the production of contemporary children's television occurs, the term 'production ecology' has been adopted in this book. In thinking of Australian children's television as a subset of a broader Australian television 'production ecology' and in considering that term to encompass 'the wider economic, technological, regulatory, commercial and cultural dynamics' of production, this book relies on work already done in this area by Jeanette Steemers (2010).

Steemers suggests that analysis is needed of the ways in which production outputs from multiple organizations and broadcasters are shaped by both internal creative and external commercial and industrial considerations, as well as the need to cater to the child audience's specialized needs. In this way, complex industrial relationships and dependencies that have recently undergone a period of rapid alteration can be better understood (Steemers 2010). In defining production as an 'ecosystem involving relationships between individuals and organizations' (p. 7), Steemers implicitly posits a balanced organic model and argues that changes in one part of the system affect everything else in that ecosystem, including interactions between the various parts (2010). She argues that:

> By examining the broader field of production including institutional relationships, dependencies, key players and professional practices, we can gain a better understanding of how media outputs change and the internal and external factors that influence them.
> (Steemers 2010: 7)

Steemers also describes the three levels at which production occurs. The macro includes the institutional, economic and political circumstances of production, for example a robust tradition of public service broadcasting. The meso-level includes the gatekeepers of production, the broadcasters and large corporations or production companies and their organizational cultures and editorial and marketing practices. At the micro-level the creative and aesthetic considerations and production practices of individuals and groups can be seen. The role and significance of the different factors affecting production can be evaluated as part of a study of a production ecology (Steemers 2010).

Australian children's television and its production ecology are themselves part of a broader Australian television culture. Tom O'Regan (1993) defines this culture as 'the ways we do things with television in Australia' and notes the complex forces at work in this 'contested terrain', such as political settlements, media policy, the means of television's delivery, the geography of production and distribution, the influence of ownership structures and the need for Australian television to fulfil a certain role in the creation of national identity. Australian television has always been considered an important nation building tool. Despite various challenges and crises since its inception, television in Australia managed to provide a common civic culture linking a diverse and physically dispersed population. It has also always been seen as a unique blend of UK and US broadcasting systems. While it may have a strong public service ethos (reflected, for example, in its treatment of children as a special audience), Australian television also has a dominant commercial sector whose ownership structures allowed two and then three channels to relegate public service broadcaster ABC to a secondary position although all are 'national' broadcasters (O'Regan 1993).

Despite the influence of the commercial sector, Australia's screen production industry is partially supported by The Australian Content Standard, a regulatory instrument that includes a 55 per cent local content quota on free-to-air commercial television. US- and UK-sourced television also makes up a significant proportion of output in contemporary broadcasting schedules. Imported content is generally much less expensive than 'home-grown' drama, and if it has rated well in other territories, can be a less risky proposition. In the mid-2000s, multi-channelling by the free-to-air commercial networks diluted Australian content as US imports were used to make up large proportions of the new multi-channels' schedules. As a result, the proportion of hours of Australian content fell from 52 to 38 per cent in 2011 (Screen Australia 2011).

In Australia considerable tension exists between support for high-quality, local content and the commercial free-to-air channels' need to maximize profit by keeping programming costs as low as possible. This tension is emblematic of the different functions ascribed to television and the need to balance commercial profitability with the provision of certain desirable forms of cultural production. The special status of the child audience ensured that, prior to Australia's transition to a digital regime, Australian children's television was reasonably well resourced and its production sheltered from some of the harsher realities of commercial profitability. This then is the television culture within which Australia's children's television production ecology sits, a culture that has tended to carefully nurture local television in the public interest while maintaining highly commercialized business models of broadcasting and a solid reliance on imports.

Despite the distinctive nature of Australian television culture, and the unique set of circumstances from which its children's television emerges, Australian children's television programmes have traditionally been a part of the global trade in television services. Export markets are a vitally important source of production funding; thus, producers have always been economically bound to make programmes that are suitable for both local markets and international media landscapes. Other internationalizing influences include the UK's public service ethos, which eventually ensured that even commercial channels in Australia have public service obligations to the child audience, in return for access to what was, at inception, rare broadcasting spectrum. American models and formats for children's television such as *Flipper* (1964–67) and *Lassie* (1954–74), have also been present in Australia since the 1950s. They gave rise to dramas such as *Skippy* and various other kinds of children's programmes including the formats *Romper Room* and *It's Academic*.

Further internationalization occurred during the digital transition as transnational super-indies that operate alongside US conglomerates in global children's television networks became a more significant part of the Australian screen production sector. Their movement into the spaces of local production often occurred through the purchase of small Australian production companies as local subsidiaries. Transnational super-indies often specialize in the international distribution and production of programme formats such as *The X Factor*, *The Biggest Loser*, *Masterchef*, *Who Wants to be a Millionaire* and *The Idol* franchise. They will therefore specialize in the localizing of international programme formats, or the globalization of television programming. The success of this strategy depends partly on having a local production company in place in major territories, because its staff will be familiar with local cultural expectations and viewing conditions (Moran 2009). The subsidiary Australian production company will be just one of many owned by the parent company in key territories.

The global nature of media distribution, including television services, and the dominance of American conglomerates in children's television markets also make it impossible to consider any one country's television industry entirely in isolation. Australia's children's television production ecology is dependent on, and affected by, changes in international markets, particularly in the UK and the US. It is particularly vulnerable to any reduction in children's television commissions caused by, for example, the UK's 2006 ban on junk food advertising. Any analysis of the production ecology of Australian children's television must therefore consider the effects of internationalizing influences on its commissioning, production values and ability to situate Australian children within Australian settings.

The Main Players in the Production Ecology

Cultural production is a collective process within which participants work both cooperatively and competitively, tailoring what they do to the response of others. Cultural products are thus social products (Becker 1982). The production ecology of Australian children's television contains a number of key players and stakeholders, not all of whom share the same beliefs about the role of children's television or an equal commitment to its production. As in many children's television production communities, at times these players work cooperatively with one another, generating resources; at other times they compete for resources (Bryant 2007). In some cases they actively work towards quite different, even incompatible agendas.

Despite Australia's medium-sized domestic market and the downward pressure on programme budgets, the independent screen production sector has numerous players – indeed an oversupply – involved in the production and distribution of children's television. Producers and distributors of Australian children's television range from small operators, some but not all of which will concentrate on children's television, to larger, often vertically integrated super-indies and US conglomerates with much broader production slates. The latter are often well placed to exploit their children's programmes in global markets. A trend towards vertical and horizontal integration as production companies were bought up, or clustered together, became obvious during the digital transition.

Among the television production companies, which tend to be based in Sydney and Melbourne, competition for children's commissions is intense. Producers compete and sometimes collaborate with one another in the pursuit of scarce resources in the field of cultural production. Established players have considerable market advantage; a track record in delivering programmes on time and on budget, and compliant with the requirements of the CTS will encourage networks to develop a small group of informally preferred providers. From 2007 to 2012 the majority of children's television was produced in Victoria, followed by New South Wales and Western Australia.

While children's television as a form of cultural production enjoys generous state supports, it is nonetheless a profit-driven business. The programmes made by production companies in Australia often circulate in highly competitive global markets in which very large, vertically integrated US conglomerates control content and carriage. The industry operates under the broad assumption that the full cost of producing children's drama will not be borne by the production company itself or the commissioning broadcaster. As the CTS limit advertising around C programming, the cost of production of C drama remains underpinned by state subsidy and is spread between producers, broadcasters and the state.

In the production ecology, individual producers and production companies operate at the micro level with creative, commercial and aesthetic motivations guiding their practice. Those working in television production in Australia—commissioning editors, producers, writers, actors, directors, craft and technical workers and administrators—are a fairly homogenous group. The vast majority are white, middle-class and tertiary educated. The large number of aspiring creative workers in the screen production industry depresses starting salaries, to the point where young people may have to work for nothing, just to get experience in the industry. This industrial practice favours workers from more affluent backgrounds who may be able to draw on family resources to survive financially (Hesmondhalgh & Baker 2011).

Most of the creative labour force working in the screen production sector in Australia is freelance and mobile. Production companies describe themselves as 'accordions', that is they hire crew and expand for a particular production, then once the production is complete, the freelancers' contracts come to an end, and the company contracts again. As a form of creative labour, the screen industry offers glamorous but insecure work, with far more people wanting to work in screen production than could reasonably be employed. The creative autonomy and satisfaction in their professional practice enjoyed by those working in the sector is frequently countered by anxiety—and emotional labour—about where the next project or contract is coming from (Hesmondhalgh & Baker 2011). Power is also very unevenly distributed in the sector. Commissioning editors who decide which shows will be commissioned have a great deal of power; freelancers working for accordion companies have rather less.

Children's television producers are passionate about their work and appear to nurture a strong sense of its cultural and social significance. Creativity is seen as being harnessed in the best interests of the child audience; reflection on their creative activities is imbued with references to the need for children to have access to Australian content and children's distinctive television needs. Yet much Australian children's television is deliberately made to avoid culturally specific Australian references that might impede its distribution in international markets while dedicated specialists in children's education or psychological needs are rarely consulted. Producers struggle to maintain quality standards under shrinking programme budgets. A widespread assumption appears to exist in the sector that the children's television produced in Australia creates public value; nonetheless the production norms that developed during the digital transition suggest this is not always the case.

Some of Australia's screen production companies are small, entirely independently owned and operated; some are effectively local branches of transnational corporations that have moved into the spaces of local production. Members of this production community, particularly company principals, are accustomed to meeting at industry gatherings, such as the Screen Producers Australia (SPA) annual conference, at the ACMA's regular industry fora or at the international television market MIPCOM in Europe. Sometimes two companies will connect to work on a particular production requiring a combination of specialized skills that each company possesses. Producers also frequently unite to lobby governments over local content requirements or other policy-related matters, under the auspices of industry organizations such as SPA and the Media Entertainment & Arts Alliance (MEAA).

Australian television channels are an important part of the production ecology as they drive much of the demand for the production of local children's television. The commercial free-to-air networks are bound by the content quotas enshrined in the CTS to transmit 240 hours of C (school-age children's) programming each year, and 120 hours of P (pre-school children's) programming. Of the C programming, 50 per cent must be Australian and 32 hours each year must be first run Australian drama (a category that includes animated drama). While the commercial free-to-air networks produce some of their children's programming in-house, drama is generally sourced from independent producers.

Considerable differences exist between the commercial broadcasters in the acquittal of their legislated commitments to the child audience; each channel's resourcing and promotion of its children's programming affects the production and popularity of particular genres. Of the three networks, Network Ten produced the widest range and greatest volume of children's television in-house and maintained the highest commissioning levels of Screen Australia-funded live action drama during the digital transition. In contrast Networks Seven and Nine began to rely more heavily on animation to fill C drama quotas during this period; animation can often be produced at a lower cost per hour than live action drama. The skewing of the ratios between live action drama and animation reduced networks' programming costs while at the same time contributing to a loss of cultural specificity in many children's programmes.

The commercial networks have no vested interest in seeing the children's drama in which they are forced to invest succeed either in Australia or internationally, because it remains the production company's intellectual property. The drive to distribute and monetize Australian children's television in international markets now comes from global media companies like Disney and Internet-based television services, all of which are accustomed to re-purposing their content across multiple platforms. Children's television can become a highly lucrative endeavour under these circumstances.

During the digital transition, Australia's limited number of free-to-air commercial licences and oligopolistic broadcasting industry continued to ensure that the CTS obligations incumbent on the commercial networks remained in place. With reduced licence fees and limited licences that prevent new competitors, the commercial networks remain under an obligation to make adequate provision for the Australian child audience in their program offerings. Nonetheless the Australian free-to-air commercial networks have lobbied long and hard to be relieved of their CTS obligations, see for example industry association FreeTV's March 2014 submission to Minister for Communications Malcolm Turnbull (FreeTV 2014).

Public service broadcaster the ABC is also an important source of commissions for local producers. From February 2014, the ABC removed its children's programmes from ABC1, to ABC2 and ABC3, mirroring a similar strategy to that adopted by the BBC in 2012, by freeing up its flagship channel for adults programming. Unlike the commercial networks the ABC is not bound by the CTS but by its own charter. As a result, although the charter implies an obligation to provide children's programmes, no content quotas for minimum amounts of local children's television apply to the ABC. Therefore no legislative safeguards exist to maintain minimum amounts of local content on the nation's public service broadcaster.

Pan-global pay-TV services operating in Australia commission only small amounts of local content, in order to fulfil their obligations under the New Eligible Drama Expenditure (NEDE) requirement. Any pay-TV channel including children's channels with a schedule that contains at least 50 per cent drama must spend 10 per cent of its total programme expenditure on new local drama programmes.

Federal, state and other agencies such as Screen Australia, Screen Victoria and the Australian Children's Television Foundation (ACTF) offer crucial production resources by providing financial subsidies and other production supports including sales, distribution and marketing services. These have all been drawn upon by children's television producers in getting up projects in free-to-air TV, particularly on the commercial networks.

In recognition of the changes that had occurred in Australia's media landscape with the introduction of digital technology, regulatory body the ACMA was created in 2005 when the Australian Broadcasting Authority (ABA) and the Australian Communications Authority (ACA) were merged. The ACMA's responsibilities include the regulation of broadcasting, the Internet, telecommunications and radio; a list that reflects the changes in the media landscape wrought by technological innovation.

The ACTF, an independent company funded by the Commonwealth government has been a particularly influential player in the children's television production ecology since its 1982 establishment under the leadership of children's television stalwart Patricia Edgar. Originally created as a catalyst to improve the amount and quality of Australian children's television in the years following the introduction of the CTS, the organization's role in supporting the creation of high-quality, culturally specific Australian children's television became more important during the digital transition.

Under chief executive Jenny Buckland's leadership, which began in 2002, the organization changed direction. It moved away from a production house model and into a more developmental role, supporting other independent producers in the sector through direct investment, distribution arrangements and indirect forms of production support. Further in-kind support is offered to producers including office space or access to particular facilities or expertise that assists in the production of innovative, high-quality children's television.

The ACTF also supplies development funding, so that producers can work up their programme proposals in order to be able to pitch their series effectively to commissioning editors and contributes to programme budgets through distribution advances. The ACTF activities support the creation of public value in children's television because the programmes with which it is involved are characterized by high production values and cultural specificity and thus speak directly to Australian children. Many also become educational resources for Australian schools.

The ACTF's reputation for quality programming and long-standing production partnerships with local and international broadcasters mean it can provide important distribution support for small contemporary independent production companies. For these companies, the financing and distribution of high-quality children's drama represent an enormous challenge. Distribution in particular is often based on a low number of long-established connections and collaborations. In the absence of direct partnerships or ownership connections to large media corporations, many Australian producers rely on organizations such as the ACTF.

The ACTF has also played an extremely important role in the development of policy settings for Australian children's television since its inception, particularly around the development of policy instruments designed to improve access to local children's television (ACTF 2013). It regularly issues discussion papers, conducts research around children's media, makes submissions to government enquiries and maintains pressure on the commercial networks to improve their treatment of the programmes they are obliged to make.

During the digital transition the ACTF's campaign for the establishment of a dedicated children's channel led directly to the 2009 launch of ABC3, which became an important if limited source of original Australian children's commissions including live action drama. The new channel also provided an outlet for what was rapidly branded 'legacy' content by the ACTF, that is, the large back catalogue of children's television made with government support and the organization's involvement since 1982.

The Production Circumstances of Children's Television

Australian children's television emerges from an unusual set of creative, economic and regulatory circumstances partly because of the special status of the child audience and partly because, with a population of 22 million, Australia provides only a medium-sized domestic market. A great deal of research has been done into the ways Australian children experience and use television, due largely to societal fears about the effects of television on this vulnerable audience (Hodge & Tripp 1986; Palmer 1986; Cupitt & Stockbridge 1996; ACMA 2007, Screen Australia 2013a). But despite the special status of the child audience and by extension, the television created especially for it, the production circumstances of Australian children's television receive far less scrutiny than its intended audience.

Little is known beyond the screen industry about the interactions between the various creative, economic, technological and regulatory factors that shape the children's television that is made in Australia. Even less is known about their combined effects on the type of children's television that is created, its production values and its ability to speak directly to Australian children. And much of what is known about the industrial circumstances of Australian children's television has come from the industry itself, through material that is published by industry bodies.

In 2007 for example the Australian Screen Council (ASC), the leading body for the independent film and television industry acknowledged the value of identifiably Australian content to children's developing a sense of cultural identity when it stated that 'Australian children's television is a vital contributor to guiding Australian children to learn about Australia, its history, its values and who we are in Australia' (ASC 2007). Yet Australian producers have little choice but to make programmes with limited cultural specificity that will appeal to international markets because without international pre-sales or co-production arrangements in place, they cannot raise production finance.

Similarly some producers' reflections on their professional practice reveal a sense of themselves in a somewhat undervalued role, whose principal reward is a contribution to the greater good of the Australian child audience. Independent producers will often refer to the precarious nature of their business and the need for increased state support for their work, particularly through the re-calibration of taxation schemes. Producers are nonetheless almost entirely driven by commercial realities to make programmes that sell well in fiercely competitive international markets and are popular with young audiences.

The television transformations that occurred locally and internationally between 2001 and 2014 meant that those producing, regulating and distributing Australian children's television operated in a state of flux. During this period international markets became increasingly dominated by a small number of global media corporations that controlled both content and carriage, with many of these well-resourced corporations producing and distributing children's television across their global networks. Nonetheless, contemporary Australian children's television continues to be largely regulated by policy settings that were conceived and developed during Australia's analogue regime, pre-2001.

How the Research was Undertaken

The research undertaken here uses semi-structured interviews conducted with television producers, regulators, channel heads and commissioning editors in Australia and the UK, economic and industrial analysis, and textual analysis of policy documents and industry publications to uncover its findings. These approaches are at times combined in the analysis of the programme case studies that inform its findings. The generously shared insights and experiences of these industry figures revealed, at first hand, the impact of Australia's digital transition on their industrial practice and production norms. These on the record interviews provide valuable insights into the values, beliefs and creative practices of Australian producers as well as their working relations with each other.

As part of this research project, additional interviews and conversations took place with a number of other industry participants. Several have worked for many years across a variety of positions and companies, regularly moving between public service broadcasting, commercial networks and pay-TV companies. They also meet regularly at industry events such as the UK's annual Children's Media Conference and MIP Junior, the children's programme markets that take place each year in Cannes. They were happy to discuss children's television, on the grounds of anonymity; their perspectives also inform the book's observations.

The line of questioning varied depending on the nature of the participant's role although each was designed to elicit information about the production and distribution process, funding models and regulatory contexts for children's drama. The research also includes findings drawn from my attendance at industry events such as a Screen Australia industry forum in May 2013, the Children's Media Conference in Sheffield, UK in July 2011 and an Academic Fellowship at the National Association of Television Production Executives (NATPE) conference in Las Vegas in 2009.

How This Book is Structured

This chapter has provided a context for this study of Australian children's television. It has explained how local children's programmes, particularly drama, are seen to play a crucial role in situating Australian children within their own culture. The inability of much contemporary Australian children's television to speak directly to the Australian child has been raised as a critical issue affecting its public value. The chapter also described some of the key trends affecting the production, regulation and distribution of contemporary Australian children's television, particularly the effects of the fragmentation engendered by the digital transition.

The concepts of public value and of a production ecology have been introduced as analytical frameworks for understanding the ways in which Australian children's television is produced and distributed. Key players and organizations in the production ecology have been introduced along with their differing attitudes and commitment to the provision of children's television. This chapter contextualizes the production ecology in its Australian setting. It also recognizes that Australian children's television is simultaneously part of an increasingly globalized, media landscape in which cultural production is dominated by a small number of very large corporations, which in many cases control both content and carriage. These companies operate in Australia providing dedicated children's subscription services as part of their Australian operations. Internationalizing influences are therefore at work both within and without the Australian children's television ecology.

After this chapter, which has outlined the key areas of investigation and the ways in which this book is structured, Chapter 2 provides a historical context by charting how public concern and activism centred on the lack of quality local television for children led to state intervention from the 1970s designed to ensure the production and distribution of high-quality children's television in Australia. It also describes the interactions between the key stakeholders involved in its regulation and production. Taxpayer investment and state interference in the free market were justified by the public value created in ensuring children's television needs were met.

In Chapter 3 the child audience for Australian children's television is considered, an audience that has always been considered special, in equal need of protection from certain forms of television and of exposure to others. Technological developments during the digital transition transformed the way children's television is produced, distributed and experienced by the child audience. Long-standing business models and industrial practices were challenged in the process. The radical changes in children's television consumption that occurred during the digital transition confirmed and indeed intensified children's status as a distinctive audience requiring special consideration and attention.

The national context of production, particularly the role of Australian broadcasters in commissioning and funding children's television is the focus of Chapter 4. This chapter highlights the differences that currently exist in Australia between the various commercial channels and their investment in and treatment of children's television. Content quotas and substantial taxpayer subvention ensure demand and funding support for local children's television yet the digital transition caused Australian children's drama to become an increasingly internationalized genre. Free-to-air commercial networks' commissioning practices contributed to the loss of cultural specificity in much contemporary Australian children's television and hence its ability to situate Australian children in their own culture.

Chapter 5 examines the international context for Australian children's television and analyses the effects of globalization on television programmes, channels and markets, particularly the economics of television production during the digital transition. It explains how an Australian television production industry that was predicated upon the achievement of the goals of national cultural representation became a serious player in global media markets, undermining the capacity of the genre to deliver culturally specific children's television and hence public value to its stakeholders. Two case studies, of *H2O: Just Add Water* (2006) and *Animalia* (2006), are used to support the analysis.

In Chapter 6 regulatory regimes for children's television are canvassed and evaluated and the policy settings that directly affect the quantity and quality of children's television produced in Australia each year are analysed. The analysis includes policy instruments and supports for children's television that were introduced during the digital transition. Some of these had unintended consequences that may eventually undermine traditional justifications for state support for Australian children's television. The ways in which the development of incompatible policy agendas for screen production contributed to an erosion of public value in Australian children's television are also explained.

Chapter 7 considers a range of production companies and the children's programmes they produce to illustrate the complexities and challenges inherent in producing Australian children's television during the digital transition. Based on interviews with independent producers, commissioning editors and distributors, this chapter outlines the interaction between the creative, economic, regulatory and institutional elements that shape the production of children's television in contemporary Australia. The interviews reveal how the fragmentation that characterized Australia's digital transition gradually reduced the ability of Australian children's television to create public value while rendering live action drama a particularly vulnerable genre.

The key trends and pressure points occurring in the Australian children's television production ecology are examined in Chapter 8. In doing so, the chapter considers how future provision might best be ensured given the transformations in children's television that occurred between 2001 and 2014 and the centrality of the provision of public value to state support for its production. It provides an overview of the key creative, regulatory and economic issues discussed in preceding chapters, in order to develop a sense of the future outlook for Australian children's television.

This is a book about the production of children's television during Australia's transition to a digital regime; it is not a book about the effects of television on children. As such it does not include any in-depth textual analysis of children's programmes, any assessment of children's cognitive development or any attempts at analysis of the effects of television viewing on children. Although this is not a book about the best interests of the child, some of the arguments about what is in that child's best interests have shaped and impacted on the mechanisms that form a part of the production ecology of Australian children's television and will be included here.

Despite the special status of the child audience and the very considerable success Australian children's television has enjoyed in Australia and internationally, a comprehensive examination of the production ecology of contemporary Australia's children's television is not available. Such a dearth of analysis is symptomatic of much of the work that has been undertaken in communication studies, which has tended to pay less attention to cultural production and organization in favour of research into the effects of the consumption of media messages on their audiences (Hesmondhalgh 2012).

The lack of attention paid to this form of cultural production means however that there is little awareness of how the creative, economic, technological and regulatory circumstances in which contemporary Australian children's television is produced and distributed were transformed during the digital transition 2001–14. So while adults may be aware that children's television viewing now occurs across a range of devices and locations, they are not necessarily aware of the effects of the digital transition on the television their children watch.

A detailed analysis of Australian children's television follows, as this book examines the ways in which its production and distribution were transformed by the transition to a digital regime, while the societal need to protect the vulnerable child was not. The role of the public as a key stakeholder in the production of Australian children's television and the importance of the creation of public value in return for taxpayer-funded direct and indirect supports are also evaluated. As this book reveals, the risk of high-quality, culturally specific Australian children's television becoming a rare commodity in digital regimes characterized by abundance and proliferation of services must not be underestimated.

Note

1 The ABC launched a children's channel, ABCkids, in 2001 but the service was axed in 2003, with a lack of government funding blamed for its demise.

Chapter 2

Shaping the Foundations: Establishing an Australian Children's Television Production Industry

This chapter reveals that although children were always considered a special audience, the quality, age-specific television that parents wanted their children to watch was not present in Australian schedules in the years following television's establishment. As television matured however, public concern and activism about the lack of culturally specific children's television, including drama available to Australian children, led to the introduction of policy settings designed to ensure that the child audience's needs were met.

These policy mechanisms included, from 1979, the CTS, which contained content quotas for children's television on Australia's commercial networks. The public value of the CTS lies in their ensuring that children can watch quality, age-specific television, including a reasonable proportion of Australian drama, made specifically for them. In this way, the child audience can identify with Australian themes, language, traditions and values.

By the late 1980s the CTS and various forms of state subsidy had helped to establish an Australian children's television production sector with a global reputation for excellence. Long-standing policy settlements and production norms in children's television were challenged however by the fragmentation that characterized Australia's digital transition from 2001 to 2014. This chapter explains how the new settlements, which were created in children's television during this period, threaten the cultural integrity and public value of contemporary Australian children's television.

The History of Australian Children's Television

In 2000, just prior to the introduction of digital transmission, Australian television could be described in four phases if viewed as a long-term business cycle (Cunningham 2000). Thus the cycle began with 'innovation' and 'diffusion' in the 1940s and 1950s as television was gradually rolled out across Australia. Television then moved into an 'establishment' period from 1964 to 1974, a time during which three networks were established, television stations enjoyed ownership stability and Australia's drama production industry began to cluster around Sydney and Melbourne. Between 1975 and 1987 Australian television reached 'maturity'. This period encompassed the arrival of colour TV in 1975, the launch of the multi-cultural hybrid station Special Broadcasting Service (SBS) in 1980 and the introduction of the domestic VCR. From 1987 to the late 1990s, a time Cunningham (2000) characterizes as 'specialization and diversification', the stock market crashed, ownership upheavals sent commercial stations to the brink of bankruptcy, pay-TV was introduced and technological change saw convergence between broadcasting, telecommunications and computing.

Digital transmission was introduced to Australia on January 1 2001. It is suggested here that Australian television entered a fifth phase, of 'digital transition', between 2001 and 2014. The digital transition was characterized by fragmentation, of audiences and advertising revenues, and encompassed free-to-air multi-channelling, abundant supply and pan-platform delivery of television services. Fragmentation of audiences and advertising revenues challenged long-established business models for television while the pressures on advertisers' budgets were amplified by the global financial crisis (GFC) in 2007. Fragmentation also led to a downwards pressure on the licence fees broadcasters were prepared to pay for children's television, locally and internationally.

Innovation and Diffusion: 1940s and 1950s

Although Australian children have always been considered a special television audience, television's earliest operations in Australia quickly revealed that specialized, high-quality children's television would not be provided if the market was left to its own devices.

Television was introduced in Australia in 1956, nearly 20 years after its on-again off-again arrival in the UK, 16 years after America and just in time for the Melbourne Olympics. After much debate and public consultation, which included a Royal Commission in 1953, a mixed model television system, considered to incorporate the best elements of the British and American systems, was eventually introduced (Curthoys 1991). The fact that two commercial stations were established in Melbourne and Sydney in 1956 and later Brisbane and Adelaide compared with only one public service broadcasting station meant that, in Australia, commercial television had the advantage from the outset (O'Regan 1993). Media ownership was also concentrated from the start; the first owners of the commercial television licences tended to be the owners of the local newspapers.

In 1956 the Australian Broadcasting Control Board (ABCB) became the first regulator of the new medium, with the power to decide what constituted suitable program content but without the power to set quotas for dedicated Australian content. Although 'localism' was the guiding principle in the allocation of licences, with local ownership intended to ensure that each licensee would fulfil the needs of their local areas, such niche programming was demonstrably at odds with television's commercial imperatives of audience maximization and cost minimization (Cunningham 2000; O'Regan 1993).

The public submissions to the 1953 Royal Commission into Television revealed societal views about children and television. Many of the concerns expressed by parents and children's interests groups portrayed children as a distinct and vulnerable audience requiring protection from the wrong sort of television but on whom the right sort of television could be a positive influence. Fears were expressed that television might harm children, and their families, by lowering their taste, encouraging delinquency and possibly even causing nervous disorders. Its viewing might also interfere with the completion of domestic chores and homework, and undermine parental authority (Royal Commission 1954).

A submission to the Commission by the Country Women's Association of Australia emphasized the need for the careful control of television schedules:

> We recommend restricted hours and one of the hours we thought was a bad time was the smaller children's bedtime, or around about 6pm [...] We do not approve of television between the hours of 6pm and 8pm: most children—those you still call real children—would be going to be bed between those hours.
>
> (Royal Commission 1954: 84)

It was believed also that television could be a strong educative and moral force that improved children's spiritual welfare, if it were appropriately delivered. With the shared perspective of children as a special audience, groups such as the Victorian Council for Children's Film and Television (VCCFT) lobbied for dedicated children's programmes. The VCCFT suggested the provision of 'programs at a suitable hour specially designed for children with the object of stimulating new interest' as well as a break in transmission after these programmes and the late scheduling of any content that might harm children even if they were not its intended audience (Royal Commission 1954: 39).

Commercial television companies, whose main interest has always been to attract audiences that could be sold to advertisers for profit, supplied a second perspective to the Commission. The Federation of Australian Commercial Television Stations (FACTS) argued for a market-led approach that allowed the audience to choose its own programming under a scheme of broadcaster self-regulation, because regulation would 'stifle the development of television from the beginning (Royal Commission 1954: 76). The Commission concluded after examining the existing evidence 'that the child is more vulnerable than the adult' but 'that there is no evidence that there is anything in the nature of television per se which is injurious' (Royal Commission 1956: 41). It recommended that the national stations (i.e. the public service broadcaster) offer regular children's programming covering a wide variety of interests and that where there was no public service broadcaster, the commercial channel should show the national station's children's programming. The Commission veered away from content quotas for commercial channels however, suggesting the broadcaster's treatment of the child audience be considered at licence renewal.

The submissions to the Commission reveal that prior to television's introduction to Australia, the public were concerned that children's behaviour, state of mind and respect for authority could be influenced negatively by the small screen. Nonetheless television was also recognized as a medium that, appropriately managed, could be of great benefit to children. These beliefs about the vulnerability of the child audience and children's capacity to benefit from appropriate television content prevail in contemporary Australia. The commercial free-to-air networks' lack of enthusiasm for state intervention in the free market has also endured.

Despite the perceived special status of the child audience, once television was introduced to Australia, high-quality, dedicated children's programming was in short supply. Without mandated content quotas in place at this stage of innovation, commercial operators were free to concentrate on attracting audiences and advertising revenue as cheaply as possible, a move that led to American content dominating the advertiser-funded networks by the early 1960s.

As Albert Moran notes:

> [T]he economics of this first stage of television were that in order to buy the necessary kind of equipment to set up television stations the commercial operators offset capital costs against the relatively cheap costs of imported American material.
>
> (1989: 3)

Thus it was not so much contempt for the local product that lay behind this practice at the time, but the need to ensure the economic viability of the new medium and profitability of stations. The use of imports sustained industry rationalization, efficient networking and cost sharing of program production between stations. As a result, demand for local content and thus investment in local production were low however; it was estimated in 1959 that only two per cent of drama was locally made (O'Regan 1993).

Despite the acceptance of the need for Australian television to achieve economic viability, the requirement to accommodate the child audience's needs was not entirely abandoned by regulators. Thus a Children's Television Advisory Committee (CTAC) was also set up in 1957 to advise the Board. The Committee created children's television's first program standards that included detailed guidelines.

These stated that:

(a) All scripts must be carefully written, having in mind the needs of the particular age groups for which the programmes are intended; adventure stories in serial form should be so concluded that no episode ends with an incident that would give rise to undesirable emotional disturbance.
(b) All stories must reflect respect for law and order, adult authority, good morals and clean living. The theme must stress the importance of mutual respect of one man for another, and should emphasize the desirability of fair play and honourable behaviour. Cowardice, malice, deceit, selfishness and disrespect for law must be avoided in the delineation of any character presented in the light of a hero.
(c) In programmes in which children appear as artists, particular attention should be directed to avoid the possibility of encouraging precocity in such children who may be tempted to 'show off'.
(d) Contests and offers that encourage children to enter strange places and to converse with strangers for any purpose present a definite element of danger to children and should be avoided.

These guidelines express faith in television's capacity to socialize children and to encourage them to develop the morals and values of the good citizen: respect for adult authority, clean living, fair play and honourable behaviour. They also reiterate the need to protect the vulnerable child, both from distressing television content and the 'emotional disturbance' that might accompany its viewing.

Content guidelines also recommended the introduction of regular sessions for children designed

(a) to impart a broader knowledge of the history and potentialities of our country and current affairs;
(b) to foster an appreciation of such cultural pursuits as music, painting, ballet, the theatre and literature;
(c) to encourage interest and active participation in simple scientific investigations, such as botanical, geological and other pursuits; and
(d) by use of great examples from the Bible, and from history, biography and literature, to impart a real appreciation of the spiritual values and of the qualities of courage, honour and integrity which are essential to the full development of the individual, and of national greatness.

(Australian Broadcasting Control Boards Program Standards 1957 p. 9 para 15 cited in Horgan 2006: 47)

These early standards articulate a view of television playing a powerful educational, moral and cultural role in Australia, for the considerable benefit of its young citizens. Due to a lack of mandated content quotas however, the children's content guidelines remained only guidelines and were not attached to particular regimes of codification and inspection. This meant various programmes and channels could claim to be meeting these ideals and providing significant prosocial benefits without any rigorous external standards for evaluating the nature, merit and amount of their children's programming.

Despite public concerns about the relationship between children and television, in the earliest days of Australian television the child audience had two principal purposes. The first was to encourage the purchase of television sets in the family home. The second was to justify the presence of inexpensive programming designed to extend commercial channels' broadcast hours at a low cost. Channels used food and soft drink companies to provide program sponsorship to fund inexpensive studio-based children's programmes in order to extend their broadcast hours into the afternoon slots (Horgan 2006). In this way, overt commercial sponsorship created an early, workable business model for original children's television production although the sponsored programmes completely failed to conform to the CTAC's guidelines.

The types of studio-based variety programmes, such as *The Happy Show, The Children's Show* and *The Tarax Show*, that emerged from these sponsorship deals were very popular with young audiences. They were however criticized by the ABCB for exploiting children's interests and leisure time. In contrast, at this time public service broadcaster the ABC placed children's programmes under 'Youth Education' and initially transmitted several programmes per week, including *Kindergarten Playtime* (1957), *Children's TV Club* (featuring Mr Squiggle) (1959) and *Partyland* (1959), (which eventually developed into *Play School*). But for the commercial networks, a workable business model for local children's television instilled with the values suggested by the board's 1957 guidelines was yet to emerge, despite the ideals expressed in early television policy-making.

By the mid-1960s, both cultural protectionism arguments and determined lobbying by the film and entertainment industry were being used to justify legislative intervention in the television industry to address the lack of Australian and children's content on air. Organizations such as the Australian Council for Children's Film and Television, established in 1957, campaigned for more local screen content for Australian children. In 1962 the senate appointed a select committee chaired by V S Vincent to investigate the amount of Australian content on Australian television. The Committee's establishment coincided with a rising sense of community dissatisfaction with the manner in which the mass media were operating in Australia, particularly their dependence on American programming. There was a growing interest also in film as an art form, and a concomitant enthusiasm for support for a local film and television production industry (Bertrand & Collins 1981).

The Vincent Report of 1963 articulated a view that Australians were receiving an inadequate picture of Australian culture through the television programming available at the time, with local drama in the early 1960s reduced to less than one per cent of the total amount broadcast by the commercial stations (Cunningham & Jacka 1996). In doing so the report provided legitimacy for increasing demands for greater levels of Australian content; particularly drama, and greater credibility for arguments in favour of government supports for a local film production industry (Bertrand & Collins 1981). Despite the fact, none of the report's recommendations were implemented; the Vincent Report remained influential and changed the terms of the debate surrounding Australian (and children's) drama.

Establishment from 1964 to 1975

As television matured, public demand for local screen content increased and a local production industry started to develop; the introduction of state support for Australian drama for adults strengthened the case for similar supports for children's television.

During this period, television started to mature in Australia, and a local production industry gradually began to emerge. Some provision was made for Australian drama for adults, the form of programming that had been most likely to be usurped in the schedules by cheap imports. In 1966 a small drama quota was introduced and followed in 1973 by the points system for drama. The formalized provision of Australian drama was justified in the interests of achieving the goals of national cultural representation while increasing the viability of a local screen production industry. A precedent for public subsidy of socially desirable screen content was set, largely due to the public's support for more Australian film and television.

At the start of this period of 'establishment', children were still seen by the commercial networks as an audience worth pursuing, despite the lack of a sustainable business model for good quality Australian children's television. The networks relied on repeats of inexpensive American animation and sitcoms like *The Brady Bunch*, *I Dream of Jeannie* and *Hogan's Heroes* and strip-scheduling shows like *The Mickey Mouse Club* (which was made for American children) in the early evening to attract the child audience with minimal outlay (Moran 1989). Despite the reliance on US imports, local children's studio-based entertainment programmes sponsored by food and drink manufacturers remained in the afternoon schedules; most went live to air.

Between 1964 and 1975, even though levels of imported programming on Australian television remained high, certain factors emerged that began to encourage local television production. A reliance on imports had enabled Australia's medium-sized television market to establish itself by freeing up funds for local programming and infrastructure. But local production remained a key to attracting audiences who would then also watch imported programmes. Having popular local content on air also made Australian channels less vulnerable to the demands of US suppliers. Further, when local content quotas were mandated, they tended to be set at levels already achieved by stations, acting as a safety net to minimum levels without placing onerous demands on the least profitable commercial stations (O'Regan 1993).

Other changes led to the increase in local production that occurred at this time. Audiences gradually grew tired of US imports; the production of Australian news and current affairs, of soaps and of Australian drama, which told Australian stories, resonated with local audiences. They contributed to the creation of an Australian cultural identity, and created a sense of place. Dramatized Australian national stories, such as the Crawford's detective series *Homicide* (1964–77), gradually became part of television's output, building a sense of national identity that was sharpened by the contrast with imported programming from the US (O'Regan 1993).

The addition of Network Ten in 1964 also led to increased demand for American programmes by the three Australian commercial networks, which forced up the prices for these programmes, making them less competitive. Once imports became too expensive, the commercial networks stopped buying US programmes while the ABC turned to the BBC as its primary supplier. Further support for local production included a content quota for Australian advertising that had been in place since 1960; the introduction of videotape, which reduced production costs; and the ABC's increased output of locally made drama. In other words it was more than simply government policy and content quotas that nurtured the Australian production industry at this time (Flew 1995).

The industrial developments that led to the increased production of Australian drama also contributed to more Australian children's television on Australian screens. In 1967 an economic model for exportable children's television programmes with high production values and a long shelf life emerged with the creation of the hugely successful live action drama *Skippy*. The story of a young boy and his constant companion, the extraordinarily talented Skippy the bush kangaroo, was filmed in the Ku-ring-gai national Park in NSW. With Australian bush settings, Australian accents and a kangaroo that could communicate with humans, play the drums, place bets and operate a radio, *Skippy* was a culturally specific Australian drama, which at the same time was deliberately produced for an export market.

The independent production company Fauna Productions made 91 episodes of *Skippy* between 1967 and 1969. These episodes were seen in over 128 countries. Fauna Productions was owned by television producer and documentary film-maker Lee Robinson and one of Australia's most prominent live entertainment promoters and producers, John McCallum. They were able to secure local finance when, after seeing the pilot episode, Frank Packer agreed to buy all the episodes they could make for Channel Nine.

Although *Skippy* was marketed as family television, appealing to adults as well as children, its funding model bore a strong resemblance to the funding model for contemporary Australian children's production. But in the absence of the state funding available to contemporary producers, a combination of local broadcasters' investment and international co-production agreements alone funded this highly successful drama. Additional revenues were generated by the merchandising of the series, which included toys, breakfast cereal, clothing, jewellery, toothpaste, comics, soft drinks and a Skippy Fan Club that had over 67,000 members.

Skippy was very deliberately made for an export rather than a local market. In order to increase its international appeal, the series had very high production values and was made in colour and filmed on 16mm at a time when Australian television was still in black and white. Most of the 91 episodes that were eventually made were written by Australians but directed by a mix of Australian and international directors due to an early skills shortage. Broadcasters in England, Holland, Canada, Japan and Belgium bought the series, representing the first time that local production companies had encountered strong success with international sales of a uniquely Australian production (Moran 1985).

Around this time another Australian drama producer also recognized that international funding was the key to making a colour series with sufficiently high production values to attract international markets. Roger Mirams, owner of independent production company Pacific Films, was one of the first Australian producers to do co-production deals with international partners. Mirams made children's drama series including *The Adventures of the Seaspray* (1965–66), filmed entirely on location in Fiji, and *The Magic Boomerang* (1964), both of which were broadcast on the ABC.

Pacific Films also worked with commercial broadcaster Network Nine, which invested in *The Terrible Ten* (1959), a show that eventually moved to the ABC as *The Ten Again*. Mirams, like Robinson, recognized the appeal of Australian scenery and exotic fauna in international markets. Actor Gary Gray who played one of the children in *The Adventures of the Seaspray* said of Mirams:

> Roger used to write a lot of the scripts on the back of an envelope, literally, and he would change it all the time during filming. He would see something interesting and decide to write it in [...] he always had an eye for what was 'commercial' so he'd change things if he saw something that he thought people overseas would like—scenery or animals or whatever.
>
> (TV Eye 1999)

However Mirams' reliance on international co-production partners meant that they, and international distributors, were able to force him to accept highly unfavourable financial arrangements. Mirams eventually gave up on his own independent productions and joined the Grundy Organisation as a producer (Moran 1985).

Small, independent Australian production companies without structural connections to larger multinational distributors have always been vulnerable in global marketplaces. Although by the late 1970s international demand for drama had dropped and McCallum and Robinson abandoned children's television production and returned to film production, the international finance and merchandising opportunities they pioneered remain crucial to the success of contemporary Australian children's television. Equally the producers' enthusiastic embrace of merchandising opportunities continues in much contemporary children's television.

The ABC was the principal source of children's drama during the mid-1960s, broadcasting several Australian drama series, including *The Magic Boomerang* (1965–66), *Adventures of the Seaspray* (1965–66), *Wandjinda* (1966), *The Stranger* (1964–65) and *The Interpretaris* (1966). These productions tended to have fairly short runs, even at times as low as six (*The Interpretaris*) or seven (*Wandjinda*) episodes. But in a blow to the local production industry, in 1975 the ABC's new controller of television, John Cameron decided to stop making children's drama and to import children's programmes from abroad because it was cheaper. The absence of quotas for local children's television in the ABC's charter permitted this institutional neglect of the Australian child audience by the public service broadcaster.

By 1971 public concern about the general lack of good quality Australian children's programmes available to Australian children was high enough to convince the ABCB to intervene. The regulator introduced a content quota for Australian children's television, of four hours in any 28 days period. This development was the first formalized recognition through content quotas for commercial networks of the special status of the child audience. Without any public investment however the quotas were, predictably, often filled with low-budget programming. Nonetheless Rex Heading, managing director of Channel Nine's Adelaide station NWS9 saw a niche market for locally produced children's television that could be sold to other stations in the network and the unaffiliated country stations that existed at the time. NWS9's children's productions included *The Curiosity*

Show (1972–90), a one-hour educational science show that went on to win the coveted international award for quality children's television, The Prix Jeunesse in 1984. NWS9's embrace of a business model for quality, Australian children's television during this period was unusual among the commercial networks; it did not however extend to the production of live action drama.

Thus at this point in Australian television history, some successful forays into drama had been made by independent producers and home-grown educational programmes by Channel Nine. Nonetheless neither Australia's commercial networks, with privileged access to a limited number of licences and rare spectrum, nor the taxpayer-funded ABC were consistently serving the child audience in ways that reliably delivered quality programmes including drama that would situate Australian children within their own culture.

'Maturity' 1975–87

At this point determined lobbying and campaigning for high-quality, locally made television for the child audience by children's advocates, combined with widespread public dissatisfaction with the quality of television on offer to Australian children, forced the Australian government to intervene in the free market operations of Australian commercial television.

This period encompassed important industrial events including the arrival of colour TV in 1975, the 1980 introduction of a new free-to-air channel in the shape of the innovative multi-cultural hybrid station SBS and the arrival of the domestic VCR in the early 1980s. The widespread availability of the VHS in the early 1980s was significant; it meant that for the first time Australian audiences had the opportunity to exert some control over their viewing schedule by recording free-to-air broadcasts and renting cassettes. It also allowed favourite children's movies and series (which were often produced in the US) to be purchased for re-viewing at home. Disney's 1959 version of *Sleeping Beauty* sold over a million copies in 1986. Australian children's television and its production industry were also transformed during this period by the introduction of the new regulatory instrument the CTS.

The development of the CTS and the C classification can be traced back to 1975 when the ABCB established an Advisory Committee on Program Standards chaired by board member and long-standing children's television advocate Patricia Edgar. The Committee made what were then revolutionary recommendations (74 in total) for Australian children's television on commercial channels. These recommendations with a distinctly public interest flavour included specified hours for children's programmes filled with programmes made specifically for them, as well as government subsidies for production and no advertising around children's viewing (Edgar 2006). The ABCB did not act on the recommendations, although children's quotas were increased to ten hours per four-week period in 1976. The report however provided a valuable model of children's television made in the public interest, designed to deliver public value.

In 1977 the ABCB was abolished and replaced by the Australian Broadcasting Tribunal (ABT), which was considered to be more distanced from the commercial channels than its predecessor. The ABT did not incorporate the ABCB's recommendations into policy either, but by this time the lack of dedicated children's television on air was becoming a source of widespread public concern. The ABT's 1977 enquiry into the Self Regulation of Broadcasting provided an ideal vantage point from which to prosecute these concerns. The Tribunal invited public participation, holding public hearings all over the country and accepting 539 written submissions. The standard of children's television programmes dominated the evidence, with public concern centred on the low budget, poor quality television on air during children's viewing times, much of which was not even made for the child audience.

The public's efforts to secure better television for Australia children paid off. Australian children's television was condemned by the Self Regulation Report 1977 as 'some of the poorest quality and most commercialised programming on television'; commercial networks were accused of demonstrating 'inadequate budgets, lack of time, and lack of personnel or management interest' in conforming to the early minimal quotas (cited in Edgar 2006: 56). The Tribunal decided that the networks' commercial imperatives were not compatible with their 'acknowledged social responsibilities' and announced it would be setting Australian and children's content quotas (Rankin 1990: 111).

The Self Regulation Report eventually proposed, among other things, the introduction of a new classification C for children, dedicated slots from 4pm to 5pm on weekdays and at least 30 minutes a day for preschool programming (AGPS 1977 cited in Edgar 2006: 57). The Tribunal considered that it was important to continue to encourage the production of Australian children's television and a Children's Program Committee (CPC) replaced CTAC in 1978. The Committee also recommended a diversity of children's programmes that should be produced, with drama as a high priority (Edgar 2006).

Leading children's television campaigner Patricia Edgar also sat on this Committee, as did Channel Nine's Rex Heading. As she reveals in her autobiography, Edgar considered culturally specific drama a vital form of cultural production for Australian children:

> It was also my strong belief—and still is—that Australian children's drama had to *be* Australian. Many critics argue that a good story works regardless of its setting and that, as long as Australians make good programs, we don't need to protect Australian culture per se. This is a fallacy. A story must first be an authentic, powerful Australian story before it will be of interest in an international marketplace.
>
> (Edgar 2006: 67)

The guidelines that were eventually produced by the CPC for the ABT referred to the role and importance of quality Australian children's television, stating:

> In our view, quality children's programs must first be entertaining television. Children's programs should fulfil some special need of childhood [...] As quality children's literature

> contributes to the social, emotional and intellectual development of children, so also should quality children's television contribute to development in these areas.
>
> (Cited in Edgar 2006: 73)

Thus historically, children's drama has always been considered to fulfil important social and cultural needs for the child audience, including that it should foster among children a sense of their own cultural identity. Its provision requires particular regulatory emphasis, because higher production costs render the genre of live action drama most at risk of market failure.

In May 1979 (the United Nations Year of the Child), in response to the CPC's recommendations, what would prove to be the most significant regulatory development for Australian children's television since television's inception, the first Children's Television Standards (CTS) were issued by the ABT. The Standards were carefully designed to improve the quality and amount of Australian children's television, with each Standard addressing certain requirements such as age-appropriateness and production values. For the first time the CTS ensured supply of local children's programmes on Australia's commercial networks. Networks had no choice but to invest in domestic production of children's television. Demand was thus created for high-quality, locally made children's programming, the single most important element in the establishment of a sustainable children's television production ecology in Australia. The public value in catering to the child audience's television needs justified this intervention in the operations of the free market, which also underpinned the foundations of the children's television production industry.

Unfortunately the networks remained recalcitrant, with cheaper magazine programmes dominating children's content and constituting 72 per cent of all C material between 1979 and 1983 (Aisbett 2000). The networks' resistance to the commissioning of quality children's television and particularly drama meant the child audience was still not being properly served with high-quality local content. Thus in 1984 and after 193 public submissions in its support, a quota for Australian-produced children's drama of six hours was added to the CTS, and the C drama classification was born. The drama requirement was increased to 12 hours in 1990, to 16 hours in 1991 and finally to 32 hours in 1996.

In the light of the demand for dedicated children's programmes created by the CTS, and following on from recommendations that emerged from a 1978 Senate Standing Committee on Education and the Arts, for an independent children's television production unit, Patricia Edgar obtained government approval to set up ACTF in 1982 and became its founding director. From its 1982 establishment, the Commonwealth funded ACTF held an enormously important position in the children's television production ecology across its various domains of responsibility. These responsibilities include investing in the production and distribution of local children's television, supplying indirect forms of production support for new, upcoming producers and sustained engagement with policy debates and development around the provision of high-quality children's television to the Australian child audience.

While it is difficult to overstate the importance of the CTS in generating demand for children's programmes in Australia, the establishment of the ACTF was also a vital development in the children's television production ecology. The existence of the ACTF ensured that demand for high-quality Australian children's television was met, initially through the organization's own production activities and later through direct and indirect support for the children's television produced by the independent production sector.

The ABT reaffirmed the importance of drama when it reviewed the Standards in 1987 stating:

> The drama format is an essential ingredient in children's television and it is important that children see a reasonable proportion of Australian drama made specifically for them so they can identify with Australian themes and language.
>
> (Cited in Mencinsky & Mullen 1999)

Under Edgar's leadership in the 1980s and 1990s the organization's activities focussed strongly on in-house production within the organization, and it quickly established a reputation as the producer and distributor of high-quality Australian children's television for local and international markets. Indeed the level of its production activities led to some tensions within the fledgling independent production sector with a number of producers complaining they were competing for commissions with a taxpayer funded organization that was not forced to carry the financial risks they faced.

The work of the ACTF and particularly Edgar's influence on the types of programmes made were crucial in shaping Australian children's television during the 1980s. Edgar had strongly held convictions about what children's television should do, above and beyond entertaining children, including that it should help situate Australian children in their own culture. Edgar also felt that children's television should reflect children's lived experiences. For Edgar, who was an enormously influential founding director of the ACTF and worked tirelessly to improve the provision and quality of Australian children's television, the child audience's needs were paramount. Children deserved the best local programming that could be made, particularly drama.

By the early to mid-1980s the commercial networks were well established and profitable, and making enough money to be able to invest in local drama production that rated well, while mandated content quotas provided additional impetus to do so. Thus economic and regulatory conditions ensured that during this period of maturity, popular local content with high production values made up a significant part of the commercial networks' schedules (Cunningham 2000; O'Regan 1993). Government intervention in the form of the 1981 introduction of tax concessions for film and television production including the tax scheme 10BA further supported local content, such as feature films and documentaries as well as the miniseries, of which 65 were made between 1981 and 1987. The establishment of the Film Finance Corporation (FFC) in 1989, a screen agency designed to support production by meeting some of the development costs and acting as a funding partner, provided further state-funded support for Australian screen content including children's television.

The creation of the ACTF, with a remit to be a source of funding, distribution and executive production for new children's C classified programmes that would attract presales from commercial broadcasters and would also qualify for government supports, led to the development of a new business model for children's television production. This model, which relied on legislated local demand from the commercial channels, government subsidies and international sales to support Australian children's television production, remains the prevalent funding model.

During this period a local children's television industry, supported by a combination of content quotas, audience demand and international investment was established in Australia. With the child audience's specialized needs as its focus, the creation of public value was integral to the Australian children's television produced.

1987–late 1990s, 'Specialization/Diversification'

At this time the production of high-quality, Australian children's television proliferated, due to the content quotas in the CTS, while the commercial networks for which much of this television was made underwent a period of chaos, disruption and financial disaster.

In stark contrast to the period of prosperity and confidence that preceded it, Australian broadcasters faced turbulent times during this phase of specialization and diversification. The 1986 Hawke government cross-ownership rules required media owners with interests in print and television in the same areas to divest themselves of one in order to specialize in the other. Opportunities for entrepreneurs to gain more market share in either print or broadcasting were created in this way.

The ensuing sales of all three commercial channels to owners who had no previous experience in television and who paid vastly inflated prices for their respective channels proved disastrous. The increasingly aggressive competition that then developed between the channels also pushed up programme costs as revenues dropped. As more was spent acquiring US programmes, less was spent on local drama production. By 1988–99 the Australian commercial television industry had made a loss for the first time since 1957. By 1990 Networks Seven and Ten were in receivership, and production costs had been slashed by as much as 40 per cent (O'Regan 1993).

Although many factors contributed to television's disastrous change in circumstances, including a stock market crash, high interest rates, crippling levels of debt in what was an extraordinarily profligate financial environment and a contraction in advertising spending, the outcomes were relatively straightforward. They included a loss of programming quality, a lack of new programmes and an increased reliance on government funding mechanisms in the shape of public service broadcasters and organizations such as the FFC to support local production. Meanwhile the commercial television stations belatedly embraced a wide range of cost-cutting measures (O'Regan 1993).

Somewhat ironically then, this was a period during which Australian children's television enjoyed increased funding and popularity as the effects of policy instruments such as the CTS began to be felt. Children's programmes also benefited from being part of Australia's agile and resourceful production culture that had honed its skills during the 1980s and understood the importance and the requirements of international marketplaces and co-production agreements (Cunningham & Jacka 1996).

While local circumstances was challenging, the CTS still led to an increase in the amount of Australian children's television being made to satisfy local content requirements but which could also be distributed internationally. In order to secure programme budgets and meet the requirements for Australian state subsidies, Australian producers had to form international connections with foreign commissioning agents. Thus despite its cultural specificity and important role in national cultural representation, Australian children's television and particularly its drama, was internationalized from the start.

One of the very first C classified dramas produced by the ACTF, *Winners* (1986), sold into 90 countries, quickly establishing a profile and reputation for quality for Australian children's television. In a pattern that would become all too familiar to Australian producers, *Winners* received critical acclaim at home and internationally but was scheduled inconsistently by Network Ten, making it difficult for its intended audience to find it in the schedule.

The financial profligacy and lack of experience that characterized television network ownership during this period helped to fund some of Australia's most well-regarded children's television. In 1988 the extravagance of Network Seven's new owner Christopher's Skase was successfully harnessed by the ACTF to invest in one of its most successful dramas, *Round the Twist*, for which Skase agreed to pay $75,000 per episode. The quirky series about the Twist Family, who live inside a haunted lighthouse, was based on the fantasy novels of Paul Jennings. Storylines included a boy giving birth, a peeing competition and a child's brain being sucked out of their nose (an episode for which the Disney Channel, unsuccessfully, demanded a refund). The first episode of the first series *Skeleton on the Dunny* set the tone—and the cultural specificity of the series.

Despite initial difficulties in securing a distribution arrangement, with the scripts declared 'too rude', 'not for television' and 'outrageous', *Round the Twist* became a global success story for the ACTF. It sold all over the world and in 1993 was the number one rating children's programme in the UK, with an audience of 5 million on the BBC. The FFC set the $75,000 Network Seven paid per episode as the benchmark price for children's drama to obtain FFC funding, thus ensuring the commercial networks invested adequately in the children's television Australian taxpayers were helping to fund. The BBC went on to become a co-production partner on other Australian productions including *The Genie from Down Under* in 1998. During this period the ACTF produced more than 115 hours of programming, won over 45 national and international awards for its production slate and began to successfully merchandise its programmes (Cunningham & Jacka 1996).

Other independent production companies also benefited from the demand created by the CTS and the supports for the genre provided by state-funded organizations like the ACTF and FFC. In the late 1980s and early 1990s producers such as Yoram Gross (the *Blinky Bill* series), Jonathan Shiff (*Ocean Girl*) and Ron Saunders (*SpellBinder*) all successfully produced and exported Australian children's television. Australian children's drama that had stood at 16 per cent of all drama hours classified from 1979–1983 rose to 69 per cent of C classified drama by 1996–99 (Aisbett 2000). The unusual levels of state support for children's television in Australia underpinned a local production industry whose programmes nonetheless sold well in international markets, particularly in Europe.

The artificial, legislated demand created by the CTS for drama and public investment and support nurtured the Australian children's production industry during the ownership paroxysms and instability of the 1980s and early 1990s. The special status of the child audience ensured that the commercial networks' privileged access to the spectrum still obligated them to provide such programming, regardless of any financial vicissitudes they might be experiencing. Even the abolition of the ABT, to be replaced with the Australian Broadcasting Authority (ABA) in 1992—a much lighter touch regulator than its predecessor—only increased the drama content quota and left the CTS unchanged.

Despite the relative stability and success for Australian children's television production during this time of specialization and diversification, technological change occurred towards the end of the period that would transform the ways in which television was produced and distributed. Pay-TV was introduced to Australia in 1995, with this 'user-pays' broadcasting model making dedicated children's channels available to Australian children for the first time. In recognition of the costs of setting up subscriber services in Australia, and in the light of the slow uptake of the services, pay-TV television enjoyed a light touch regulation with negligible local content requirements.

Internationally the advent of digital technology, introduced to the UK in 1998 by Rupert Murdoch's pay-TV operation BskyB, expanded the bandwidth. Digital technology undermined commercial broadcasters' public service obligations, the traditional justification for which was spectrum scarcity. The end of spectrum scarcity also led to a proliferation of new services in the UK, leading to audience and advertising fragmentation and challenging the business model for free-to-air commercially funded television. The circumstances surrounding long-standing co-production arrangements between Australia and the UK were irrevocably altered by these technological developments.

In Australia this period of specialization and diversification saw certain regulatory and production norms develop. These norms were grounded in the creation of specialized content that would speak directly to the Australia child audience. The high production values and cultural integrity of these programmes justified the state subsidy and intervention in the workings of commercial television they required. After decades of neglect, the Australian child audience finally had high-quality, culturally specific drama available, paid for by a combination of broadcaster licence fees, taxpayer funds and international distribution arrangements.

The CTS ensured that state support for children's television carried its own set of obligations, with a set of quality standards and cultural specificity expressed through the requirements for the C drama classification. Thus the Australian children's television production industry prospered during this period of specialization and diversification, while consistently delivering public value to its key stakeholder, the Australian taxpayer.

2001–14 The Digital Transition

Television broadcasting was transformed at this time by the introduction of digital transmission, which led to a rapid increase in the number of free-to-air channels. The end of spectrum scarcity created abundant supplies of television delivered across multiple platforms, while fragmenting the audience and advertising revenue.

Between 2001 and 2014 Australian television entered a fifth phase, of digital transition. This period was characterized by audience fragmentation, downwards pressure on licence fees and the increased internationalization of both Australian children's television, and the independent production sector responsible for its creation. Australia's digital transition encompassed the establishment of new regulatory and screen bodies, the ACMA and Screen Australia respectively. This period also included two important reviews, the ACMA's review of the CTS in 2007 and the 2012 Convergence Review, an independent enquiry undertaken through the Department of Broadband, Communications and the Digital Economy intended to prepare Australian media for its digital future. Internationally, new models of television allowed global media conglomerates such as Disney, Time Warner and AOL, which controlled both content and carriage, to position themselves strongly in the market as providers of children's services.

Industrial and technological developments during the early 2000s in Australia led to increased television provision and, inevitably, audience fragmentation. The 2001 introduction of digital broadcasting enabled multi-channelling by free-to-air broadcasters, heralding the end of spectrum scarcity in Australia. Australian media policy, with its emphasis upon high-definition digital broadcasting, ensured digital broadcasting in Australia got off to a slow start. Nonetheless digital offerings from both the commercial networks and the ABC (but not from any new market entrants) eventually began to appear. By 2014, the number of free-to-air channels in Australia had increased from 5 to 20.

The new multi-channels offered by Australia's commercial networks proved popular with local audiences, despite their reliance on inexpensive US programming rather than any home-grown product. Without content quotas on commercial free-to-air multi-channel offerings, Australian content was proportionally reduced in their schedules. The pay-TV industry also matured during this period; increased market penetration meant that by 2007, 32 per cent of Australian homes were paying for multiple channels including dedicated children's channels. Providers (of which the largest is Foxtel) finally made a profit. With a regulatory obligation to spend only ten per cent of their programming budgets on local content, pay-TV children's channels were also largely filled with US programming, which was generally supplied by the parent company.

The Internet also contributed to the audience and advertising revenue fragmentation that occurred during Australia's digital transition. In a return to their role of marketers of new technology, children were drivers of Internet take-up in Australian homes. Homes with children were more likely to have an Internet connection than those without. By 2012, 79 per cent of Australian homes had Internet access and by 2013, 98 per cent of all Internet connections in Australia were broadband connections (ABS 2013b). As more Australian homes obtained broadband connections, audiences were able to view increasing amounts of self-scheduled television online including via broadcasters' own catch-up players.

While online services provided opportunities for broader distribution of all types of television including children's programmes, the challenge for all media content producers during this period was how to effectively monetize new means of distribution that did not rely on subscription or advertising models. In the early 2000s the arrival of the DVD saw television series become more widely available for purchase while the revenue raised became an important part of the funding model for adult and children's drama. The introduction of online catch-up players and TiVo and the T Box during the mid-2000s reduced demand for the DVD. This previously lucrative form of merchandising became a less significant part of the local drama production funding model, including for children's drama, as a result.

The transition to digital meant that for the first time since television's introduction, dedicated channels provided by both commercial organizations and the ABC served the child audience. The end of spectrum scarcity enabled the ABC to venture into multi-channelling with offerings that included, from 2009, a dedicated children's channel. After a false start that saw the ABC launch two digital channels in 2001, including the children's channel ABCKids (only to discontinue them two years later), the ABC had, by 2009, four digital channels on air including its children's channel, ABC3. The existence of ABC3 owes much to the ACTF, which was keen to take advantage of the opportunity for a niche service for the child audience facilitated by the digital transition.

The ACTF campaigned from 2006 onwards for a dedicated free-to-air children's channel in Australia, which would provide a specialized broadcasting outlet for both new and legacy Australian children's television. The status of the child audience and the perceived public value in this kind of children's channel enabled Jenny Buckland and the ABC's director of television Kim Dalton to persuade two successive and politically opposed governments to support the proposal. ABC3 was launched in November 2009 with an extra $67 million in tied taxpayer funding, although budget constraints meant the new channel relied heavily on imported programmes and repeats.

Meanwhile Australian advertiser-funded networks continued to schedule children's television programming at times when children were generally not watching television while becoming increasingly reluctant to pay the minimum licence fees required for programmes to be eligible for Screen Australia funding. Industry organization FACTS (later FreeTV) continued to put the case to government for the dismantling of the content quotas. The arrival of ABC3 provided additional impetus for the commercial networks to press for changes to their obligations to the child audience, despite advertiser-funded, free-to-television continuing to operate in an oligopolistic Australian market. A permanent 50 per cent cut to the licence fees commercial networks pay for spectrum access was made in 2012. This substantial cost reduction was not however accompanied by any meaningful requirements for increases in local content, including children's television.

The repeal of the Hawke government's cross-ownership rules was an important regulatory event that occurred just after the ACMA's establishment. The policy change precipitated a modest version of the sale of overpriced television assets, last seen when the same rules were first implemented. Barely had the legislation been passed when James Packer (who had inherited Channel Nine on his father Kerry Packer's death in 2005) sold half of PBL's assets including Channel Nine to investment company CVC Asia Pacific for $4.5 billion. Kerry Stokes swiftly divested himself of half of his media interests including Channel Seven into a new media company he co-owned with investment group KKR, in a deal which valued Seven's media interests at $4 billion (Schulz 2007).

Several important regulatory developments occurred during the digital transition that directly affected the capacity of Australian children's television to fulfil the functions with which it was invested by the public campaigns of the 1970s. First, the ACMA was established in 2005 as the Commonwealth organization responsible for the regulation of Australia's converged media environment, which includes broadcasting, telecommunications, radio communications and the Internet. The need for a deliberately converged media regulator confirms the rapid pace and the scale of the industrial, technological and economic changes that occurred during the digital transition.

The ACMA's duties include the implementation and policing of the CTS, a role which encompasses the classification of the C drama used to fill the networks' quota obligations. As a consequence, the organization plays an influential role in the production ecology, interpreting the criteria contained in the CTS and in this way setting the standards and production norms for C classified drama in Australia. The ACMA also has the power to penalize networks for non-compliance with their quota obligations, with the ability to fine or even suspend the licences of networks which fail to conform to the conditions of the licences.

The new ownership structures meant that Networks Seven and Nine were owned by equity investors whose sole interest in television was its ability to return a profit to its shareholders. The ownership changes coincided with both networks' increased use of animation to fill C drama quotas rather than live action drama, which tends to be a much more expensive genre. Network Ten however maintained its long-term commitment to live action drama and various amounts of in-house children's television production during the digital transition. A further refashioning of screen bodies occurred in 2008 when screen agencies the Australian Film Commission (AFC), the Film Finance Corporation (FFC) and Film Australia were replaced with new screen body Screen Australia, which is responsible for supporting Australian film, television, documentary and digital media makers.

As regulatory and screen bodies evolved during Australia's digital transition, long-standing policy settlements were also reshaped by technological change and industrial change. The Convergence Review of 2012 represented an attempt to reconsider and reframe Australia's media policy settings in digital regimes. The decision to allow the commercial networks to shift their children's quota obligations onto their multi-channels from January 2013 emerged from the recommendations of the Review.

Although the proliferation in television services in Australia led to an abundance of supply of programming including children's programmes, multi-channelling meant broadcasters had more schedules to fill. The increased need for content was accompanied by a downturn in advertising revenues that led to a concomitant reduction in programming budgets. Demand for Australian co-productions in the UK market contracted with the 2006 junk food advertising ban, which saw the UK's ITV withdraw entirely from commissioning new children's content and left the BBC as the main provider of new children's programmes in the UK.

In the mid-2000s as the UK production industry contracted, reduced licence fees led to an increased need for international co-production partnerships and presale agreements for Australian children's television. Producers became accustomed to having to stitch together complex funding arrangements during this period, arrangements which often led to a loss of creative autonomy as broadcasters in other territories became more involved in the production process. In these international market conditions, pan-global children's channels with access to their parent company's libraries operated from a position of strength, while exerting further downward pressures on licence fees. The trend towards globalized media industries encouraged the vertical integration of the screen production sector internationally and in Australia, as media companies attempted to manage the effects of digitization on their operations.

Conclusion

Since television's inception in 1956, Australian governments of various political persuasions have consistently but reluctantly intervened in the free market operation of the commercial television industry to ensure the provision of certain types of content that would not exist otherwise. They have often used 'honeymoon' periods to allow a service to establish, develop and pay for its infrastructure and set up costs before requiring more of stations. Post-establishment, governments have used mechanisms such as content quotas and financial subsidies to achieve cultural goals and safeguard supplies of content that the market would not otherwise support.

Public activism and the public's willingness to fund the measures required to ensure its production through their taxes, have guaranteed supplies of culturally specific, high-quality Australian children's television since the late 1970s. The public value of this television lies in its ability to situate Australian children within their own culture by providing identifiably Australian content and taking into account their development within society. Given the importance of the special status of the child audience to producers, broadcasters, regulator and the Australian public, children and their relationship with television are the focus of the next chapter.

Chapter 3

A Very Special Audience: Children and Television

The proliferation in television services and platforms that occurred during Australia's digital transition transformed the ways in which children watch and engage with television. The radical changes in children's television consumption during the digital transition did not and could not change the child audience's continuing and special status as a distinctive audience requiring special consideration and attention. Indeed they intensified this. In stark contrast to 1970s Australia however, contemporary children's television is characterized by abundance, rather than shortage of supply, with eight dedicated children's channels accessible across a variety of platforms. The Internet also became widely available from around 2006 onwards; children's use of the Internet quickly became an additional source of optimism, and anxiety, for adults.

This chapter considers in more detail the child audience in Australia and internationally, and the ways in which children's uses of television were transformed from 2001 to 2014 by the transition to a digital regime. Unlimited spectrum has considerable benefits for television and its audiences; nonetheless the fragmentation that characterized the digital transition reduced the ability of Australian children's television to situate Australian children within their own culture, leading to a reduction in its public value.

The Child Audience

One of the defining characteristics of contemporary western society is the construction of 'childhood' as a special psychological and physical developmental phase during which children can be protected from the more demanding conditions of the adult world (Aries 1962; Buckingham 2000; Postman 1994). Although globally, many children's lived experiences in poverty, war zones and refugee camps expose them to very different childhoods, the construction of the vulnerable child who requires adult protection is broadly accepted:

> There does seem to be agreement that in all societies round the world children are perceived to be the most vulnerable members: they are smaller and physically weaker, they need protection, care, feeding, fostering and socialization to the adult world; they lack life experience and knowledge; they think differently than do adults and they lack social and economical resources.
>
> (Lemish 2007: 70)

While this book has adopted the ACMA's definition of a child as under 14, childhood remains a contested state. Indeed the construction of childhood upon which Australian media policy relies has been criticized for its reliance on a dichotomous sense of the child as both vulnerable and in need of protection, while at the same time as highly corruptible (Hodge 1989; Keys 1999).

The corruption of children—through their commercialization, sexualization, obesity or exposure to pornography—is regularly exposed by media industries amid calls for their greater protection, while the same media industries are often blamed for their part in the corrupting processes (Buckingham 2000). The corrupted child quickly becomes an object of suspicion while retaining (if not increasing) their value to these media industries. No appalled commentary on Miley Cyrus's performance at the 2013 VH1 awards is complete without a reference to her former status as a Disney child star and fears about the effects of her behaviour on her impressionable young fans. Most, if not all, of the commentaries and analyses feature footage or stills from the same performance, while Cyrus's music dominates the charts.

The special status of the child audience and children's rights to certain types of media content have been enshrined since 1989 in the *UN Convention on The Rights of the Child*, which maintains that all governments should 'encourage the mass media to disseminate information and material of social and cultural benefit to the child' (UNESCO 1989). Nonetheless concerns about children and television often focus on the need to limit children's access to certain forms of television—through for example banning junk food advertising—rather than in safeguarding supplies of socially and culturally beneficial content. The CTS are unusual in their emphasis on providing television for children, rather than constraining their viewing

Despite the changes in television that have occurred since the CTS were first introduced in 1979, the felt need to protect the vulnerable child while providing children with culturally specific screen content continues to feature prominently in Australian policy discourse. The final report of the 2012 Convergence Review outlined three key areas in which government intervention in the media is justified, two of which specifically mention children. The report notes that regulatory intervention is required and justified in the public interest and to ensure provision of 'culturally significant forms of Australian content,' including children's programmes. Regulators should also act to prevent harm and ensure public expectations are met through the protection of the child from 'inappropriate content' (Convergence Review 2012: 30). The report noted, too, that during the consultation process, public submissions clearly conveyed a felt need to shield children from 'harmful or inappropriate content' (2012: 53).

While content may have replaced 'television' in policy discourse, in acknowledgement of the converged, multi-platform nature of television made for digital regimes, the report also reminds us that free-to-air television remains the most dominant form of television viewing and that 'viewers expect commercial and public broadcasters to provide content suitable for younger audiences at particular times' (2012: 54). Clearly children continue to provide powerful justification for regulatory intervention in the operations of the newly converged national media, just as they did in the earliest days of television in Australia.

Screen Australia reiterates the cultural value of Australian television in its 2011 *State of Play* report into the fate of local screen content in Australia's converged media environment. The organization maintains here that 'The delivery of quality drama, documentary and children's programming is seen as essential to the health and vitality of Australia's cultural life' (Screen Australia 2011: 19). Societal norms about children and Australian television are similarly reflected in Screen Australia's 2013 children's television research project *Child's Play* with:

> It is a community expectation that children have access to content that deals with stories, concepts and ideas relevant to them, including content that presents a uniquely Australian point of view.
>
> (2013a: 1)

Clearly children's needs remain central to any re-evaluation of policy settings for a converged media environment. Thus the special status of the child audience, and public expectations that regulators will ensure that audience's needs are met, continue to legitimize state intervention in television's free market operations. The cultural integrity of much of the children's television produced in Australia's converged and fragmented television system is proving difficult to retain however.

The International Context

Despite the importance of its role in situating children within their own culture, Australian children's television has been internationalized from the outset. As children's television fragmented across multiple platforms, international sales and co-production arrangements for Australian children's television became increasingly important during the digital transition. At the same time, highly commercialized, globalized children's television services distributed by large US-based corporations Nickelodeon, Disney and Cartoon Network increased their market penetration in international territories. The ways in which the US and the UK regard and make provision for the child audience are particularly important because of the effects they have on Australian production practices and norms.

Australia is not unique in its treatment of the child audience as a special and distinctive audience. Similar debates about the meaning of childhood, the child audience and the regulation of children's programming occur in the US and the UK, both key sources of the children's television that circulates in global markets. Although Australian, UK and US television cultures share the general principle that the child audience is a distinctive one, their broadcasting systems, regulatory regimes and the programmes that have emerged as a consequence differ from each other (Kunkel 2007; Lisosky 2001; Steemers 2010). The transition to digital regimes accentuated the differences between their respective television systems; the extent to which Australian policy-makers are prepared to commit direct and indirect state support to ensure supplies of local children's television is particularly unusual.

In America children were first constructed as a distinct audience by early radio advertisers to whom they were valuable because of their influence on their parents' purchasing decisions. They then became an equally valuable audience for emerging audio visual markets during the 1930s, including for the Disney Corporation. Thus US children's primary construction as an audio-visual audience was as consumers rather than citizens (Pecora 1998). Once television was introduced to America in the 1940s, the child audience was regarded by marketers as little more than a marketing tool to encourage families to buy television sets. As a result, programming designed to appeal to children and their families was scheduled in prime-time slots.

By the mid-1950s however Americans had bought 16 million television sets and children's television had moved out of prime time. The early 1960s saw Saturday morning schedules filled with inexpensive animations instead. The child audience was lucrative and much sought after here, on the grounds that children would tolerate endless repeats and children's programmes could be profitably syndicated. Best of all, children could be ruthlessly targeted by advertisers who wanted to sell products to their parents, through their nagging power (Melody 1973).

During the late 1960s, broader societal concerns about violence swept the US, exacerbated by the assassinations of President Kennedy in 1963 and both Martin Luther King and Robert Kennedy in 1968. The Dodd Senate Subcommittee Hearings 1961–64 investigated concerns about the violent television content produced by US networks and the business practices that accompanied them. Fears were also expressed to the hearings about the image of the US created abroad by its programme exports. Despite Dodd's high media profile, no final report or recommendations emerged from his investigations (Boddy 1997). In response to public disquiet about violence, President Johnson set up the National Commission on the Causes and Prevention of Violence in 1968. Its duties included examining the effects of television violence on audiences.

During this period, concerns about the child audience's unrelenting exposure to violent cartoons and the lack of quality children's television on offer to the child audience saw the creation of advocacy groups including Action for Children's Television in 1968. Public activism combined with the newly launched Public Broadcasting Service (PBS) and a more general fear among broadcasters of federal intervention led to the introduction of some better quality, innovative, child-centred programming such as *Sesame St* and *Mister Rogers' Neighborhood* (Mitroff & Herr Stephenson 2007). Children were still primarily regarded as consumers in America, however, with toy companies such as Mattel producing programmes like *Hot Wheels* (1969) in order to market their toy cars directly to children (Pecora1998). An Federal Communications Commission decision to lift restrictions on commercial airtime led to a rapid rise during the 1980s in the production of inexpensive animation featuring licenced characters, including *The Care Bears, My Little Pony* and *G.I. Joe*, programmes which were designed purely to sell merchandise (Mitroff & Herr Stephenson 2007).

It was not until 1990, after a decade of deregulation and heavily advertiser-sponsored children's programming, that the Children's Television Act required US networks to provide three hours a week of children's content, although it was only in 1996 that these requirements were formalized. Children's television is the only area where specific quotas are enforced on US broadcasters. Despite the historic lack of legislative attention paid to the networks, by the mid-2000s over 1,000 hours a week of children's content were transmitted in the US, most of it on cable channels. These subscription services pursue the contemporary child audience in the US, with abundant supplies of children's television available to homes which can afford to pay for it. On the other hand, the 15 million US homes without cable access rely on PBS and three hours a week of mandated content for their dedicated children's programmes (Mitroff & Herr Stephenson 2007).

Children's television in the US is dominated by media conglomerates and commercial television systems, with 77 per cent of children's viewing taking place on cable television. The involvement of vertically and horizontally integrated conglomerates, which frequently control content and carriage, makes the production of children's programmes a much more lucrative endeavour than it is in Australia. The ability to obtain revenue streams through subscription, advertising and merchandising while distributing programmes through global television networks increases profits (Alexander & Owers 2007).

US business models for children's programming are driven by companies like Disney whose capacity for branding, merchandising and encouraging the hybrid consumption of its products underpins the success of its children's programming (Bryman 2004). As Pecora notes, without significant public investment, children's television in the US will always be driven by commercial imperatives:

> The idea of children as a special audience, though historically important to American culture, simply cannot be supported in an economic system that allows no consideration for public service.
>
> (1998: 155)

With its commercial ethos and poorly funded public service television, the US provides models and processes for children's television that undermine Australia's treatment of children as a special audience deserving of free access to high-quality programming made with state support. The influence of US models of children's television can be seen in the popularity and proliferation of dedicated children's subscription services in both the UK and Australia. In an echo of the child-centred marketing strategies of 1950s America, children also play an important role in driving the uptake of pay-TV services in the UK, the US and Australia, making them an audience to be carefully courted.

In contrast, in the UK the dominance of a public broadcasting ethos ensured the presence of high-quality children's programming on first the BBC and later the free-to-air commercial network ITV from the 1950s onwards. Indeed the provision of specialized children's television is considered a defining principle of public service broadcasting. Although initially the BBC displayed a somewhat paternalistic attitude to the child audience accompanied by a 'widespread suspicion of the popular pleasures that television can afford' by the late 1960s a more child-centre concept of programming had emerged (Buckingham et al. 1999: 73). Despite its public service ethos, the BBC has never been reluctant to embrace merchandising opportunities, with *Muffin the Mule* generating £0.75m in revenues in 1952 (Oswell cited in Steemers 2010).

The BBC's larger funding base and increased capacity for risk-taking as a public service broadcaster have supported the provision of much grittier children's drama in the UK than might be seen in Australia. Long-running series include *Grange Hill* (1978–2008), which at its peak was watched by millions of children a week, and *Byker Grove* (1989–2006). Both these children's dramas dealt with confronting issues, including drug addiction, homosexuality, teenage pregnancy and rape (Messenger Davies 2010). Both were aimed at older children and both were axed in the mid-to-late 2000s.

The BBC remains the key provider of children's programming in the UK with two dedicated children's channels on air since 2006, CBBC and CBeebies for school-aged children and preschool children respectively. Since January 1 2013 the BBC has shown children's television only on its dedicated children's channels and their websites, with 1.8 million children aged 6–12 watching the CBBC channel and 900,000 accessing its website each week. The children's channels commission 45 per cent of their programmes from the independent production sector, investing over £100 million in UK-made content (Godwin 2013).

A belief in the capacity of children's television to positively influence the child audience is reflected in BBC controller of children's services Joe Godwin's claim that 'I want our content to inspire children to think or do things differently and to be active citizens' (2013: 20). With 30 dedicated children's channels on air in 2013, UK children are well served by both free-to-air television, particularly the BBC and by pay-TV services. In contrast, the commercial networks have had no content quotas for local children's television since these were removed by the Broadcasting Act 2003. The lack of quotas and the 2006 introduction of the junk food advertising ban in the UK dramatically reduced production levels of children's television during the mid-2000s. Nonetheless the UK remains a key source of the children's television appearing on Australian screens and an important co-production partner and market for Australian television producers.

Issues surrounding the need to situate children within their cultural context do not affect UK broadcasters as they do their Australian counterparts, due to local content being the norm on the UK public service channels. UK producers, then, can only dream of the levels of regulatory support and government funding enjoyed by their Australian counterparts while Australian producers may dream in turn of the BBC's £100m annual spend on children's television. The absence of state subsidies and content quotas (until the introduction of the animation tax scheme in 2012) mean the BBC is likely to remain the most important source of funding and air time for UK children's drama.

While childhood may be a constructed and contested state, legitimate concerns about television's effects on vulnerable children and the provision of age-appropriate content to the child exist in Australia, the UK and the USA. But different reinventions of broadcasting emerged in these television markets as their traditional services (and audiences) fragmented across multiple platforms. While some similarities can be seen between these various reinventions including downwards pressures on licence fees paid for children's programmes, each country's market is developing in a distinctive and non-coincident way as it embraces its multi-channel and digital future. Indeed digital regimes have underscored rather than reduced country by country differences. Given the interconnection and integration between programming production and distribution, the nature and scale of these adjustments are increasingly important for Australian producers producing television for these new digital markets.

Children on Television

Of course, children do not only watch the programming made especially for them, they also appear in these television programmes. Some of Australia's earliest children's variety programmes such as *The Happy Show* (1957–60) and *Channel 9 Pins* (1958–71) were filmed in front of a child audience with whom the presenters frequently interacted. Quiz shows, like *It's Academic* featuring school children, have been on air in Australia since the 1950s while Australia's most successful television export of the 1960s, *Skippy*, starred child actor Garry Pankhurst alongside its eponymous kangaroo.

In contemporary Australia children continue to appear as both fictional characters in live action drama (although in many children's dramas the actors playing children are not children at all but are in their late teens or early twenties) and as themselves in game shows, action, factual, and adventure programmes made for children.[1] Many children's shows that feature ordinary children, as opposed to child actors, fall in to the category of ordinary television, which can understood as television that is popular, unscripted, addresses the audience and which often features ordinary people doing fairly mundane things. Reality television can be seen as one element of this sort of television (Bonner 2003).

Australian policy-makers have always privileged drama over other genres, such as game shows or sport, in the achievement of national cultural representation. Drama, particularly live action drama, is also likely to be rarer and less supported without specific regulatory focus, because of the costs associated with its production. The privileging of the genre led to the creation of specific drama quotas in the CTS, while Screen Australia funding is only available for children's drama projects. Nonetheless television that is made for children and stars children who are not acting professionals has a strong presence in contemporary television schedules and is extremely popular with the child audience. Historically these forms of television did not exhibit some of the same characteristics of market failure as drama however and could be relied upon to be provided without the need for especial support.

In contemporary Australian schedules, series such as *Prank Patrol, Escape from Scorpion Island* and *Bindi's Bootcamp* on ABC3, *Kitchen Whiz* on Network Nine and *Camp Orange* on pay-TV channel Nickelodeon can all be classified as ordinary television made for the child audience. Ordinary television often rates well; children enjoy watching their peers on television. Indeed *Prank Patrol,* which is based on a Canadian format and features real children carrying out pranks on their unsuspecting peers, is the most popular programme on ABC3. The series also generates extensive audience engagement, with the ABC's online children's forum Chat-A-Box hosting an extensive *Prank Patrol* thread with over 800 users in 2012. The vast majority of children contributing to the thread are searching for information about how to appear on the show, although considerable online discussion surrounds the relative hotness of the host Scotty and the merit of the various pranks he organizes.

The societal need to protect the vulnerable child as television viewer applies equally to the vulnerable child on television, particularly children taking part in ordinary television. Thus in contrast to the role of much of the ordinary television made for adults, the intention of which is to expose, humiliate and shame those taking part (Turner 2010), the role of children's ordinary television is quite different. Australian children participate in ordinary television for fun, to prank their specially chosen friend in an amusing episode, or as competitors in activities that are often team-based, where loyalty, friendship and teamwork are highly valued. Children are not deliberately set up to fail, or to clash with other participants or to share something deeply revealing about themselves, which will then generate media content beyond the real time transmission of programme content.

In the interests of protecting the vulnerable child, television producers of ordinary television that features children assume certain gatekeeping responsibilities. Monica O'Brien, executive producer of Ambience Entertainment's *Kitchen Whiz* explains her production practices:

> We have a duty of care to the children who appear in our shows. We never penalise children for getting a question wrong, we never penalise them for trying. We are taking children out of their comfort zone and putting them on national TV and exposing them to potential ridicule if we're not careful. So we make sure they're appropriately dressed, we give them the best opportunity to come across at age appropriate levels, to not stand out as a genius nerd or dummy loser.
>
> (Personal communication June 12 2013)

Efforts to ensure children are protected extend to the auditioning process, when the production team are not deciding whether or not children should appear on the show, but are instead making efforts to fairly match them 'so they have the best opportunity to shine'. Similarly, according to O'Brien, the whole class takes part in filming, 'so that they've all participated and to reduce chances of kids being bullied for having taken part in a TV show'. As executive producer, she also makes changes in the edit suite to ensure children are not ridiculed, saying 'If a kid's pulled a weird expression, I cut it out even if it's good TV, because I don't want a child tormented (personal communication June 12 2013).

A similarly protective attitude towards the child participants prevails in the action and adventure competitive shows *Escape from Scorpion Island* (of which 112 episodes were made in Australia) and *Camp Orange*. Michael Bourchier, executive producer of *Escape from Scorpion Island* spoke to all the participating children's parents to make sure the children could cope with the programme's activities:

> Certainly we were very careful about who we chose. We not only interviewed the kids, I then flew all around the country and interviewed the parents as well and just had an absolutely open meeting with them saying 'I am here to tell you everything about what's going on, although there are some things to do with the games that I don't want you to tell your kids'. But I showed them what we would be doing and how the kids would be living. If any of them felt their kids couldn't handle it, then was the time to speak up.
>
> (Personal communication 23 April 2013)

Bourchier is clear that the activities and competitions in the show were designed to build resilience and confidence in the child participants:

> What the show really felt to me to be very much about was developing team work. Sure there were winners and losers on the day. One team would win and feel really proud of themselves but if you look at those episodes, the other team may be down at mouth but one of the kids would say 'but we can do better and tomorrow we will' so it was really about resilience.
>
> (Personal communication 23 April 2013)

As part of the activities in the series, children arrive from the UK (the cast is made up of a mixture of Australian and UK children; 10,000 application forms were downloaded for its first series) and are dropped by plane on to a North Queensland island the next day. The producers have a deliberate policy of non-elimination because the process is seen as being too hard on the children, so 'we never had people being voted off which would have been humiliating for kids. There was no humiliation' (Michael Bourchier personal communication 23 April 2013). Friendship and team work are encouraged, with cross-cultural friendship and understanding seen as a key outcome of children's participation in the show. Bourchier nonetheless describes producing the show as 'very nerve-wracking' because:

> You never entirely know what's going to happen. What you do want to make sure of is that everything is going to work, that the games we have constructed are actually do-able and that the team of people that you put together which you do in the innocence of

pre-production are not going to just swamp the other team. So you don't want one to be completely great and one to be absolutely hopeless if you're making 52 shows!

(Michael Bourchier personal communicaiton 23 April 2013)

A corresponding sense of needing to protect children and make sure their appearance on ordinary television is a positive one shaped the production of Nickelodeon's *Camp Orange*. As Nickelodeon Australia's head of network Hugh Baldwin explains

> The show features four teams of best friends, it's kid friendly and nobody gets voted off. We're very careful; it's about you and your best friend having a really good time playing a game, with challenges. But it's not about being the survivor. So the values are friendship and teamwork.
>
> (Personal communication June 12 2013)

As a result of their protected status and the particular values producers want their shows to convey, children do not fit nearly as usefully into what Mark Andrejevic (2004) describes as the symbiotic relationship that exists between entertainment coverage and the culture industries. This is partly because when children do appear in ordinary television, they are not subjected to the same processes of celebretization as adults. Children's television appearances rarely result in national fame, fleeting or otherwise and tend not to stimulate the creation of further media content.

So unlike adults in reality television such as the *Big Brother* or *MasterChef* franchises, children do not generally become the subject of tabloid press and television gossip stories, neither do they anchor advertising campaigns or provide marketing endorsements. They tend not to launch their own ranges of merchandise, release albums or write their autobiographies. Further, children's ordinary television (unlike animation or some live action drama) does not generate substantial ancillary revenues from merchandising. Neither does it lend itself to the pan-platform revenue raising enjoyed by ordinary television made for adults, such as voting costs, premium content subscriptions and i-tunes sales.

When children's celebrity has been amplified and commoditized, for example as Bindi Irwin's was in the months following her father Steve Irwin's death, these processes of celebretization tend to be accompanied by criticism and calls for protection of the vulnerable child. As Bindi Irwin was seen to replace Steve Irwin as the public face of Australia Zoo, media commentators wrote columns expressing concern for her well-being and decrying the heavy responsibility that lay on her young shoulders. This example from News International's now defunct online site *The Punch* is typical of the discourse at the time about the need to protect Bindi Irwin from exploitation:

> Bindi has been encouraged since the day her father was tragically killed, to be a Wild Life Warrior, to carry on his legacy, to keep the Australia Zoo running and send a message to an international public, that she is now the face of a going commercial concern. What

> an enormous weight for a ten year old girl. Where is her self-exploration, the whims and flights of a child's imagination that allow a kid to hanker to be a fireman one day and a world class gymnast the next? Where are her immature, messy, exploring the REAL world, childhood days?
>
> (Pascari 2009)

Such commentary assumes that the state of childhood uniformly provides children with opportunities for daydreaming, self-exploration and flights of imagination. For children living in poverty, slavery or war zones, Bindi's home-schooling and life in a zoo in the bosom of her family, interspersed with television filming and red carpet appearances, must appear positively utopian.

One Australian child subverted the production norm of protecting children on television when she used her appearance on an episode of Series Two of *Prank Patrol* in 2011 to celebretize herself. The child in question, Stevie-Lou, was introduced by the show's host as a 'singing, sewing, hand-standing all-rounder who can't wait to add pranking to her list of achievements'. Although Stevie-Lou was presented throughout the episode as an ordinary child whose appearance was due to her writing in to the show like everybody else, she was in fact a child actor who attended stage school in Melbourne.

After her appearance on *Prank Patrol*, Stevie-Lou adroitly used YouTube to help launch her career by posting a range of self-publicizing clips. These included the video of her appearance on *Prank Patrol*, a personal audition reel, a video of her singing live at a televised sporting event in Melbourne and a video of her debut single. So while the convention of protecting the child is maintained by the gatekeeping practices of programme producers, in this case the child herself bypassed adult controls. She used her television appearance to celebretize and promote her nascent career, choosing a transnational television distribution platform on which to do so.

Despite certain children's obvious resourcefulness, the opportunities for the monetization of additional content across multiple platforms are reduced when children are the stars of ordinary television. Without recourse to these increasingly common practices in contemporary media industries, much of the value of the programming in which children appear lies in its capacity to fill quota obligations and in its future iterations as a programme format. Ordinary television series and their formats will often work in international markets, thus increasing their potential revenues for the production company.

The *Camp Orange* (2005–) format was developed in Australia (and made in-house by the Nickelodeon production team) but has been used by Nickelodeon to make localized versions in other territories including the UK. Both the *Kitchen Whiz* format and Australian episodes of the series circulate in international markets including Asia and Europe. Some ordinary television series have been the subject of international co-productions, such as *Escape from Scorpion Island* (2006–13), which aired on the UK's BBC1 (and originated in the UK) as well as ABC3. Others, like *Bindi's Bootcamp* (2012–), a wildlife game show starring Bindi Irwin have achieved significant international distribution, in this case on the Discovery Channel.

The budgetary pressures producers face and the media globalization that facilitates trade in programme formats encourage the production of ordinary television for children over live action drama. This is particularly true when there are no quotas to fill or when drama quotas have been reached. Additional value for channels (and particularly for ABC3) from a format like *Prank Patrol* is derived from its capacity to introduce a young audience to the broadcaster's brand and ensure its relevance in a multi-channel environment and centrality as national broadcaster.

Despite the privileged status in national cultural representation accorded to live action drama, these other forms of locally made television featuring real children also instil a sense of cultural identity in young Australian audiences. Thus Australian state supports for children's television, including the CTS, recognize the role played by other forms of television including quiz shows in situating Australian children in their social and cultural context. Indeed programmes such as *Kitchen Whiz*, which use Australian children and questions from the Australian national curriculum, are frequently very culturally specific and thus speak directly to the Australian child audience.

In addition to the entrenched production norms around the protection of the child, other industry views affect the production of children's television. Children are widely believed to enjoy 'aspirational' viewing, or watching programmes featuring characters older than they are. Programmes made for the ABC do not require a C classification, and can therefore be more robust and less age specific. But programmes made for commercial networks must be age-specific in order to receive a C classification, without which they lose their value to a network only interested in filling its regulatory obligations. Producers maintain that the ACMA's insistence that C programmes should be age appropriate limits opportunities to increase programme audiences by producing television for family viewing (Screen Australia 2013a).

In an Australian television regime characterized by fragmentation, abundance of supply and the development of niche audiences, the special status of the child continues to shape regulatory instruments and programme production. The effects of a growing platform-agnosticism among Australian children on the public value of Australian children's television are considered next.

Children's Use of Television

The transformations in children's television that occurred during Australia's digital transition saw the child audience fragment across multiple platforms. Prior to this, the introduction of the VCR in 1980 and of pay-TV in 1995 had provided some freedom and niche television offerings for viewers. But it was Australia's transition to a multi-channel and multi-platformed digital regime from 2001 to 2014 that caused widespread and sustained fragmentation of audiences, of all ages, challenging long-standing business models.

In recognition of children's status as a special television audience and the impact on this audience of new media technologies, Australian regulators have paid close attention to the ways in which children and their families use electronic media since the early 1990s. In 1993 just before the introduction of pay-TV and in Australia's 'Year of the Family', the ABA released a report called *Living with Television*. The report provides a snapshot of Australian television on the brink of transformation, with free-to-air television the only form of television on offer at the time and VCRS in 83 per cent of homes. With the introduction of pay-TV and hence multi-channelling imminent, three out of four Australian viewers who had seen, read or heard something about the new service appeared suspicious of its offerings, with one respondent observing, 'from what I've heard of it, a choice of about 46 channels and overall the quality of it is very poor and tending towards pornographic' (Aisbett, Sheldon & Gibbs 1993: 29). Despite a lack of enthusiasm about subscription television that saw pay-TV services in Australia lose $3 billion in their first three years of operation, the report's authors turned out to be right in their cautious prediction that soon, 'television schedules may no longer determine when we get news and when we will be entertained' (Aisbett, Sheldon & Gibbs 1993: 1).

Three years later in 1996 free-to-air television still dominated children and teenagers' media consumption, although computers and computer gaming were gaining popularity. Another report commissioned by the ABA into children's and teenagers' use of electronic entertainment *Families and Electronic Entertainment* found children were watching 125 minutes a day of free-to-air with peak viewing time between 6pm and 9pm. At this time social networking was unknown in Australia; Messenger, MySpace and Facebook had yet to enter the vernacular. Mobile phone ownership was not even measured. The lack of viewing devices and platforms meant it was harder for children to escape the confines of broadcast television, and adults were able to exert some control over the television they watched. Seventy nine per cent of parents had rules that attempted to control their children's access to certain forms of television content, with sex and violence causing most concern (Cupitt & Stockbridge 1996).

Just over ten years later a report by newly created regulatory body the ACMA reflected the seismic shifts occurring in the media landscape during Australia's digital transition. The report's findings paint an extraordinarily different picture: by 2007 children's overall media consumption was up, but their free-to-air television viewing had declined. Ninety-eight per cent of Australian homes had at least one computer, and 97 per cent had at least two DVD players. The average Australian home also contained three mobile phones. Further, 90 per cent of homes had Internet access, with one in 10 children having Internet access in their bedrooms. Pay-TV was at 32 per cent market penetration with six dedicated children's services available to Australian audiences, including the BBC's CBeebies. Not only were children watching pay-TV, a further 24 minutes of their time was spent watching videos or DVDs. Children also dedicated 77 minutes a day to messaging, visiting social network sites and emailing (ACMA 2007a).

As a result of this audience fragmentation, while Australian children watched more television than ever in 2007, an erosion of the free-to-air broadcasters' analogue-era dominance of their viewing patterns occurred. From 2001 to 2006 in the 4–5pm slot on the commercial networks, when children's programmes are usually shown, the

0–14-year-old-age group dropped by 48 per cent, with children's drama attracting particularly low audiences. Children's programmes were watched on the ABC however, which had a dedicated children's 'block' or destination in the schedule every afternoon. Indeed in 2005 the top 20 rating children's programmes were all on the public service broadcaster. Of these top 20 programmes, 18 were animations; the only local live action drama the ABC was airing at the time was *Blue Water High*, which was produced by Noel Price and Southern Star Entertainment (now Endemol Australia).

The introduction of additional new services during the digital transition encouraged further changes in children's television consumption and increased fragmentation. Multi-channelling by free-to-air broadcasters saw the introduction of ABC3 in 2009; by 2011 Australian children were also enjoying the new free-to-air advertiser-funded multi-channels introduced by Networks Seven, Nine and Ten, including 7Mate, Gem and Eleven. Indeed in the 4pm dedicated children's timeslot, children were watching *The Drew Carey show, I Dream of Jeannie* and *The Ellen Degeneres Show* on these multi-channels, rather than the programmes made especially for them (Screen Australia 2011).

Australian children watch television in greatest numbers in the early evening, when most television is rated PG, although this is not the television made specifically for them. Most children, it seems are co-viewing with family members at this time, watching programmes like *The X Factor* and *Big Brother* (Screen Australia 2013a). From January 1 2013 as a result of recommendations that emerged from Australia's Convergence Review, the commercial networks were allowed to fill their children's quota obligations on their new channels, a move that created dedicated destinations for children's viewing on commercial networks for the first time.

Despite the frequency with which children watch television made for adults, contemporary Australian children still prefer to watch television made especially for them. They are not however, as concerned about its provenance as adults are, with 84 per cent saying they do not care if children's television is Australian or not. Nonetheless older children enjoy seeing places they recognize, characters that are like them or their friends and stories that could conceivably happen to them or their friends (Screen Australia 2013a). So in Australia's digital regime, localized, culturally relevant television programmes continue to appeal to the child audience and not just to the adults creating media policies for that audience.

During the digital transition an increasing number of children also began accessing programmes on multiple platforms, such as mobile devices and tablets. This platform mobility, combined with widespread access to broadband internet services, allowed channels including subscription services, to offer children's content online and on the move. In 2012 for example a quarter of all viewing of the second series of the live action drama *Dance Academy* took place on the ABC's online catch-up service iView. As Endemol Australia's head of children's production Noel Price explains:

> Basically you have three major windows with children—one is in the morning before school, the second is when they get home and the third is weekend mornings. It's clear that when you look at the total numbers viewing during these windows (on all free-to-air

> and digital channels), that the audience isn't there in significant numbers anymore. Even allowing for the addition of 'Catch Up' viewing on the various ABC and commercial network internet services (and it's not clear how many of these are new viewers or repeat viewers), total viewing numbers are dramatically down.
>
> (Personal communication June 12 2013)

From the mid-2000s the Internet also afforded the child audience new, transnational opportunities for viewing and interacting with television and its audiences, including access to social media and other forms of interpersonal communication, games and programme applications (apps). By 2010 there were 10.45 million Internet subscribers in Australia and children had become accustomed to multi-tasking, using computers, mobiles and tablets to access games and social media while watching television. Thirty one per cent of the older children engaging in second screen activities selected activities related to the series they were watching (Screen Australia 2013a), suggesting the Internet is contributing to an increased engagement with children's television, in digital regimes, even as the viewing figures decline.

For specialized children's channels, their online offerings are important for reinforcing their distinctive branding while retaining children within the channel's orbit. Since its 2009 launch, ABC3 has made multi-platformed delivery a priority, to the extent that Australian children can engage with ABC3 programmes and other content through the broadcast channel, the ABC3 website, its downloadable programme apps, online gaming, social media such as Twitter and Facebook and a dedicated YouTube channel. Merchandising, which includes DVD sales, offers an additional means of distribution, while raising revenue for the broadcaster. According to then controller of ABC3 Tim Brooke Hunt in 2013, children have very specific reasons for accessing online services:

> We find our audience goes online for two reasons. One is for catch-up TV; the other is to play games [...] So when we launch a new drama like Matchbox Pictures' *Nowhere Boys*, it will be accompanied by an interactive stand-alone game that is related to that series, made with a significant budget contributed by the distributor, ABC TV and Screen Australia.
>
> (Personal communication May 2 2013)

Joanna Werner, producer of ABC3's *Dance Academy* was aware of the importance of a web presence to the series and partnered with Brisbane-based Hoodlum Entertainment to produce extensive online resources. The website material features the series' actors, in three different versions representing first, second and third year, because the characters and their rooms change in each series. The resources also include dance tutorials, behind-the-scenes segments and days in the lives of the actors. *Dance Academy's* online resources won two Kidscreen awards for Best Television Companion Site for creators Hoodlum Entertainment in 2011 and 2013 respectively.

Children's subscription services in Australia also devote considerable resources to the multi-platform distribution of their offerings. In order to create brand familiarity among non-subscribing families, Disney and Nickelodeon make most of their short-form content freely available on line, along with games, apps, competitions and behind-the-scenes content. While these free offerings do not generate revenue, they raise the channel's profile among Australian children. According to Hugh Baldwin of Nickelodeon Australia:

> The kind of experience we provide doesn't stop with TV. Multi-platform is incredibly important. There's long form programming which is our priority content on the Foxtel platform and consists of full episodes of shows like *SpongeBob* and *Big Time Rush*. They might also be on other paid environments, like i-tunes. But typically those things are monetised. But clip based content and short form content, animation, live action, behind the scenes content always does really well. The website and our apps and games are out there for anyone. The long form content lives behind a wall.
>
> (Personal communication June 12 2013)

Children's pay-TV channels also use their 'second screen' offerings to retain viewers beyond the reach of the linear channel while reinforcing their brand. As one executive explains:

> We're always thinking about our non-linear strategy. We're always thinking multi-platform, we're always thinking second and third screen when developing ideas internally or when we're talking to producers about programme ideas. In Australia, the majority of viewing on tablets is still within the home. Children are still watching TV on the linear channel, then other content on the second screen, on tablets and mobiles if there's competition for the remote control. As content creators, we want to keep viewers within the world or our characters and stories; so online you've got extra, unique content, games, activities, etc. Most of our locally produced programming lends itself extremely well to being viewed on non-linear platforms like our own website and on YouTube as it's short form and bite-sized.
>
> (Personal communication June 12 2013)

Online offerings are also used to create visibility and brand awareness for the channel in Australia, with a view to attracting new subscribers. According to one executive:

> Our bread and butter is Foxtel subscribers, but reach and awareness is a challenge and you've got to get talked about in different ways. So you can watch most of our short form content on our website as it's promotional for the subscription TV platform and gets kids talking about our brands and our programming. And most of our Australian content is short form and perfect for non-linear consumption. We believe it drives subscription acting as a taster and helps build awareness.
>
> (Personal communication June 12 2013)

Dedicated children's services have embraced the opportunities created by the end of spectrum scarcity, to retain audiences within their world, by extending their offerings across multiple platforms. These changes in delivery have made it easier to retain the child audience on one platform or another. They have also, suggests one executive, affected the production of children's programmes:

> The tablet and mobiles have changed everything. There's concern that it cuts down on TV screen time, but much research suggests it's additive. Maybe children are watching the main telly less, but they're consuming more television content through another device. You always have to think of multi-platform—shows are being constructed with that in mind, being developed with companion apps in tandem; it's all about immersion with the world of our characters and stories.
>
> (Personal communication June 12 2013)

Clearly then during the digital transition, niche children's channels including subscriber services enthusiastically embraced digital strategies to pursue the child audience and strengthen their brands, using their multiplatform offerings to do so. Children, in turn, welcomed the opportunity for greater involvement with their television programmes and online interactions with one another. They also enjoy additional resources including games associated with that programming.

When multiple means of distribution become the norm for the child audience, individual television channels assume less relevance, and Australian children in future may look for programming by brand, rather than channel. According to Noel Price:

> Free-to-air TV is still a strong and highly influential medium but it's less and less so for kids in the 6–14 age group. As long as the free-to-air sector continues to perform healthily and quotas are in place there will continue to be Australian content on Australian television. But certainly in the teenage and children's area, the Internet is where they're all migrating. The Internet is still a work in progress. But there's absolutely no doubt that it's demanding that content creators think about different kinds of content presented in different kinds of ways and based on a very different relationship with the audience.
>
> (Personal communication June 12 2013)

As children's television in Australia became increasingly associated with platform-agnostic viewing practices, the lack of interest in the child audience shown by the commercial networks became even more noticeable. While Network Ten offers some of its children's programmes for catch up viewing, few additional online resources are provided for the child audience while Networks Seven and Nine do not offer catch up service for children at all.

None of Australia's free-to-air commercial networks appears to devote any resources to digital offerings for the child audience beyond their CTS mandated broadcasts. With little interest in capturing the child audience, or in establishing networks as branded destinations for young audiences, the lack of multi-platform activity by the commercial networks is unsurprising. It is also symptomatic of an inability to conceive of the child audience as anything other than a burden to broadcasters, in the face of global trends to the contrary.

Public Value and Fragmentation

Public agreement that children require protection from harmful television as well as the provision of age-appropriate, culturally specific television legitimizes public funding for the production of Australian children's television. But a platform-agnostic child audience with access to transnational television and other media content poses significant challenges to Australian policy-makers and programme producers. Yet a sense emerges in Australian regulatory reports that current ways of acting at policy level in children's television are susceptible to path dependency, that is, conditioned by long-standing corridors of thought where 'what has already been constructed shapes both what can be imagined and what can be achieved' (Murphy 2010: 452).

The contributions the CTS make to quality in children's television and to the achievement of the goals of national cultural representation are fundamental to their legitimacy. They are predicated on the understanding that '[c]hildren should have access to a variety of quality television programmes made specifically for them, including Australian drama and non-drama programmes' (ACMA 2009). While the CTS were created, in part, to help nurture Australian's developing television production industry, this policy instrument was designed primarily to ensure the child audience's particular needs were met and to contribute to the achievement of the goals of national cultural representation. So amid the transformations of the digital transition, the CTS arguably became one or both of an increasingly anachronistic measure and an increasingly important mechanism for safeguarding the production of Australian children's television in the new television settlements.

Despite the challenges to policy regimes and long-standing broadcasting and business norms presented by Australia's digital transition, convergence and the expansion of the bandwidth brought many significant benefits to the child audience. These included abundant supply, freedom from a linear schedule, multiple add-ons to the viewing experience, a dedicated public service broadcaster children's channel and a change in status to a highly sought after audience in the digital space. The introduction of ABC3, a free-to-air children's channel, meant Australian children had eight dedicated children's channels from which to choose by 2014.

On the other hand a number of developments that transformed Australian television during the digital transition were less advantageous for children's television. Multi-channelling led to audience fragmentation across all genres and a concomitant reduction in licence fees and programme budgets. Pressures on advertising revenues were compounded by the GFC in 2008. All networks became increasingly cost conscious in the acquittal of their C quota obligations, particularly Networks Seven and Nine. For some independent producers, any obligation to deliver public value in return for taxpayer-funded state support for children's television became subordinated to the need to secure programme commissions and production budgets. The rhetoric of national cultural representation as justification for increased state support for children's television at the time in fact masked an absolute commitment to internationalization and a need to make children's television that would circulate freely in global markets.

While producers and television markets struggled to adjust to the new circumstances of broadcasting, the introduction of ABC3 and increased pay-TV market penetration appeared to indicate that the child audience was benefitting from the digital revolution. Unfortunately abundant supply masked the subtle and gradual erosion in public value in Australian children's television, as much of the children's television produced from the mid-2000s failed to situate Australian children within their own culture. The use of animation rather than more expensive live action drama to fill C drama quotas on the commercial networks accelerated this loss of public value.

The special status of the child audience has not changed in Australia since the 1950s. The television produced for that special audience has. Much contemporary Australian children's television is less culturally specific than the television produced before the introduction of digital transmission, most notably the television used by the commercial networks to fill their C drama quota obligations.

Conclusion

The vulnerability of the child and the importance of the goals of national cultural representation remained a constant theme in policy debates during the digital transition. At this time however, regulatory and societal concerns shifted towards children's broader use of media, particularly the internet and the material (and individuals) to which children are exposed online. The loss of the separation of spheres of communication between adults and children led to fears that went beyond simply the access to unsuitable content such as pornography that the Internet facilitated. The loss of separation of spheres also changed the nature of communication between broadcasters and the child audiences, as well as between children and their peers, and children and adults.

In digital regimes adults remain preoccupied with the need to protect children from television just as they did in the 1950s. But the shift in attention from controlled sites, like television, to the less-controlled Internet and advertising sites demonstrates how some important elements in the relationship between children, broadcasters, producers and regulators changed during the digital transition. The target of parental, civic and regulatory concern became a broader mediasphere, with concerns about broadcast and subscription television far less prominent in these debates than they were before the creation of the online environment.

Nonetheless television remains central to Australian children's lives, regardless of the means of its distribution. The public value of high-quality children's television that speaks directly to the Australian child audience and situates them in their cultural context continues to legitimize taxpayer-funded state support for the genre. But this support entails a reciprocal obligation, that the production sector should ensure the cultural integrity of their children's programmes. The public as a key stakeholder in Australian children's television has the right to expect and indeed demand the creation of public value in children's television, in return for the state subsidies that continue to underpin its production in digital regimes.

Note

1 Children also appear in reality programming made for adults such as *SuperNanny, Toddlers and Tiaras, Wife Swap* and *Junior MasterChef,* however programmes made for adults are not the focus of attention here.

Chapter 4

The National Context: Australian Broadcasters, Children's Television and Public Value

This chapter's focus is the relationship between Australian broadcasters and local content for the child audience, particularly the ways in which institutional commissioning and scheduling practices affect the production slate and public value of Australian children's television. First the influence of the commercial networks on the production ecology is examined, and then the impact of fragmentation on the production and cultural integrity of Australian children's television. This chapter explains how the inability of the CTS to guarantee that programmes will be adequately resourced, combined with a certain lack of rigour in their application, undermined their efficacy as a policy instrument during the digital transition. The effects that the specialized children's channels supplied by both public service broadcaster the ABC, and pan-global commercial providers such as Disney and Nickelodeon, have on the production ecology also form part of the analysis.

The Broadcasters

At the end of Australia's transition to a digital regime, free-to-air broadcasting consisted of three advertiser-funded networks Seven, Nine and Ten and two public service broadcasters, the ABC and SBS. These broadcasters each provide at least two multi-channel services including, in the ABC's case, a dedicated children's channel. Pay-TV providers, of which the largest is Foxtel, offer eight children's services; these include local offerings from pan-global providers Disney, Nickelodeon and Cartoon Network. All the children's channels supplement their linear schedules with extensive multi-platform offerings and, in the ABC's case, the online catch-up player iView.

Although the digital transition led to abundant supplies of multi-platform, self-scheduled, interactive television for Australian children, the free-to-air commercial networks remain at the heart of the production ecology, because of their legislated need for children's television. Multi-cultural public service broadcaster SBS has a different remit and tends not to show children's content. Indigenous service NITV broadcasts as a channel of SBS, screening very small amounts of children's content, aimed specifically at an Indigenous audience. The pay-TV channels are obliged to spend just 10 per cent of their programming budgets on local content, if they are primarily drama channels. They produce and acquire only small amounts of local children's television, relying on the resources of their US-based parent companies for their programming needs.

In contrast to Australia's commercial networks, the ABC is not bound by the CTS, although catering to the child audience's needs is seen as an important part of its public service remit.

The ABC's charter is generally considered an adequate safeguard for its obligations to the child audience, although children are not mentioned specifically. Neither does the charter contain any quotas for children's content or specific provision for Australian drama. It proposes instead that the ABC should broadcast programmes 'that contribute to a sense of national identity and inform and entertain' and are 'of an educational nature' (ABC 1983). The ABC's Code of Practice, the document which contains its editorial guidelines, suggests children's programmes should be enjoyable and enriching but contains little in the way of concrete detail. So while the code emphasizes the need to protect children and young people and to take care of their dignity, and physical and emotional welfare, it does not contain any specific requirements for particular amounts of genre-specific content (ABC 2014).

In Australia then, in contrast to the UK and US, public service broadcasting ideology is expressed and applied to commercial free-to-air channels through the CTS, rather than to the country's public service broadcaster. Since the 2009 launch of its dedicated children's channel however, the ABC has been the local broadcaster with the greatest need for children's content. Therefore the ways in which the ABC commissions and acquires Australian children's television also have a direct bearing on its public value.

Australia's Commercial Networks and Children's Television

Australia's free-to-air commercial networks are all bound by the conditions of their licences to conform to the CTS quotas for C classified content. They are obligated to transmit 240 hours of C programming each year, and 120 hours of P programming. Of the C programming, 50 per cent must be Australian, 32 hours each year must be first-run Australian drama and eight hours can be repeat C drama. Demand for Australian children's television is thus entirely artificially created. Although networks consistently conform to their quota requirements, no commercial network exceeded its mandated obligations to the child audience between 2003 and 2008 (Screen Australia 2011). As reluctant institutional gatekeepers responsible for the commissioning, financing and scheduling of C classified children's programmes, Australia's commercial networks are enormously influential in the shaping of contemporary production norms.

The business model upon which Australian free-to-air commercial television was built relies on advertising spot sales as its primary source of revenues. Under such a business model, market failure for children's television is inevitable, given the costs involved in its production and the lower audience numbers it attracts. The child audience on free-to-air commercial channels simply does not generate sufficient advertising revenue to make children's drama attractive to these broadcasters, with most Australian children's drama costing over $500,000 per hour. Existing difficulties in generating advertising revenue are compounded by the advertising restrictions the CTS place around children's television, with no more than seven minutes of commercials, station promotions and identifications permitted in each 30-minute programming block (ACMA 2009).

Unanimous agreement exists among regulators, producers and the networks themselves that without the CTS in place, demand for local children's content, particularly drama, would plummet. Indeed a 2012 modelling exercise undertaken by PriceWaterhouseCoopers to evaluate the impact of content quotas on the local production sector concluded that 'without the requirements [of the CTS] no Australian children's programming would be funded by the commercial FTA operators' (PriceWaterhouseCoopers 2012).

The commercial networks' quota obligations for first-run Australian drama can be filled using either live action drama (one of the most expensive genres to produce) or animation (one of the least expensive genres to produce). The CTS, the Australian Content Standard and Screen Australia all include animation within their definition of drama, a definition that became extremely significant during the digital transition. As audiences and advertising revenues fragmented across multiple platforms, commercial networks reduced the licence fees they were prepared to pay for children's television. As animation is generally less expensive to produce than live action drama, animation immediately gained a competitive advantage.

From January 1 2013 Australia's commercial networks were given permission to schedule the children's quotas mandated by the CTS on their multi-channels, rather than their main channels, for the first time. Prior to this, advocates of children's television, including the ACTF, consistently argued that commercial networks poorly promoted and scheduled their mandated children's offerings in order to confuse and discourage the child audience. They were then able to advance the argument that children's content quotas are pointless, because children do not want to watch the type of programmes created by the CTS.

Mixed reactions greeted the decision to give networks permission to move their children's programming from their main channels. Some initial concerns were expressed in the production industry that networks expect to pay reduced licence fees for their multi-channel programming and this regulatory concession would further drive down the cost of children's programmes. In contrast Stuart Paul, assistant manager of content monitoring and review at the ACMA suggested that the creation of dedicated children's destinations would allow the child audience to benefit from consistency and predictability in the scheduling of children's programming.

> Once the shift goes across to the non-core channels we're envisaging there will be stability for those C and P programmes. And it really does create a time and a place where parents and children can watch this content.
>
> (Stuart Paul, personal communication May 2 2013)

Cherrie Bottger, head of children's television, Network Ten agrees that the decision was helpful because:

> It gives flexibility, allowing a network to create its own children's block. Now we're permitted to transmit on multi-channels, you can create a destination for the kids and they'll find you. It's been an excellent decision that's evolved out of the Convergence

> Review. In the past major sporting and news events also displaced kids' programming but not anymore. The created destination airs without disruption and I think that's very important.
>
> (Personal communication October 3 2013)

The Convergence Review's other recommendation for children's television, to double the quota requirements, was ignored entirely. The 50 per cent licence fee reduction the networks were granted in 2012 was widely seen however as further justification for their public service obligations, even though the cut was not accompanied by any formalized provision for local content.

Australia's free-to-air commercial networks have little interest in exploiting their children's programmes and brands through, for example, multi-platform distribution, merchandising or the repurposing of content. As television providers like Disney and the BBC, which are not directly funded by spot advertising, responded to multi-channelling and fragmentation by maximizing opportunities to monetize their children's television properties, Australian free-to-air commercial networks pursued the very opposite end. They effectively rented transmissions of Australian children's programmes, particularly drama, to exactly fill their quota obligations. In these economic circumstances the production company is left to monetize their C classified drama series through multiple windows, as opposed to the local broadcaster.

The artificial demand generated by the CTS underpins the production of the majority of the Australian children's television produced each year. While some children's programmes are produced in-house, particularly by Network Ten, drama is generally sourced from specialized independent production companies. These arrangements mean that the burden of organising production funding falls largely on the producer but the financial risk is spread between the producer, distributor, network and taxpayer. In spite of their status as reluctant investors, the networks are crucial to the viability of the children's production sector in Australia both because of their initial investment and because their involvement also triggers the essential state-funding supports that underwrite production.

Direct investment funding for children's television (excluding reality and factual) is provided by organizations such as Screen Australia and the ACTF, through direct investment and distribution advances, once the series has secured a presale to an Australian broadcaster. Children's television is only eligible for Screen Australia funding if the networks agree to pay minimum licence fees, which were \$105,000 per half hour in 2013. Available funding is capped at \$3 million on a 26 x half hour episode series or \$1.6 million for 13 episodes. Screen Australia and ACTF investment is a vital part of the stitching together of production budgets and the financing of locally produced children's television. The involvement of these state-funded agencies is also a marker of quality; it suggests minimum licence fees have been paid and the production is better resourced as a result.

Further support for Australian children's television is provided through the tax scheme the producer offset, which is not associated with a requirement for minimum licence fees but is based on the Qualifying Australian Production Expenditure (QAPE) component of the production budget. In practice, for children's television this is slightly less than 20 per cent of an Australian budget, and can be claimed for 65 hours of programming. The producer offset is widely regarded in the industry as an effective and important form of state subvention for all local content production, but is set at only 20 per cent for children's television, as opposed to 40 per cent for Australian films.

The introduction of the producer offset in 2006 enabled productions, including cheaper forms of children's drama (primarily animation), to access a form of state subsidy. (Pre-2006 they were not eligible for Screen Australia funding because the broadcaster did not pay the minimum licence fee.) Despite the importance of the producer offset in subsidizing Australian children's television, the new arrangements had the unfortunate effect of contributing to the erosion of its public value. Once the animation deliberately designed for distribution in global markets became eligible for state subsidy, live action drama was rendered an even more vulnerable genre.

Under the current funding model local broadcasters and state agencies usually provide approximately half the necessary production finance, so further private and public service revenue must be obtained by producers. Such finance generally comes from co-production, presale and distributions arrangements with pay-TV and public service broadcasting channels. Thus policy coexists with generous financial state support designed to lead to further private investment from local and international broadcasters and distributors.

Content Quotas and Public Value in Children's Television

Despite the uniformity of the CTS quotas and associated funding structures, considerable network-by-network differences exist in the acquittal of CTS quota obligations. These differences are symptomatic of the levels of investment networks were prepared to put into children's television during the digital transition. A network's institutional priorities therefore have a profound impact on the range, quality and public value of Australian children's television. A number of factors contribute to the differences in the children's programmes that are made by each network in the fulfilment of ostensibly identical quota obligations, and hence their public value. The network's willingness to pay minimum licence fees for C drama is a critical factor; it is extremely difficult to produce children's live action drama without Screen Australia investment. A network's commitment to investing in the production of its own children's television in-house will inevitably affect the quality and cultural specificity of its children's offerings. Finally the networks' scheduling and promotion of children's television directly affect the ability of Australian children to find programmes in the schedules and hence those programmes' cultural visibility.

Since the 1980s, live action drama has most often attracted minimum licence fees from commercial networks and direct state investment from screen funding bodies. Drama enjoys a superior status in the achievement of the goals of national cultural representation but has higher production costs, while production itself can be difficult to divide across several territories. For many years following the introduction of the CTS, Australia's commercial networks commissioned award-winning, high-quality live action drama as part of their C drama obligations. Examples of culturally specific children's drama with high production values include *Round the Twist* (1989–2000) for Network Seven; *Saddle Club* (2001–07), *Mortified* (2006–07) and *Lockie Leonard* (2007–10) for Network Nine; and *Wicked Science* (2004–06), *H2O: Just Add Water* (2006–08), *Me and My Monsters* (2010–11), *The Elephant Princess* (2008–10) and *Mako Island of Secrets* (2012) for Network Ten.

These series went on to sell to broadcasters all over the world and generated significant export revenues. Many also received critical acclaim and national and international awards. They offered Australian children the culturally specific television with high production values demanded by the Australian public prior to the introduction of the CTS. Their demonstrated ability to fulfil Australian cultural policy objectives meant the state investment that underpinned their production secured public value for the Australian taxpayer, even if the networks' scheduling and promotion practices reduced their audience numbers. During the digital transition, however, new patterns emerged in the commissioning behaviours of Australia's commercial networks. The networks' reduced institutional commitment to the child audience helped shape new settlements in Australian children's television characterized by lower licence fees, increased production levels of animation as well as the need for greater international investment in programmes.

The reluctance of Networks Seven and Nine to pay Screen Australia minimum licence fees causes significant network-by-network variations in the commissioning of C drama. While Network Ten's commitment to high-quality, Screen Australia funded live action drama endured, the other networks' attempts to minimize programme costs encouraged the production of animation, rather than live action drama, during the digital transition. The 2006 producer offset taxation subsidy reinforced this market trend, rather than containing it, by providing tax relief for the first time for the production of inexpensive animation.

For networks which simply want to fill the C drama quotas as cheaply as possible, animation is a much more competitive product than live action drama. Animation is often cheaper to make while production can be split easily across two or more countries, making investment easier to secure. According to ABC3 controller of children's television 2010–13 Tim Brooke Hunt:

> There are two categories of animation producers in this country. There are those who want to make high-quality animation, with a majority of creative Australian elements, while others are happy to be a minority partner in the production of international animated series where they might be spending around 35% of the budget here. Most Australian commercial broadcasters are happy with the latter approach.
>
> (Personal communication June 12 2013)

Thus policy settings that were designed to achieve the goals of national cultural representation began, during the digital transition, to facilitate the production of animation often deliberately designed to circulate in international markets.

Analysis of the children's television commissioned during the latter half of the digital transition reveals the various ways the networks filled their C drama quotas. Between 2006 and 2013 Network Ten invested in ten live action drama series made with the Screen Australia funding[1] that suggests minimum licence fees were paid. While Network Nine maintained a clear commitment to live action drama between 2006 and 2009, only three titles *Stormworld* (2006), two series of *Lockie Leonard* (2007/8) and *A Gurlswurld* (2009) accessed Screen Australia funding. Network Nine also paid Screen Australia licence fees for four animated titles from 2006–09.

Between 2006 and 2011 Network Seven relied heavily on animation in the acquittal of its C drama obligations. During this period, the network commissioned only three live action dramas, *Castaway, Timetrackers* and *Trapped* with a fourth series, *In Your Dreams*—Network Seven's only Screen Australia-funded series—in 2013. Two animated telemovies, *Gumnutz* and *The Adventures of Charlotte and Henry* also received Screen Australia funding in 2006 and 2007 respectively; no minimum licence fees are attached to telemovies, and each hour is weighted at three hours of the C drama quota.

Network Seven is recognized in the industry for its consistent refusal to pay Screen Australia minimum licence fees, while Network Nine has not accessed Screen Australia funding for any of its children's C drama series since 2009. The absence of Screen Australia funding suggests Network Nine has made an institutional decision not to pay minimum licence fees for its C drama quotas. Animation is therefore likely to become Nine's preferred means of filling its C drama quota. Networks Seven and Nine's enthusiasm for using animation to fulfil their CTS C drama obligations led to a slow decline in the levels of live action drama commissioned by Australia's advertiser-funded broadcasters from the mid-2000s.

Analysis of the ACMA C drama classification data from 2006 to 2012 reveals that the first release Australian C drama quota across all three commercial networks was filled with 274 hours of live action drama, and 312.5 hours of animation, with live action drama production clearly in the minority (ACMA 2011). Network-by-network analysis suggests Network Ten used 64 per cent live action drama and 36 per cent animation; Network Nine used 58 per cent live action drama and 42 per cent animation; and Network Seven used 14 per cent live action drama and 86 per cent animation in the filling of their C drama quotas.

The animation that is increasingly relied on in the filling of C drama quotas is almost always made with international partners for a global market. Canada has been a prominent co-production partner for Australian producers of live action drama and, particularly, animation for many years. The Canadian production industry benefits from domestic production incentives, a well-developed local skills base and expertise, robust local broadcasters and an effective co-production treaty with Australia. Malaysia, Korea and Singapore have also more recently become key partners on Australian animation productions. They have been encouraged to do so by their own governments' investment in digital production industries and their increasing skills bases. For these countries, Australia is well positioned to offer both financial investment and production expertise for their developing industries, while their investment and lower labour costs offset Australian production costs.

As independent producer Patrick Egerton explains:

> Off shoring is just a reality for most people and traditionally those kinds of co-productions occur between Europe and Australia, or Canada and Australia, where you have treaties in place and subsidies in each of those territories so everyone can bring their own pile of cash to the table. Increasingly people are looking to offshore in to Asia because there's an emerging skill base; in some places a growing skills base and some pretty attractive subsidies as well.
>
> (Personal communication June 12 2013)

The animated series engendered by these kinds of international partnerships will generally avoid Australian references and will be made to circulate easily in international markets. Even when animation is based on Australian books, for example *Animalia* and *Pearlie*, the characters in the series frequently are given American accents—the price the producer has to pay in order to secure the production funding. So co-production arrangements can mean that the animation used to fill C drama obligations may lack overt markers of Australian-ness even when it is based on original Australian ideas. Original Australian ideas do not necessarily form the basis, however, of many of the animated dramas used to fill C drama quotas during the digital transition.

Many of the animated series commissioned by the commercial networks from 2006 onwards as part of their C drama content obligations are not based on Australian stories. Network Nine's *Dennis and Gnasher* (2009) animation is based on UK comic *The Beano's* longest-running comic strip *Dennis the Menace* and was made in partnership with the BBC. Network Seven's C drama animation *Sea Princesses* (2009) (also known as *Princesas Do Mar*) is based on Brazilian picture books and is a co-production with Spain. Similarly *Sally Bollywood Super Detective* (2009), also on Network Seven, is based on French picture books and is a co-production with France. In these sorts of cases the majority of the production funding is likely to be provided by the international partners, further reducing the creative autonomy of the Australian producer and the likelihood of the series having any culturally specific relevance to Australia.

These sorts of internationally funded animations, which do not make any obvious contributions to the goals of national cultural representation, nor speak directly to the Australian child audience, nonetheless qualify for a C drama classification. They can therefore be used to fill quota obligations, in what those who lobbied and campaigned for high-quality, culturally specific content for Australian children might consider something of a remodelling of the rules. According to Jenny Brigg, manager of content and review at the ACMA, creative control is more significant as a marker of Australian-ness than the accents children hear because:

> Australia is a multi-cultural country. It's entirely possible for someone to be Australian and have an accent of any kind you can imagine. So we have taken the approach both for children's and for adult that it is about who's creating it—creative control as well as creative talent, rather than legislating for accents.
>
> (Jenny Brigg personal communication May 2 2013)

The ACMA appears to be resigned to the commercial networks' use of deliberately internationalized animation to fill their C drama quotas, which removes one important mechanism that is intended to create and safeguard public value in children's television.

Tensions inevitably exist between producers of live action drama and animation in the competition for commissions and resources in the field of cultural production, where suppliers vastly outnumber outlets for children's television. Producers of animation and studio-based entertainment question the culturally superior status that years of government subvention have afforded to live action drama. Live action drama producers recognize the genre is threatened by the networks' reluctance to pay minimum licence fees and the ease with which animation can be used to fill quota obligations. Further, without regulatory intervention, the economics of contemporary children's television production and commercial television suggest the skewing of the ratios between animation and drama is likely to become more, rather than less, pronounced in future. As independent producer Donna Andrews observes, '[I]t's getting harder and harder to do the high-end Australian only productions. Financing continues to be an ongoing challenge as commissioning dollars decline or are divided further between more projects' (personal communication May 3 2013).

The practice of Networks Seven and Nine of consistently reducing their investment in C drama during the digital transition appears similarly entrenched. The impact of reduced funding levels suggests the production of live action drama will decline further. According to Noel Price, producer of Endemol Australia's *In Your Dreams*:

> The networks are increasingly reluctant to pay the sorts of licence fees that trigger Screen Australia subsidies and without healthy levels of both sources of funding the great tradition of Australian live action children's drama looks precarious to say the least.
>
> (Personal communication June 12 2013)

Network Ten's sustained commitment to the provision of high-quality, culturally specific children's television led to the creation of internationally successful live action drama with public value, but much depends on the network's resourcing of the genre in a digital regime. As Price observes:

> How long things can continue as they have in the past has a big question mark over it, particularly as the audience for post pre-school TV is moving with increasing rapidity away from free-to-air TV and onto the Internet. The basic TV model we've known for

> the last 30 years is unravelling at a rate of knots and somehow we'll all have to adapt to that fact.
>
> (Personal communication June 12 2013)

Network Ten head of children's television Cherie Bottger is widely regarded in the industry as a steadfast advocate and supporter of Australian children's television, particularly live action drama. She describes the realities of filling children's television quotas in contemporary Australia:

> We commission a project at least 18 months to 2 years out. That's how long it takes to get your financing, series break down, casting, synopsis of all episodes, production and then post production. So I've got to work that far ahead to make sure I get my delivery of quota in my triennium. It's very costly to produce a television series and nobody is sitting out there today with a series on the shelf waiting for a broadcaster to come along.
>
> (Personal communication November 13 2013)

In 2013, Ten remained the only network to supplement its commissioned programmes with the in-house production of two children's series, *Totally Wild* (1992–) and the science series *Scope* (2005–). Both are made in Ten's Brisbane studios, as is the preschool programme, *Wurrawhy*. The Network also plays *Toasted TV*, which consists largely of studio-based hostings and imported animation for three hours each morning on its multi-channel 11. Network Ten's treatment of its child audience for many years provides a model for the provision of high-quality, Australian children's television by the commercial networks. It also illustrates the profound impact that institutional decision making has on the filling of CTS quotas.

The cost squeeze on children's television is however a feature of digital regimes. Broadcasters are exerting a downward pressure on licence fees for children's television, because of fragmentation and the propensity of large US production studios to flood the market with their branded programmes. At the same time, budgets have gone up due to increased costs and the networks' expectations for high-quality programming. The resultant cost squeeze combined with the networks' refusal to commit to more than one series at a time made raising production funding increasingly difficult and complicated during the digital transition.

Budgets are also affected because Australian children's television (with the notable exception of preschool properties such as the ABC's *Bananas in Pyjamas* and *The Wiggles*) generally lacks sufficient production volume to achieve the brand recognition that underpins successful merchandising. This lack of brand recognition is compounded by the commercial networks' reluctance to promote children's programmes on air, further reducing their cultural visibility and producers' opportunities to monetize content through merchandising.

The production and classification norms that developed during the digital transition suggest that the C drama classification is no longer synonymous with high-quality

Australian content. Indeed from 2001 to 2014 Screen Australia involvement began to indicate high production standards and cultural specificity more reliably than the policy instrument specifically designed to create public value in children's television. The use of live action drama to fill C drama quotas declined inexorably during the digital transition, as did the public value of much of the children's television produced to fill C drama quotas. The likelihood at this stage of either of these trends being reversed appears unlikely.

The ABC: Public Service Broadcasting and Public Value in Children's Television

Further state support for Australian children's television is provided by the publicly funded ABC, which relies on government support and revenue from its commercial arm ABC Commercial to maintain its services. The ABC has struggled with limited funding to fulfil the myriad obligations of its charter for many years (Given 2003). In 2013–14, the ABC received funding of $1.05 billion, as part of its base funding of $2.5 billion over the next triennium funding period, including $30m over three years to meet the growing demand for its digital services. In January 2014, communications minister Malcolm Turnbull announced a review into the ABC and SBS's efficiency, with the review expected to clarify the costs of the broadcasters and 'provide options for more efficient delivery of services' (Department of Communications 2014). By May 2014, cuts to the ABC and SBS's budgets of 1 percent had been announced, cuts which were described by Malcom Turnbull as a 'down payment' on the efficiency review's recommendations.

The ABC has been able to supplement its government funding to some extent through ABC Commercial, although only $1.1 million was generated for the broadcaster in 2012–13, compared with over $19 million in 2005–06 (ABC 2013). Commercial activities include DVD sales; however a softening of demand occurred with the increased popularity of PVRs and iView during the digital transition. The merchandising of preschool properties, including *Play School, Charlie and Lola* and *Bananas in Pyjamas,* provides other revenue streams. So the ABC, like the BBC, relies on sales and merchandising of its programmes to partially fund its operations, although these opportunities appear to lie largely with its established preschool properties.

The ABC's existing funding pressures were compounded by Australia's digital transition and the need to deliver its content across multiple platforms. These platforms eventually included four digital television channels, digital radio, the online catch-up player iView and extensive news and current affairs online services. The ABC's multi-platform services illustrate how the digital transition enabled the public service broadcaster to increase the range and reach of its content. Australian audiences embraced the new platforms, with an average of 5.3 million monthly plays on iView in 2012 when, for the first time, the majority were on mobile devices (ABC 2013). From February 2014, when the ABC moved all its children's programming from ABC1, the broadcaster's children's offerings consisted of the school-aged children's channel ABC3, on air from 6am to 9pm and preschool service ABC4Kids on ABC2 from 6am to 7pm. In 2012–13 ABC3 was the number one ranked channel among children aged 5–12 years during the day, with a 30.6 per cent metropolitan free-to-air daytime share and a regional daytime free-to-air share of 33.8 per cent (ABC 2013).

With its own children's channel and a significant preschool presence on ABC2, the ABC became, during the digital transition, the Australian broadcaster with the greatest need for children's programmes. It, therefore, has a very influential role in the production and cultural visibility of Australian children's television. Despite limitations on its ability to acquire and commission local children's television due to budgetary constraints, and a concomitant reliance on repeats and imports, by 2012 the broadcaster announced it had achieved its initial goal of 50 percent Australian content on ABC3 and 25 per cent on ABC4kids (ABC 2012). With a programming budget of around $21 million per annum, the ABC tends to outsource most of its children's commissions to independent producers. Its in-house production consists of relatively low-cost preschool shows such as *Play School* and hosted segments such as *Giggle and Hoot*. The channel also endeavours to secure international co-financing for all of its commissioned content, further reducing its cost to the broadcaster (Tim Brooke Hunt personal communication May 2 2013).

The ABC's charter is considered an adequate safeguard for its children's content, despite the absence of quotas for children's television. During the digital transition but prior to the establishment of ABC3, the ABC produced much smaller amounts of first-run children's programmes each year than its commercial counterparts, relying heavily on imports and repeats to fill its two-hour afternoon children's block. An apparent reluctance to commit resources to the production of local children's content also characterized the ABC's initial foray into multi-channelling for the child audience.

In 2001 the ABC launched its first children's channel ABCKids and a second youth channel, Fly TV, both of which used the same spectrum at different times of the day. The broadcaster allocated only $7 million in additional funding for both channels, which meant ABCKids' schedule was filled largely with acquired rather than commissioned content and relied heavily on repeats. Producer Donna Andrews, who was recruited from a background in commercial and pay-TV to establish ABCKids, explains how innovative the channel was, despite its lack of resources:

> At the time there was no packaging around children's programs, they didn't call themselves ABC Kids. The ABC just went to children's programs, and then went off again. So we packaged and branded for the first time and created a dedicated destination. In the end you had Nick, Disney and Cartoon network here, all of which branded themselves very strongly. And the ABC had the parents' blessing but didn't necessarily have the kids! So it was important to package and brand the kids destination.
>
> (Donna Andrews personal communication June 12 2013)

ABCKids represented the first time the ABC had deliberately branded its children's programmes and repurposed existing content in the creation of a destination for the child audience. In doing so, the ABC started both to mimic and to compete with dedicated children's subscription services in Australia.

Despite the high level of repeats, the ABC's children's channel attracted 500,000 viewers per month in the early 2000s, a significant number given the low digital market penetration at the time (less than 3 per cent in Australian households). Digital uptake was slow in Australia due to policy settings designed to appease pay-TV operators and which prevented the ABC's digital channels transmitting news, drama or sport (Inglis 2006). ABCKids was taken off air in 2003 with the ABC blaming its demise on a lack of money, after a $17 million request for extra funding was rejected by the government. The ABC was however able to reuse its strategies of audience capture when ABC3 was launched in 2009 (Donna Andrews personal communication June 2 2013).

During the early 2000s the ABC did invest in some Australian drama for children, although at levels below those required by the commercial networks. Live action drama series included co-productions with the UK's BBC, such as *Jeopardy* (2002); *Bootleg* (2002); two series of *Out There* (2003), a BBC-Sesame Workshop production; and with the ACTF's involvement, *Noah and Saskia* (2004). The ABC also invested in live action drama series *The Saddle Club* (2001–03), a co-production with Canada. By 2004 however ABCKids had gone and local children's drama levels on the ABC declined significantly, with only two series of Screen Australia-funded drama, *Blue Water High* and 13 x 5-minute episodes of *Five Minutes More* commissioned in two years. The broadcaster did not invest in any of the 40.5 hours of children's television funded by Screen Australia in 2006. It commissioned only one live action drama, a third series of *Blue Water High*, in 2007.

So, prior to the launch of ABC3, the ABC commissioned only minimal amounts of local drama for the child audience, particularly live action drama. The ABC's lack of Australian content quotas also affected local content for adults at this time; in 2004–5 the ABC made only five hours in total of adult drama (Inglis 2006). It appears then that the lack of content quotas in the ABC's charter enabled an institutional neglect of drama for both the adult and the child audience early in the digital transition and one that could recur in future, were funding levels to decline again. As the ABC's head of television 2006–12 Kim Dalton observes:

> The ABC doesn't have any rules and doesn't have to meet any Australian content quotas, full stop. And prior to ABC3, the ABC was nowhere near meeting the quotas the networks had to make. That was something one has to assume the senior management and board of the ABC were completely comfortable with as they allowed it to happen.
>
> (Personal communication 11 June 2013)

In 2006 the appointment of Kim Dalton as the ABC's head of television heralded a push for greater funding and increased commissioning of Australian content, including children's drama. Dalton, a former chief executive of the AFC with extensive experience in the independent screen production sector, was widely recognized for his commitment to Australian drama. His appointment also added momentum to the ACTF's campaign for the ABC to take advantage of the digital transition to properly serve Australian children by establishing a dedicated children's channel and home for Australian content.

A sustained lobbying campaign by the ACTF's chief executive Jenny Buckland and Kim Dalton saw the ABC secure $67 million in tied funding to launch its dedicated children's channel in 2009. ABC3's launch gradually increased investment levels in local children's programming including live action drama, although the channel also relied on imports and repeats to fill the schedule. Controller of ABC3 2010–13 Tim Brooke Hunt admitted prior to the channel's launch:

> The issue is one of cost [...] we pay significantly more per half hour for local content than we do for overseas content. And the reality is that the ABC can only put on as much Australian content as we are funded to do, and the biggest problem that has existed over recent years has been lack of funding which has inevitably diminished the level of Australian content.
>
> (The Media Report 2007)

The 2009 introduction of ABC3 demonstrated nonetheless an ongoing commitment to the Australian child audience, and created a concomitant need for children's television including local drama. It also demonstrated an astute institutional awareness that a children's channel could be a key driver of expansion and underpin the ABC's continued relevance in multi-channel markets. The ABC took advantage of the digital transition and the special status of the child audience to ensure its centrality in Australia's contemporary media landscape.

As the ABC prepared for the 2009 launch of ABC3, it began to commission local programmes for its new children's service, with 13 hours of Screen Australia funded drama in 2007–08 increasing to 32.5 hours by 2010–11. Since its inception ABC3 has commissioned several series of high-quality live action dramas, including *My Place* (2009), *Dance Academy* (2009–12), *Nowhere Boys* (2013) and *Worst Year of My Life, Again* (2013). All the channel's drama commissions since its establishment have been made with Screen Australia investment, which suggests ABC3 is consistently paying Screen Australia minimum licence fees.

One of ABC3's showcase dramas at its launch was the historical drama *My Place*, an adaptation of Nadia Wheatley and Donna Rawlins' book, about the various children who lived in one Sydney home from 1888 to 2008. The fig tree in the garden of the house represents the continuity in the storylines, symbolizing each child's place of belonging. Two additional characters Lily, the daughter of Vietnamese boat people and Mohammed, an Islamic boy and keen cricketer, were added to the storylines of the drama series, boosting its prosocial credentials and sense of inclusivity.

My Place was very unusual in that it was 100 per cent funded by Australian organizations, including ABC Commercial, Screen Australia, the ACTF, Screen Tasmania and the New South Wales Film and Television Office (NSW FTO). The ACTF is also its international distributor but unlike most children's television, the series did not need to secure an overseas sale to secure Screen Australia funding. *My Place* consisted of 26 episodes, which cost $12 million to make; the ABC provided approximately 25 per cent of the series' budget. Commercial broadcasters would not have tackled *My Place* because it would have been impossible for its producers to raise international presales with such a culturally specific programme, thus substantial investment was needed from the ABC to fund its production.

Despite its lavish production values, high profile cast and the publicity that surrounded its production and launch, *My Place* did not, it appears, resonate with either the child audience or its parents. Although it was critically acclaimed, the ratings for Series Two on ABC3 were particularly disappointing, with one episode dropping to 28,000 (Knox 2011).

Reflecting on the series' ratings in 2013, Tim Brooke Hunt said:

> We didn't commission *My Place* to get a huge audience. We supported *My Place* because we needed a landmark show that would set a standard of quality, Australianness and relevance. And I believe the ABC will still be broadcasting *My Place* in 10 and 20 years' time—it has long term value to Australia, and to the ABC and the fact it doesn't get a big audience every time it broadcasts really isn't important.
>
> (Personal communication May 2 2013)

As a landmark show for ABC3, the value of *My Place* appears to lie in its creation of reputational capital for the newly established public service broadcaster, and its educational capacity, rather than ratings, distribution or merchandising opportunities. *My Place* has a strong educational remit; the ACTF created extensive online educational resources for teachers in addition to ABC3's multi-platform offerings that accompanied the series broadcast.

Most of the culturally specific live action dramas commissioned by ABC3 between 2009 and 2013—*My Place, Dance Academy, Worst Year of My Life, Again* and *Nowhere Boys* were also made with ACTF involvement. Their cultural specificity ensures they speak directly to the Australian child audience while Screen Australia and ACTF investment underpins the production budgets required for high production values. *Worst Year of My Life, Again* was also made with the involvement of UK public service broadcaster CBBC, which was described as a 'co-financing partner, contributing a significant acquisition fee' by ABC3's Tim Brooke Hunt (personal communication May 2 2013).

From 2008, the increased amounts of live action drama commissioned by ABC3 masked to some extent the decline in Network Nine's investment in live action drama series over the same period. The addition of a dedicated children's channel did not, therefore, increase the amount of culturally specific high action drama available to Australian children, although it did help prop up existing demand. The willingness of ABC3 to pay minimum licence fees for culturally specific live action drama series with high production values did however increase the public value of the children's television being made with state investment. Its presence on ABC3, a dedicated children's channel, led to more Australian children viewing these series as well.

Prior to Australia's digital transition and the introduction of ABC3, the CTS ensured that Australia's commercial networks supported the vast majority of the live action drama produced in Australia. ABC3 was established in 2009 as a direct result of the increased spectrum engendered by Australia's digital transition. At around the same time, Networks Seven and Nine moved away from live action drama and the payment of Screen Australia minimum licence fees. All broadcasters' actions at this time were a response to Australia's digital transition, although fragmentation facilitated an increased commitment to the child audience by Australia's public service broadcaster the ABC, in stark contrast to the commercial networks' reduced resourcing of the genre.

As the commercial networks continued to prefer to use animation rather than live action drama to fill their CTS quotas, the ABC became virtually the only source of live action drama commissions for Australian producers. Nonetheless animation is also a key part of the ABC's programming strategy, with more money allocated to its production in 2013–14, 27 per cent of ABC3's $21 million local production budget compared to 23 per cent earmarked for comedy and drama. Further encouragement for the production of animation is provided by ABC3 entering into co-production and co-licensing arrangements with the commercial networks on animation series.

As Brooke Hunt explains, there are advantages to both broadcasters in these financing arrangements that can help resolve the problems associated with reduced licence fees and hence production budgets:

> ABC has approached this problem differently by entering into co-commissions with commercial broadcasters which means that the commercial broadcaster still only pays a lower fee (say $75k per half-hour) and the ABC pays the same amount thereby providing a decent combined licence fee that helps to fund majority local elements.
>
> (Personal communication May 2 2013)

When these co-licensing deals are struck, ABC3 contributes $70,000 rather than $120,000 per episode, enabling the broadcaster to almost double the number of shows it can commission each year. The transmission of the resulting animation series on both commercial networks and public service channels delivers a larger aggregated local audience (Brooke Hunt personal communication May 2 2013). The commercial networks receive first rights for these co-productions with the ABC, which can then be counted towards their C drama quota obligations.

The ABC's involvement acts as a degree of quality control on production while at the same time reducing the amount that individual channels have to pay for children's series.

While this arrangement may result in higher licence fees being paid and auger well for the quality of the animation that is produced, it also means the ABC has to settle for secondary transmission rights. They can only air these shows after the commercial free-to-air networks have broadcast them as part of their quota obligations. There is a slight sense then that in investing its funds in these types of productions while agreeing to forgo Australian television first rights, the ABC is effectively subsidising the production of the commercial networks' content quota obligations.

The introduction of ABC3 into the production ecology clearly led to extra funding and additional demand for Australian children's television. On average between 2008 and 2011, the ABC spent $7 million per annum on children's drama. This investment meant that for the first time the public service broadcaster virtually matched the commercial networks' annual $22 million investment in children's over the same period (Screen Australia 2011). The amount of Australian drama produced for ABC3 since 2009 has tended to reflect the levels of Australian drama mandated on the commercial networks by the CTS. But a key difference in commissioning behaviours between the ABC and the commercial networks is the ABC's commitment to live action drama, for which it pays Screen Australia minimum licence fees. As a result, ABC3's live action drama has high production values, cultural specificity and speaks directly to the Australian child audience. The involvement of Screen Australia and the ACTF in these live action drama commissions is further evidence of their public value.

ABC3 also competes for audiences and content with the pan-global providers offering dedicated children's channels to subscribers in Australian markets. Prior to ABC3's emergence as an outlet for legacy Australian children's television, much of which was originally produced with taxpayer subsidies, pay-TV channels had been able to acquire these programmes at fairly low cost. The ABC and pay-TV channels would also share rights for children's programmes, although ABC3 now prefers to have all rights. Hugh Baldwin Nickelodeon Australia's director of television and digital content believes ABC3's demands for exclusive deals have reduced the amount of funding available to Australian producers:

> It's no secret that we used to share content with the ABC but now the ABC are demanding exclusivity but not paying any more, so the producer can't exploit that bit. So previously it might have been 80 percent and 20 percent [of the licence fee] from us, but now the producers are only getting the 80 percent. So they have to try to get it somewhere else, privately or Screen Australia or somewhere else, but the margin is now very skinny for Australian producers.
>
> (Personal communication June 12 2013)

The arrival of ABC3 in the market also meant increased demand for acquired children's programmes sourced from international markets. Distributors often prefer to supply ABC3 with their children's content because of the channel's greater audience share in Australian markets, and hence opportunities for merchandising revenues. The increase in competition of children's programmes led to some resentment among pay-TV operators, but was welcomed by distributors like the ACTF and local producers.

It is important to remember that prior to the establishment of ABC3, levels of local children's content and commissions, particularly live action drama, were extremely low on the nation's public service broadcaster. They could conceivably fall again if the institutional will to allocate resources to children's television weakened or the ABC had its funding sharply reduced. No quotas apply to ABC3 to safeguard local levels of Australian children's television, just as no requirements for minimum levels of drama made for adults apply to the nation's public service broadcaster. The ABC's charter alone cannot prevent local commissions dropping back to their low levels during the early stages of the digital transition.

Pay-TV, Children's Television and Public Value

Pay-TV was first introduced to Australia in 1995. Despite slow uptake rates, by 2014 eight dedicated children's subscription services were available to the child audience, including offerings from pan-global channels Disney, Nickelodeon, The Cartoon Network and CBeebies. The majority of these services include two channels, one aimed at school-aged children and one aimed at pre-schoolers, a pattern which the ABC replicates with ABC3 and ABC4Kids.

The arrival of pay-TV did not lead to a local production boom in Australia however. Initially high-infrastructure costs, an overcrowded, medium-sized market and government policy designed to protect the free-to-air incumbents combined to make pay-TV's early years unprofitable (Flew & Spurgeon 2000). As a result, pay-TV children's services were spared the requirements of the CTS. Children's subscription services in Australia participate instead in the New Eligible Drama Expenditure (NEDE) scheme, which was introduced in 1999 after the failure of self-regulation to secure local programme investment. Under this scheme, channels whose output is primarily drama must spend 10 per cent of their programming budgets on local Australian content.

In order to reduce their local content costs, pay-TV children's channels tend to prefer to share rights to programmes with Australian free-to-air channels. In this way a subscription channel will get the rights to a series soon after its free-to-air transmission as part of a commercial network's CTS quota obligations. Under these arrangements, the Disney Channel Australia invested in Jonathan Shiff's *H2O: Just Add Water* while Shiff's live action drama series *Lightning Point* and *Mako Island of Secrets* aired on Nickelodeon Australia after Network Ten. As Hugh Baldwin explains:

> We don't contribute enough to be the primary partner. So there'd be a first window for Channel Ten say and six months later we'd premiere it. It's a similar model with animation, for Nickelodeon Australia to fully fund an animation the production level is too high.
> (Hugh Baldwin personal communication June 12 2013)

Pay-TV channels' investment in live action drama that was originally commissioned by a free-to-air network is an astute acquisitions strategy. The live action dramas will often rate well on subscription channels where, as one pay-TV executive observes, 'there is an expectation now of a certain amount of quality in kids TV, especially drama' (personal communication June 12 2013). Many Australian children will not have seen them previously, due to their lack of promotion or poor scheduling on free-to-air networks with little interest in attracting the child audience.

In addition to their investment in shared rights to the local live action drama commissioned by networks to fill their C drama quotas, children's subscription services will also commission or produce in-house small amounts of first-run Australian programmes. These will help to localize their offerings while acquitting their ACMA-mandated ten per cent spend. Such productions might take the form of local versions of international scripted formats, such as The Disney Channel's *As the Bell Rings* (2006–10), of which four series were made by Fremantle Australia. This interstitial live action comedy originated in Italy; versions have been made in multiple territories, including Australia.

The Disney Channel Australia also sometimes produces its own scripted drama in-house, such as *Mind over Maddie* (2012), a ten-minute scripted drama series, which was made by the channel's production team at its Sydney headquarters. According to one pay-TV executive, although children's channels in Australia do not transmit large volumes of local content, series such as *As the Bell Rings* and *Mind over Maddie* are useful because they can be used to 'pepper the schedule, and provide that Australian flavour' (personal communication June 12 2013). Local pay-TV channels may also create a format in Australia that will then be exported to other territories in the pan-global parent company's network. This occurred with Nickelodeon Australia's original format *Camp Orange* (2005), which was then used to make local versions in Italy, Asia and the UK. Nickelodeon also localizes its offerings by producing live television events, such as *The Kids Choice Awards* and, its replacement from 2012, *SlimeFest*.

Both Disney and Nickelodeon have specific additional strategies of localization that do not count towards their quota but give their channels an Australian patina without incurring high production costs. Strategies often consist of links produced in the studio or out on location, local competitions and short-form content that may include pranks or gags. A pay-TV executive agrees that investment in strategies of localization is important for pan-global channels in attracting and retaining Australian audiences, stating:

> We've got two local presenters who are really connecting well, and while that hosted block programming doesn't count towards our quota, it services the schedule and our audience. We're always thinking about what our schedule needs, our affinity with our viewers and how we're connecting with kids' lives. We need to reflect what they're talking about on YouTube or in the playground. That kind of daily hosted block in post school primetime is very immediate and important in establishing our connection with Aussie and Kiwi kids. (Personal communication June 12 2013)

As Hugh Baldwin explains, localization efforts also go beyond the linear schedule to Nickelodeon's multi-platform offerings, 'The digital side is big for localization. We create games based around our properties, so kids feel engaged, as well as competitions and messaging' (personal communication June 12 2013).

Pan-global subscription services invest in various forms of local production intended to localize the Australian channel, some of which will also contribute to the filling of quota obligations. Series that are made for the local version of the channel will generally be culturally specific, with a first and final market in Australasia, although a format may travel to other countries. These series do not have much of an impact on the production ecology however, as they are generally produced in-house or with limited resources.

Despite the obvious commitment of their Australian staff to strategies of localization and their enthusiasm for local content, the reality of pan-global channels operating in niche markets with limited quota obligations is a reliance on the parent company's products. These are also the most popular programmes with the child audience; as one executive concedes, '[T]hose half hour comedies from the US drive the schedule' (personal communication June 12 2013). The pay-TV children's channels' absolute commitment to multi-platform also hints at the impending redundancy of policy settings like the NEDE scheme:

> Program apps are more and more important, including in the preschool space. That's what's shifting everything. There's concern that it cuts down on screen time, but overall it's additive. Maybe children are watching the main television less, but they're consuming the stories and characters through mobile devices. We always have to think of multi-platform consumption of content when evaluating our properties.
>
> (Personal communication June 12 2013)

The proliferation of dedicated children's television services and their use of multi-platform distribution changed the character of the global and local components that make up the output of these television channels, without obviating the necessity for either. The 'local' is being reinvented in various ways, with market-led demands for localized content (which might take the form of local presenters hosting programmes and providing links between programmes, dubbing programmes or running competitions open only to that country's audience) giving channels local relevance without necessarily localizing the actual programmes they transmit.

These strategies of localization are quite different from the type of local content that is generally supported by media policies via mandated quotas such as the ACS, which states that 55 per cent of all prime-time programming on free-to-air commercial networks must be locally produced. These different characteristics of the local must be considered when surveying the new television settlements and when reimagining any media policy that seeks to attain the cultural goals of supporting local content and a local production industry while engaging audiences with Australian content. These goals would probably not be sustained in a purely market-driven television landscape.

Conclusion

Australia's commercial networks remained absolutely central to the production of Australian children's television throughout the digital transition, a role that was first thrust upon them in 1979. While local broadcasters may only supply a maximum of approximately 30 per cent of production budgets, they underpin demand for Australian's children's television. The networks are under no obligation however to spend any minimum amounts on its licence fees. They can therefore reduce their financial commitment to local children's television by choosing to rely on animation to fill their C drama quotas, rather than live action drama.

Animated series made for global markets often do not speak directly to the Australian child audience; thus the reduction in the ability of C drama to situate Australian children in their own culture reduced its public value during the digital transition. This loss of value was exacerbated by the 2006 introduction of the producer offset, which made state subsidy available to programmes with lower budgets and production values. The decline in the public value of much of the CTS-mandated children's television made for digital regimes is inevitable in a broadcasting system where policy objectives for children's television are largely removed from the means of achieving those objectives.

Continuing the practice of allowing the commercial networks to fill C drama quotas with animation, without any requirements for minimum spending levels, is likely to have disastrous consequences for the production of the high-quality live action drama for which Australia is renowned. Although ABC3 has become an important source of live action drama commissions in the production ecology, the absence of content quotas suggests changes in the channel's funding allocations could see its live action drama commissions fall again. If the ABC's resources are diverted away from children's television to its news and current affairs divisions, live action drama for children is likely to be one of the first casualties.

The creation of public value in CTS-mandated television requires urgent reconsideration by broadcasters, producers and regulators, to ensure that Australia's free-to-air broadcasters adequately serve the child audience and that the ABC can continue to do so. Without measures to address the loss of public value in drama that occurred during the digital transition, the CTS will become nothing more than an industry protectionist measure. Their original purpose—to guarantee quality and cultural integrity in Australian children's television—may be forgotten entirely.

Note

1 *Wormwood, K9, H2O: Just Add Water series 1 & 2, Elephant Princess 1 & 2, Lightning Point, Mako Island of Secrets, Sam Fox: Extreme Adventures.*

Chapter 5

It's a Small World After All: The Internationalization of Australian Children's Television

A key justification for the state support enjoyed by Australian children's television remains the contribution this television makes to the goals of national cultural representation. The effects of the trend towards increased internationalization in Australian children's television that developed during the digital transition, therefore, merit close scrutiny. This chapter examines Australian children's television as a global enterprise, analysing two case studies of children's drama in order to describe and explain the effects of internationalization. Both case studies are emblematic of the various ways in which internationalization affected the production of children's television during the digital transition. Its considerable benefits included the opportunity for distribution arrangements on pan-global children's channels and increased cultural visibility, while less welcome consequences of internationalization included a loss of cultural specificity and a reduction in producers' creative autonomy.

Globalizing the Local

Although local broadcasters play a crucial role in its production, Australian children's television has always been subject to powerful internationalizing forces. From television's inception, Australian schedules were filled with children's television from other countries, particularly the US and UK. Broadcasters relied on cheaper imported programmes to attract the child audience, scheduling series such as *Lassie, Rin Tin Tin* and *The Mickey Mouse Club* alongside inexpensive locally made entertainment. The use of transnational formats such as *Romper Room, Play School, It's Academic* and, more recently, *Prank Patrol* and *As the Bell Rings* also has a long history in the production of children's television in Australia.

The economics of programme production in a medium-sized television market have always obligated Australian producers to integrate their work into larger globalized television systems, through exports and international co-productions (Cunningham and Jacka 1996). Children's television is no exception, with local producers forced to partner with Australian and international broadcasters to raise sufficient finance to fund their children's television. Producers are accustomed, therefore, to having to integrate their work into both local, and international, television systems and have been straddling different market ecologies for many years. These market ecologies include the dominant mass broadcasting model in the Australian domestic market in which the CTS suggest the child viewer is an unwanted obligation. They also include multi-channel environments in other territories, where the child audience is highly sought after, particularly by dedicated children's channels.

The internationalization of Australian children's television, which saw co-productions and presales with UK and other partners assist in the creation of C drama during the 1980s, assumed different proportions during the mid-1990s. At this time the pace of media globalization accelerated, due largely to a worldwide trend towards the deregulation and privatization of media industries and the liberalization of the regulatory regimes in which they operated (Cunningham and Jacka 1996). Industrial and technological developments further transformed media operations, particularly ownership structures and broadcast capabilities.

Concentrated, vertically integrated ownership structures characterize media production and distribution in contemporary markets. During the mid-1990s a series of mergers and consolidation of ownership among the world's largest media corporations led to ten global media companies, of which six are American, dominating world media markets. The second largest of these companies is the Disney Corporation (Thussu 2006). This period also saw the rise of the pan-global channel, with channels such as MTV, CNN and Discovery (all distributed by global media corporations) charging subscribers for thematic content designed to cross national borders (McMurria 2004).

During the 1990s, satellite and cable technology sustained the global expansion of these pay-TV services, which included dedicated children's television services. Ownership of the children's channels was dominated by three key players—Disney, Nickelodeon/Viacom and Cartoon Network/Time Warner. Their pursuit of the child audience saw children's television and its associated merchandising became a very lucrative endeavour. As a result of these trends towards concentrated ownership and vertical integration, Australian producers now operate alongside well-resourced conglomerates that not only produce most of their own content, but also control its distribution, carriage and merchandising revenues in a global market place. These industrial arrangements, the control of content and carriage, give US conglomerates considerable market advantage.

The 1995 introduction of pay-TV to Australia saw these pan-global subscription services enter the spaces of Australian television for the first time. With minimal local content quotas, pan-global channels tend to commission only very low levels of original Australian content. They excel however at making and distributing their own content such as Disney's *High School Musical* (2006). Produced on a budget of US $4 million, the made-for-TV movie generated over US $500 million in revenues for the Disney Corporation and has been viewed by an estimated 300 million children worldwide.

Australian producers depend for their survival on their capacity to straddle two entirely different market ecologies, that is the local and the international, so the operations of conglomerates like Disney and Nickelodeon can represent great opportunity, as facilitators of the international distribution of Australian children's drama. If Australian producers can sell their programmes to a global channel in a particular territory, its success in that territory can lead to much wider distribution across other channels that form part of the same global network. As one pay-TV executive explains:

> Vertical integration brings access to distribution. Obviously for kids content, local free to air exposure is important to reach the broadest audience possible, but international distribution is also important to make a programme a bigger success. Australia is known for making quality kids TV and there is some great content coming out of here. But being part of a large, commercial organisation gives you a global scale leading to merchandise opportunities, particularly in the preschool space.
>
> (Personal communication June 12 2013)

On the other hand, US models of subscription television simultaneously pose a high degree of risk to the local regulatory and broadcasting systems that have traditionally supported Australian children's television. They suggest subsidy-free, sustainable business models for children's television that is enormously popular with the child audience. The structural and industrial conditions that support these business models encourage production norms that are shaped by the generation of merchandising revenues and rely on programmes' capacity to travel in international markets. These production circumstances are quite at odds with the creation of culturally specific Australian children's television made with state-funded subsidies, particularly live action drama.

From the early 2000s onwards, the world markets in which Australian producers circulated their programming underwent a period of rapid evolution largely due to the introduction of digital technology. The multi-channelling engendered by digital transmission led to audience and hence advertising revenue fragmentation. With new global children's channels launching or expanding their reach and programming budgets fragmenting, the prices for children's television in global markets dropped. The US conglomerates that provided these dedicated children's services had large programming libraries from which to draw, further reducing demand for new content (Thussu 2006).

While multi-channelling drove down the prices networks would pay for children's television in the early 2000s, the creation and maintenance of a strong brand, to help children's channels stand out in crowded and fragmented markets, became increasingly important. Uniquely and demonstrably Australian content was not always the best programming with which to establish and reinforce a US channel's branding. In order for Australian producers to continue to distribute their work in these transforming markets, they were forced to adapt their production practices to the new economic conditions and media systems.

Producing programmes for children in such a highly competitive market where many programmes are required to work in several territories is challenging. Independent producers have to create programmes that are obliged to meet myriad market requirements while stitching together complicated production budgets. The general need to go offshore for production partnerships also reduces cultural specificity in children's programmes.

As independent producer Patrick Egerton explains:

> Generally speaking you are putting together a mixture of three different territories increasing up to 10 different stakeholders to try and put the financial jigsaw together. So unless there's really compelling reason for it, you can't make something that is really openly Australian or looking only to engage an Australian audience because you only get between 20 and 30 percent of your budget from the local broadcaster.
>
> (Personal communication April 29 2013)

Programmes produced as a result of these internationalized funding models are likely to have to fulfil the programming needs of multiple co-production partners in several territories, including at times both public service broadcasters and commercial channels. Programmes should ideally have merchandising potential and be able to attract the viewing loyalty of the child audience in a multi-platform world of viewing abundance (Ward & Potter 2009). At the same time these productions generally constitute the Australian children's television mandated and supported by policy settings and funding arrangements grounded in the achievement of the goals of national cultural representation.

The pressure on all producers to limit the cultural specificity of their children's television is the perfectly logical outcome of the globalization of children's television in which very large US corporations play a leading and extremely influential role. Nonetheless, the capacity of these programmes to speak directly to Australian children and, in doing so, to achieve the policy objectives that underpin the justifications for their state subsidy may be compromised in the process. Any reduction in these programmes' ability to help situate Australian children within their own culture affects their public value.

Globalization and the Creation of Public Value in Children's Television

The internationalization of children's television and the proliferation of dedicated children's channels engendered by technological and industrial change during the digital transition present certain benefits for Australian producers. Successful partnerships with international broadcasters can help secure global distribution and favourable scheduling arrangements for Australian programmes, while increased investment by multiple partners supports the high production values on which Australian television built its reputation. A global hit can further bolster Australia's reputation for producing high-quality children's programmes (or Brand Australia) and at the same time reinvigorate an individual production company's reputation as a supplier of versatile, high-quality children's content.

On the other hand, the new production and distribution circumstances of children's television can bring certain disadvantages. Drawbacks may include a loss of creative autonomy in the negotiation of differences in production cultures between various production partners, skills shortages and disagreements about where production should occur. The need to accommodate the different programme expectations of public service and commercial operators further complicates the process. If things do go wrong, producers may struggle to recoup their production budgets and face a loss of reputational capital as well as the prospect of reduced licence fees for their programmes.

In addition to the creative challenges posed by internationalization, the children's television produced for global markets can struggle to speak directly to Australian children. The ability to contribute to national cultural expression has come under particular pressure since 2001, due to the emergence of a global trend towards the production of animation. Animation is generally cheaper to produce, less culturally specific and has a longer shelf life than live action drama (Steemers 2010). Although animation is a perfectly legitimate genre and enormously popular with the child audience, Australian cultural policy has tended to privilege live action drama in the achievement of the goals of national cultural representation. Live action drama remains also the genre most at risk of market failure. Policy settings and state-funding mechanisms were never intended to support the production of animation to the extent that they did during the digital transition.

From 2001 to 2014 the effects of far-reaching changes in the circumstances of international children's television began to be felt and the patterns of the new settlements in children's television began to establish themselves firmly. Halfway through the digital transition, two Australian production companies made programmes that became emblematic of the influences that were shaping the production ecology at this time. The production companies, Jonathan M Shiff Productions and Burberry Productions made *H2O: Just Add Water* (2006) and *Animalia* (2007) respectively.

These Australian dramas are used as case studies in this chapter, to illustrate the form and scale of the new settlements in Australian children's television as they began to emerge. At around the same time these examples of Australian children's television were produced, Disney's made-for-TV movie *High School Musical* (2006) became an unexpected hit for the company. Disney maximized new means of distribution and marketing in children's television to amplify the success of this low-budget movie, locally and globally. Disney's adroit harnessing of the new markets in children's television is also worthy of analysis, because of its implications for Australian children's television.

H2O: Just Add Water

Jonathan M Shiff Productions is an Australian production company that has experienced considerable success in international markets with C classified live action drama. The Melbourne-based company has developed a reputation for producing high-quality programming for Australian and international markets, including global networks like Disney and Nickelodeon. It has long-standing production partnerships with local and international broadcasters that, most unusually, supported the creation of both public and private value in the children's programmes produced by the company during the digital transition.

For the past 23 years Jonathan M Shiff productions has supplied Network Ten with C drama enabling the network to fulfil its quota obligations for which Ten contributes between 10 and 20 per cent of the production budget. The live action drama produced by the company is generally produced with Screen Australia funding, as Network Ten has a long track record in paying minimum licence fees for its drama commissions. Jonathan M Shiff Productions also has an output deal with ZDF Enterprises, the commercial branch of Germany's public service broadcaster ZDF, which buys all the children's series that Shiff produces.

Jonathan M Shiff Productions was launched in 1988 leading with documentary series productions *In Search of the World's Most Secret Animals* and *The Pandas* before moving into children's television drama with *Ocean Girl* (1994–97). The series was identifiably high-quality and original and won a BAFTA Award for Best Children's Television Programming. It sold to 130 territories worldwide including The Disney Channel in the US (and Australia), Discovery Kids and the BBC in the UK, NHK Japan and ZDF in Germany grossing over $50 million in export sales.

Following *Ocean Girl*, Shiff produced three seasons of the dark, futuristic and post-apocalyptic series *Thunderstone*. That series also won industry accolades including a BAFTA award and Australian Teachers of Media (ATOM) award. Shiff continued to make quality live action drama, including *Horace and Tina* (2001), *Cybergirl* (2001) *Pirate Islands* (2003), *Scooter: Secret Agent* (2005) and Pirate *Islands: The Lost treasure of Fiji* (2006). These series were eclipsed by the commercial success of the teen mermaid series *H2O: Just Add Water* (2006–09). After the production of three series of *H2O: Just Add Water*, Shiff went on to make *The Elephant Princess* (2008), *Lightning Point* (2012) *Mako Island of Secrets* (2013) and his first series aimed at an adult market, *Reef Doctors* (2013), all for Network Ten.

Unlike other Australian companies that build a profile within the domestic market before going international, Jonathan Shiff purposely launched the company as a global producer. His drama and documentary series have sold to more than 160 territories worldwide. For Shiff there are only two options—'You're either driven as a local business (and paying the negative costs) or operating as a global business with 12% from the local partner but the rest is international' (Shiff personal communication September 3 2008). In 2013 Shiff pioneered a completely new global distribution model for Australian children's television when he entered into a distribution arrangement with US-based Internet TV network Netflix, which saw the renamed *Mako Mermaids* made available to audiences in 51 countries, on the same day. The purchase represented Netflix's first investment of children's live action drama and demonstrates the demand for high-quality children's content created by new television services.

H2O: Just Add Water, the first series of which was produced in 2006, became one of Jonathan M Shiff's most successful children's series ever, and went on to be viewed by over 300 million children worldwide. The live action drama is based on the lives of three teenage girls, Rikky, Cleo and Emma. After swimming in a hidden grotto at the height of the full moon the girls find themselves morphing into mermaids every time they come in contact with water. *H2O: Just Add Water* was a Queensland production, and was largely filmed on the Gold Coast at the theme park Underwater World.

H2O: Just Add Water sold in 150 countries including the US, where Series One was the first non-American drama to be bought by Nickelodeon in America and screened every Sunday night (Shiff personal communication September 3 2008). Series One was also the number one live action show on Nickelodeon UK. Yet in Australia the programme was variously scheduled on Network Ten at 4pm on Fridays and at 7am on Saturdays, as part of the network's C drama quota obligations. In these slots it attracted between 300,000 and 400,000 viewers. These are strong ratings for children's television in Australia but they illustrate the chasm between a domestic broadcaster's scheduling and promotion of its C drama and the practices of pan-global channels which avidly pursue the child audience in prime time.

The success of *H2O: Just Add Water* demonstrates the importance of branding and brand management on a number of levels in multi-channel environments where form, content and business models are evolving in digital regimes. For production companies in the business of creating content for the media marketplace for which they need to attract considerable finance either as licence fees or as equity investment, branding is equated with an established and trustworthy reputation based on a record of performance.

Australian children's television has been branded as quality since the late 1980s, thanks to the requirements inherent in the CTS and Shiff's series have historically formed part of this quality output. Trust plays an important role in the production ecology as commissioning editors will tend to use preferred providers for much of their children's television. A company which can be trusted due to their track record in delivering on time, within budget and with programmes that will encounter no difficulties achieving a C classification from the ACMA develops considerable reputational capital (Cherrie Bottger, Network Ten, personal communication October 3 2013).

A large part of Shiff's success as a content producer has been founded on his ability to, first, create a presence within the market place for his particular style of programme—to create what he terms as 'the Jonathan Brand' and, second, based on this trusted brand presence to gain entry to networks that facilitate the flow of his content across national borders. Compatibility across corporate brands also facilitates the creation of mutual alliances between broadcasters and distributors which enables the process of international syndication or co-productions arrangements to take place.

When asked to define 'the Jonathan Brand', Shiff lists the following characteristics: family, heart-warming, important social values, good role modelling, adventure, transporting to a higher plateau, high concept fantasy (Shiff personal communication Sep 3 2008). It is also clear that Shiff's productions have always been characterized by high production values, including an attention to visual spectacle in art direction, in the use of landscape, and in costly special effects.

Water has also become a central motif in *H2O: Just Add Water* in narratives that centre on mermaids, in the use of the Gold Coast's beachside settings, and in film-making infrastructure such as custom built studios that include water tanks. The theme park SeaWorld with its tropical aquarium and trained dolphins continues the watery theme. So too do specializations such as underwater cinematography (evident in frequent camera framing that sits half submerged in the water, collapsing the audience's view with the mermaids' point of view). Water is also evoked through special effects in digitally simulated waves, bubbles, and in the watery swish of a mermaid's tail used to mark major scene changes.

Attention to narrative and screen aesthetics works to Shiff's commercial advantage by creating 'must see' television that international distributors 'must have' because of the ratings these programmes attract and because of their status as quality children's content. *H2O: Just Add Water* also prompted fervent fan behaviour, either as fan fiction, or in the uploading of small re-edited video clips to YouTube attracting in excess of ten and a half million hits to date. These clips are tolerated in the interests of viral marketing, as opposed to the illegal sharing of *H2O* episodes on torrent sites, which is not tolerated (Shiff personal communication September 3 2008).

The programme also demonstrates a stylistic intentionality—in the tonal qualities of the image, in art design, and in the use of settings and landscape that feature many of the seductive features of a Gold Coast lifestyle. As the show's director Colin Buddes explains:

> I stayed away from pastels and beige and went for the primary colours, and given that our biggest audience is in landlocked Europe, they love to see the crashing surf, blue skies and palm trees [...] I wanted to keep it energized, and I didn't want a lot of 'suburban' or middle-of-the-range lenses. It was 'see the real sunny Gold Coast' [...] i.e. wide and tight without the middle ground.
>
> (Cordaiy 2007: 152–53)

Hence characters are either immersed in glorious subtropical environments of beach and rainforest, or the built environments of the Gold Coast (beach esplanades, marine harbours, and canal estates) that are designed to be and are marketed as signs of a pleasurable middle class lifestyle as per its role as a tourist destination. As Shiff suggests, the main driver of *H2O*'s international appeal is this aspirational lifestyle.

A focus on fantasy and science fiction genres also enables a degree of narrative transparency. As Shiff observes, 'universality widens as you get into fantasy because it's really hero's journey material or its quest driven—they're universal templates'. So while Australian audiences may engage with the setting of *H2O: Just Add Water* as the Gold Coast (though the locality is never mentioned by name), Shiff acknowledges that half of the US audience may think it is filmed in Florida. Hence the Gold Coast as production location functions as a non-specific sunny, safe, charismatic place that resonates in different ways for Australians, US or a landlocked European audience experiencing the cold depths of winter. Its meaning is determined by its audience's own cultural backgrounds (Olsen 2004).

Despite the success of Series One, Series Two of *H2O: Just Add Water* was less popular with US audiences. The drop in ratings led to Nickelodeon's decision not to buy Series Three, although Series Three did sell into 130 other countries. Series Three was also ineligible for the Australian funding support mechanism, the producer offset, as Screen Australia guidelines

Figure 1: L-R: Scottie Tweedie, Mitch Tomlinson, Amberley Lobo, PM Kevin Rudd, Kayne Tremills, Hannah Wang & Ben Crawley at the launch of ABC3. © ACTF.

Figure 2: ABC head of television 2006–12 Kim Dalton and ACTF CEO Jenny Buckland at the launch of ABC3. © ACTF.

Figure 3: Brooke Harman, Thomas Lacey and Clapper Loader Max Seager in the Werner Film Production *Dance Academy* Series Three Behind the Scenes. Steve Brack © Werner Film Productions.

Figure 4: Cast and crew in the Werner Film Production *Dance Academy* Series Three Behind the Scenes. Steve Brack © Werner Film Productions.

Figure 5: Group still Keiynan Lonsdale (Ollie), Dena Kaplan (Abigail), Xenia Goodwin (Tara), Isabel Durant (Grace), Jordan Rodrigues (Christian), Alicia Banit (Kat) and Thomas Lacey (Ben) in the Werner Film Production *Dance Academy* Series Three. Alyce Corbett © Werner Film Productions.

Figure 6: *Lockie Leonard* Series One: Set up director and co-producer Tony Tilse at Salmon Holes beach. David Dare Parker © Goalpost Pictures (2007).

Figure 7: *Lockie Leonard* Series One: Director Wayne Blair gives directions to Sean Keenan (Lockie) and Gracie Gilbert (Vicki) with 1st AD Mark Boskell. David Dare Parker © Goalpost Pictures (2007).

Figure 8: Nicholas Dunn (Hector) and Marny Kennedy (Taylor) shooting on location, Gold Coast, Queensland for *Mortified*. Jimmy Malecki © Mortified Productions (2006).

Figure 9: *Mortified* crew on location, Gold Coast, Queensland. Jimmy Malecki © Mortified Productions (2006).

Figure 10: Jeffrey Walker (Bronson, "Ice Maiden"), *Round the Twist* Series Two. Greg Noakes © Australian Children's Television Foundation (1992).

Figure 11: The Twist Family L-R: Sam Vandenberg (Pete), Richard Moir (Dad), Tamsin West (Linda), Front: Rodney McLennan (Bronson), *Round the Twist* Series One. Greg Noakes © Australian Children's Television Foundation (1989).

Figure 12: Cast and crew on *Lightning Point* 2011. © Jonathan M Shiff Productions.

Figure 13: Clare Holt (Emma), Phoebe Tonkin (Cleo) and Cariba Heine (Rikki) in *H20: Just Add Water.* © Jonathan M Shiff Productions.

Figure 14: "George" from the series *My Place 2* (played by Michael Cochrane). © Mark Rogers.

Figure 15: A member of the make-up team with "Alice" from the series *My Place 2* (played by Victoria Shaw). © Mark Rogers.

Figure 16: Bindy Irwin and the teams during the making of an episode of *Bindi's Bootcamp*. © Fremantle Media.

at the time only funded the first two series (or 52 episodes) of any local production. While ZDF supplied the funding for the third series to bridge the gap in funding previously provided by the producer offset, the strength of the Australian dollar meant this funding was worth less than Screen Australia's contribution had previously been worth. Series Three was completed for a cost of $12.7 million for 26 half-hour episodes.

H2O: Just Add Water and its successful circulation through global networks and European markets suggest that public broadcasters like ZDF, which distributes Shiff's children's content, may have a leading role in ensuring original quality children's content with public service values. This role was first played by the BBC in its early co-production arrangements with the ACTF in the 1980s; the BBC continued to co-produce or acquire some Australian live action drama during the digital transition such as *Bootleg* (2002), *Noah and Saskia* (2004), *Mortified* (2006), *Dead Gorgeous* (2010) and *Worst Year of My Life, Again* (2013).

The success of *H2O: Just Add Water* demonstrated that high-quality, culturally specific Australian children's television can be profitably distributed internationally on a mix of free-to-air and dedicated subscriber children's networks that all adhere to similar social values. Merchandising and the repurposing of content for different platforms will often also be an integrated feature of the financial resources underpinning high profile, quality drama made for digital markets. A programme that can work across these different channels and platforms then becomes a desirable commodity for broadcasters.

The relationship with German public service broadcaster ZDF has benefited Jonathan M Shiff Productions in several ways. First, ZDF buys all the drama that the company makes. This means Shiff has the crucial international presale in place in order to access Australian funding mechanisms. As a result, Shiff spends less energy on difficult and time-consuming funding negotiations and discussions to raise finance for his programmes:

> It's a guaranteed pre-buy finance deal, we will be doing a show and they will finance it, in order to trigger it through deficit finance in other sources such as Screen Australia. ZDF provided a lot of fuel to add growth in the last few years because it allowed us to know we've got frequent work, it allowed us to step up our volume of work, it allowed me to then concentrate more on the creative area.
>
> (Shiff personal communication September 3 2008)

Second, the German relationship has been an important part of Shiff's success by providing market intelligence and contacts with internationally distributed dedicated children's channels. Speaking about the success of Series One of *H2O: Just Add Water* in 2008, he described how his relationship with ZDF had helped him as a producer: 'I got a lot of market information first hand. I was able to connect directly with the head of Nickelodeon international, the head of Cartoon network, of Disney international' (Shiff personal communication September 3 2008).

Shiff was able to access the means of securing the presence of his programming on global distribution networks, and in doing so benefit from the industrial constellations that favour

US conglomerates which control both content and carriage of their children's programming in subscriber markets. ZDF has also been invaluable in tailoring content to the cultural nuances of individual markets.

> [O]ur German partners often say keep away from the high rises. I go—well that's the Q1 building; and they say well it looks like a Russian housing commission block of flats.
> (Shiff personal communication September 3 2008)

Finally, Jonathan's relationship with ZDF enables him to retain his creative autonomy and exert an extraordinary degree of control over every aspect of his productions. In doing so he is able to conform to the authorial function of producer/director (Caldwell 2008). This is very much a privileged position for Australian producers who frequently have to accommodate the needs and wishes of multiple production partners in their efforts to build sustainable funding models for their productions. In doing so, Australian producers can suffer a loss of creative autonomy and control in the programmes they are making.

Speaking in 2003, Shiff was at that time concerned about the degree to which he oversaw every detail of production, and questioning whether his innately cautious gate keeping might have had a negative impact on some of his drama productions. He said then:

> The ABA have had very few issues in the last few years because I tend to be much more stringent. In fact as we grow now into doing different genres and different budget level shows, I'm being encouraged to let go of some of that gate keeping because it's actually acting as a blocker [...] I'm actually becoming a little less hands on because I've acted as a creative gatekeeper so much, we've overcompensated and it's stopped us diversifying.
> (Shiff personal communication December 8 2003)

However in 2008 Shiff admitted that his attempts to delegate more of the producing and directing of his programmes to other members of his team had been unsuccessful. They had led to budget overruns on one project and the need to reshoot another because of quality-control issues, devaluing the Jonathan brand and cutting into programme profit margins. Further, his German partners at ZDF wanted to deal with Jonathan in person, and not his representatives, necessitating his involvement in all the production decision and deal making (Shiff personal communication September 3 2008).

Shiff admitted in 2008 that he had made a complete return to his producer/director authorial role: 'I would be lying to you if I didn't tell you that I'm still over-editing and re-scripting. I'm still hands across every hairstyle, every frame that's shot'. Shiff's ability to retain control over every aspect of his production output might be personally taxing but ensures that the Jonathan brand is undiluted and that the final programming conforms to his traditionally high-level production values. The fact Shiff is also a qualified lawyer means he has an unusual skill set, encompassing the financial negotiations with ZDF and the producer/director's role.

So for Shiff, *H2O: Just Add Water* affirms 'the Jonathan Brand' earned through consistency in performance and industry accolades since the 1980s. It is a corporate identity that facilitates alliances such as the ZDF arrangement that leads to company growth and expansion across a range of activities including the development of new programmes, websites and gaming. Shiff acknowledges that being an Australian producer of children's content creates tactical advantage in that the country of origin brand (or Brand Australia) reaffirms 'the Jonathan Brand'.

Australia is known for its stunning landscapes, for certain cultural sensibilities, and especially for its content regulations and government funding for quality children's content. As early as 2003 Shiff recognized the importance of the quality demands in the C classification, saying 'We like the fact the C structure nursed high-quality, that's why it's been good. It's QC [quality control], like someone saying you can't do rubbish' (Shiff personal communication September 3 2003). The private value in international markets of Brand Australia—which was initially created by the ACTF's C classified live action drama portfolio and increased by Shiff's live action drama output—is entirely compatible in these cases, with the creation of public value.

Clearly the key benefits for Jonathan M Shiff Productions from the relationship with ZDF are significant. Not only does ZDF provide the presale that triggers local production funding subsidies in Australia, it also has a vested interest in selling the resulting programmes as widely as possible, under a commissions-based sales structure which ensures the global visibility of Shiff's programming on the most popular of the dedicated children's channels such as Nickelodeon or Disney. Shiff is given complete autonomy as producer/director, while his partners provide high level contacts with international partners and information about the cultural nuances of European markets.

Shiff's ability to ensure his children's programmes benefit from both Australian and German state support contributes to its high production values and ease of circulation in international markets. Unfortunately for other Australian production companies, the kind of partnership that exists between Jonathan M Shiff Productions and ZDF is unusual. There are no other public service broadcasters like ZDF in terms of wealth and a willingness to partner with Australian producers in, for example, France or Spain.

Jonathan Shiff's live action drama series are unusual too in their ability to combine the creation of both private and public value. Shiff has developed a sustainable business model, underpinned by careful brand management, strategic partnerships and the pursuit of innovative distribution practices. At the same time, series such as *H2O: Just Add Water*, which was commissioned by Network Ten to fill its C drama quotas, benefited further from state support through access to Screen Australia funding and the producer offset taxation subsidy.

As culturally specific live action drama with high production values made especially for the child audience *H2O: Just Add Water* fulfils the policy objectives for Australian children's television, returning public value to its taxpayer investors. Network Ten's sustained commitment to paying minimum licence fees for Shiff's live action drama series are vital to the creation of its private and public value, despite the low viewing figures *H2O: Just Add Water* achieved in Australia in comparison with its international distribution.

Brand Australia and the Jonathan Shiff Brand, both of which are associated with quality children's live action drama contributed to *H2O: Just Add Water's* international success and its private and public value. Although the processes of internationalization were a significant advantage for *H2O: Just Add Water*, not all Australian children's television made with international involvement experiences this kind of alignment of the planets. Indeed for some producers, internationalization and media globalization created significant creative and economic challenges during the digital transition, affecting both the private and public value of their programmes.

Burberry Productions and *Animalia*

Prior to its 2010 purchase by European transnational All3media, Melbourne-based independent production company Burberry Productions, which was established in 2000, had been making programming across a range of genres including prime-time drama, comedy and miniseries. Former Burberry Productions and now Burberry Entertainment's managing director Ewan Burnett has over 30 years' experience in the industry across commercials, documentaries and drama, and worked for both the pioneering Australian television production company Crawfords and the ACTF. Burnett has also produced stage plays and hosted radio programmes.

In addition to its programming for adults, Burberry Productions made award winning drama for children that sold well internationally, particularly to the UK. These programmes included *The Wayne Manifesto* (1997) *Bootleg* (2002), *Short Cuts* (2001) and *The Sleepover Club* (2003–07). Prior to Burnett's company's purchase by All3media, Burnett had to enter into individual presale, co-production and distribution arrangements for every children's series he produced in order to secure local funding subsidies and the production budget.

The need to secure multiple funding partners is time-consuming and diverts producers' energies from the creative production processes. It also means producers are obliged to juggle and accommodate the creative wishes of diverse production partners, each of whom has an executive producer credit and a financial interest to protect. As a result, the producer's authorial role is diluted and shared.

Although Burberry Productions had a long track record in the production of children's live action drama, *Animalia* was the company's first attempt at making animation. The television series is based on the very successful illustrated children's book by Graeme Base, which was first published in 1986 and sold over three million copies worldwide. The picture book won several awards including the Young Australia best book award and the Children's Book Council picture book of the year in 1987. Base's book was described in a review by *The Sydney Morning Herald* as:

> The ultimate alphabet book, loved for its look and playful language. Base is known for his beautiful, detailed illustrations and *Animalia*, populated mostly by animals, is his best known and most loved book.
>
> (Schiavone 2009)

However because the television series was to be sold in multiple territories, a key element of the book, that each illustrated object and animal corresponded to a particular letter of the alphabet, was dropped.

The main characters in the book and series are 11-year-old Zoe and Alex who find themselves in a world of talking animals when they stumble across a magic portal hidden in their local library and enter the kingdom of Animalia. Animalia's ruling heart, the magic core, is not functioning properly and the children must solve various mysteries in order to help the animals save the core and safeguard Animalia's future.

While the success of the illustrated book meant there was already an international awareness of the Animalia brand, Base's reputation for high-quality, exquisitely illustrated work meant there were also certain levels of audience (and author) expectations surrounding its television incarnation. Base's role in the production (he had an executive producer's credit) was not an entirely happy one for the self-confessed 'control freak'. He described television production as 'a different type of creativity, that hasn't come naturally to me [...] I would live longer if I wasn't at the table. I passionately argued for my ideas [...] not all were acted upon and that was occasionally difficult to say the least' (Kizilos 2007).

Although Burnett first acquired the television rights to the story in 1999, it took five years to put together the deal to secure sales and funding with Burnett describing the process as 'enormously difficult' (personal communication September 5 2010). The UK government's decision to change a key taxation law meaning a series had to be produced in the tax year for which it was claimed delayed funding further. Eventually Burnett entered into production partnerships with multiple partners, including Channel Ten and Nickelodeon in Australia, the UK's public service broadcaster the BBC, which provided a vital international presale, the Canadian public service broadcaster CBC, the US production company Porchlight Entertainment and the US public service channel PBS.

Distribution rights were acquired by BBC Worldwide in the UK, New Zealand and Australia, and Porchlight Entertainment in North America. Porchlight, which was established in 1995 and is based in Los Angeles, had significant influence over the series' production as well as distribution rights. For example, Porchlight put together the writing team and cast in Los Angeles. High production costs contributed to the number of production partners with which Burnett had to work, and led to five executive producers, including author Graeme Base.

Production on the series eventually began in 2005. Forty half-hour episodes were made, at a cost of $20 million. The series is an early example of Australian computer-generated imagery or CGI animation. Production took almost 18 months, and employed 45 animators as part of its production crew equivalent of 150 full time jobs. The series was directed by first-time director David Scott who had previously worked on *Superman Returns*, *Harry Potter and the Goblet of Fire* and the *Lord of the Rings* trilogy and also for the art department on *Happy Feet*. The animation was made by two production houses, Photon VFX on the Gold Coast and Iloura-Digital Pictures in South Melbourne.

One contributing factor to the high budget was the series' use of 'pre-visualization' techniques, which meant creating a rough animation using proxy models prior to producing the final version (Kizilos 2007). Thus *Animalia* cost half-a-million dollars per episode, slightly more than each episodes of *H2O: Just Add Water*. While the cost per half hour difference is not substantial, animation traditionally is much cheaper to produce than drama, which suggests costs were unusually high for this production from the outset. As Burnett concedes, 'It was a huge show and a very expensive show, because it was such high end feature quality animation' (personal communication September 5 2010).

The cost per episode of *Animalia* made it difficult for Burnett and his partners to recoup their investments, as animation generally attracts much lower licence fees than drama in international markets. For example, according to its producers, the rights to new high-quality episodes of a 2010 UK preschool CGI animation that had played on CBeebies and the US channel Sprout were bought by ABC3 for licence fees in the very low hundreds of dollars per 15-minute episode.

While *Animalia* is high-end quality animation, the series suffers from comparisons with other CGI animation examples of children's programming made by better resourced conglomerates, such as Pixar-Disney's *Toy Story* franchise, the first of which was released in 1995 with a production budget of $30 million. *Animalia* is also inconsistent in its tone—at times it adopts a worthy, environmentally friendly, slightly preachy stance and extols the merits of inclusivity and tolerance. For example, the humans, Zoe and Alex, are initially feared and perceived as a threat to Animalian society. They are painted as ugly intruders by foolish tabloid-esque TV reporters who whip up public fears about their arrival in Animalia, rumours which quickly trigger demands to hunt down the intruders and remove them from the kingdom.

Environmental concerns are voiced in the key plot line featuring the problems with the core, the living heart of the Kingdom of Animalia. These problems are leading to a loss of sunlight, and thus threatening life in the jungle and the animals' food supply. While the animals are confused about what is causing the core's problems, the need to safeguard the environment means every effort must be made to find a solution to its ills. At the same time, there are large amounts of dialogue and side storylines which slow down the action, interspersed with bursts of slapstick, gags and comic chases which are much more reminiscent of light-hearted comedy based animation. The uneven tone and pace reflects the input of a large number of production partners—including two public service broadcasters—all of whom had differing expectations for the series.

Although 40 episodes of *Animalia* were eventually completed and aired by all the channels that had invested in the series (*Animalia* premiered in Australia in 2007), the production process was difficult. Initially, differences in production cultures complicated the early development of the series. For example, all members of the Los Aangeles-based writing team selected by Porchlight with responsibility for all scripts had formerly written for Warner Brothers. As a result they were unaccustomed to the Australian tendency to use character-driven storylines, and were also unfamiliar with Australian humour.

A further problem was that the same writers had also been used to writing for 2D rather than 3D animation. As Burnett explains:

> 2D is about big action, big voices, but with 3D our director said 'give me some space for my characters to act', and we said 'what do you mean, act? This is animation'. He just showed us how much could be done in terms of getting into their faces and seeing that emotion.
>
> (Ewan Burnett personal communication September 5 2010)

The country-by-country variations in programme style, pace and dialogue that can cause cultural discount of the eventual programming in international markets (Hoskins & Mirus 1988) also complicated the production process. For example, the BBC 'wanted it to be character driven, almost like English dirge drama whereas the Americans wanted us to be fast moving and funny' (Burnett personal communcation September 5 2010).

While the script writing and voice recording was largely completed in Los Angeles with a cast that was half Australian, in order to conform to Australian content requirements, 93 per cent of the production budget was spent in Australia, with most of the animation being created in Queensland. Unfortunately a skills shortage at the time, and the sheer scale of the project, compounded by the newness of CGI technology, held up production and increased costs. As Burnett explains:

> There had never been a pipeline put together for that kind of volume of material and so we had two previous teams working in our office in the studios in Queensland, we had 20 extra animators down here, and all of the lighting and rendering and compositing was done in Queensland as well as the score and things.
>
> (Ewan Burnett personal communication September 5 2010)

However due to 'a great lack of skills' among Australian animators, Burnett had to bring in a line producer from overseas, as well as animators from Argentina, New Zealand, France and Spain even though the presales for the series were to the BBC, Channel Ten, Nickelodeon Australia, and America. In fact, as Burnett admits, '[T]he facility we had in Queensland was grossly inadequate in terms of equipment, personnel and skills'. The need to import animators increased production costs while further complicating the production process as Burnett was forced to recruit from countries that had different production cultures again.

There are also certain cultural differences between each of the investing country's public service broadcasting systems, and concomitant differences in the expectations surrounding the role of their children's programming. In the US, where public service broadcasting has scant resources, children's programming for PBS tends to be curriculum driven, creating programmes like *Sesame St* or *Mr Rogers' Neighborhood* (Kunkel 2007).

On the other hand, the affluent BBC's children's channels are popular with parents (and children) because they are advertising free, have significant levels of high-quality UK content and contribute to the BBC's stated public purposes of 'promoting learning, creativity, diversity and emerging communications' (Steemers 2010: 59). Thus the BBC's children's television has a much wider remit than America's PBS. In contrast, in Australia *Animalia* was made for advertiser-funded Channel Ten and subscription service Nickelodeon. It therefore needed to conform to the requirements of the C classification, unlike the children's television made for the ABC.

Differences in production culture and programme function between Australia and the US and the skills shortage Burnett describes were exacerbated by a change of staff at the BBC during the drawn out production process. Thus while Michael Carrington, who at the start of production was controller of CBeebies, had been pleased with the style and pace of *Animalia,* his successor wanted it to be more dramatic and more character-driven. On the other hand, the Americans wanted the series to be more humorous and fast-paced.

The fact *Animalia* was made for public service broadcasters, advertiser-funded and pay-TV channels complicated the production process as the various executive producers attempted to ensure it was appropriate for their respective channels. Thus production and cultural difference was compounded by differing expectations among broadcasters (and their audiences) about the role and responsibilities of children's programming.

While *Animalia* served a public service ethos for CBC and the BBC, for Nickelodeon its primary purpose was to brand the channel and attract audiences. Due to *Animalia*'s large team of production partners, encompassing four countries, three public service broadcasters and a commercial broadcaster, managing these incongruities was extremely difficult for Ewan Burnett who has stated categorically that he would never attempt a similar project again (personal communication December 5 2010).

Despite production tensions and budget over-runs, the completed series of *Animalia* was shown at the Melbourne International Film Festival in August 2007 before launching on Channel Ten on November 11 2007. To Burnett's disappointment, Channel Ten scheduled it in a Sunday lunch time slot, rather than in the 4pm weekday slot, making it difficult for children to find in the schedule. The series also did less well in Australia because Channel Ten has a very limited budget and air time for promoting children's material despite the wishes of its producers and regulators.

The lack of on air promotion was frustrating for Burnett:

> I mean, it broke my heart with *Animalia*; there were a few promos on air but these shows just aren't publicised. ACMA tried to instil a way of forcing broadcasters to publicise but there's just no interest, because they don't see it as a commercial audience.
>
> (Burnett personal communication 2010)

Notwithstanding the lack of on-air promotion, *Animalia* achieved modest ratings in the Sunday midday timeslot, with an average of 328,000 viewers. Overall it was tenth out of the top 20 children's programmes on Channel Ten in 2007 while *H2O: Just Add Water* was number five, with 419 000 viewers (Free TV 2007: 26). On dedicated children's channel Nickelodeon *Animalia* was number two in the week of its premiere on Nickelodeon, after only *SpongeBob Squarepants*, in November 2008 with 57,000 viewers (MCN 2008). Despite being Nickelodeon's number two programme that week, the levels of audience fragmentation on children's services are clear from the low numbers of children watching. Low numbers also mean a series rarely gathers sufficient audience volume to achieve any level of merchandising.

Animalia still sells in international markets although it is sometimes bundled with other children's programming by its distributors. Nonetheless its production process and funding basis were fraught with difficulties for Australian producer Ewan Burnett, and the financial repercussions were extremely challenging for his small production company. Since 2010 Burberry Entertainment has been owned by UK transnational All3media.

In addition to the challenges inherent in funding and monetising the series, the need to accommodate the demands of multiple production partners also compromised the public value of *Animalia*. Although the series was based on an Australian book, the inclusion of characters corresponding to letters of the alphabet proved impossible for international audiences while in order to ensure the series' global circulation all the characters spoke with an American accent. *Animalia's* ability to speak directly to the Australia child audience and contribute to national cultural expression therefore remains doubtful, despite the importance of state subsidy and content quotas in its production.

High School Musical

Originally produced as part of Disney's annual slate of eight to twelve TV movies used to distinguish its children's channels from competitors like Nickelodeon and the Cartoon Network, *High School Musical* became an enormously successful made-for-TV movie franchise. Over 295 million people worldwide saw the original made-for-TV movie, while its sequel, *High School Musical 2* was watched by 18 million US viewers on its television premiere, making it the highest rating telecast of all time.

The story of high school students Troy and Gabriella and their attempts to fit in with their respective peer groups while following their passion for singing in musicals (and for each other) attracted very high audiences to Disney's international and local subscription channels. Indeed it made the Disney Channel US the number one basic channel for prime time viewing in US homes in 2007. Disney made the final in the series, *High School Musical 3*, for initial theatrical rather than television distribution. In cinemas it was the highest opening musical of all time, taking $42 million on its opening weekend in October 2008 (Child 2008).

The movie's message of the value of fun, friendship and self-belief clearly resonated with a transnational child audience. Possibly locating the narrative in the universal setting of a school, which reflects the experience of its audience and in doing so appeals to a wide range of children, was key to its success. The social tensions generated between the various cliques within the school would also be familiar to children in most countries. A familiar narrative of romance-based conflict underpins much of the storyline and plot development; the two lead characters are from opposing social groups, of athletic and academic students. The lead male character Troy is a local boy and basketball hero while Gabriella is portrayed as an academically talented outsider who has only recently moved to the school.

The relationship between Gabriella and Troy takes a fairly conventional and easily recognizable path, culminating in the characters' musical performance that unites the various social groups within the school. The movie's musical numbers including its signature 'We're All in This Together' embody feelings of acceptance, inclusion, unity and generosity and in doing so appear to resonate with a young audience's yearning for what Dyer has identified as a utopian, better and fairer social order (Dyer 1993).

Despite its conservative storyline, *High School Musical*'s cast, which included a Hispanic and black actor in key roles, as well as a lead character, Ryan, who can be read as gay and is only ever partnered with his sister Sharpay, underscores the film's message of inclusion and acceptance through the uniting force of music. So although ostensibly *High School Musical* pays little heed to the public service view of children as a special audience entitled to high-quality drama programmes, its messages of inclusion and acceptance are positive ones and the movie, with dance routines choreographed by Kenny Ortega, has high production values.

While the decision to make a musical for the tween audience was at the time an unusual one, once Disney realized how popular *High School Musical* was with children, the company was able to use its distribution and merchandising capabilities to capitalize on its success. Thus the movie's merchandising potential, backed by the might of Disney's synergistic, horizontally integrated parent company has produced substantial revenues, estimated at upwards of $500 million, far beyond what could have been predicted when the movie's $4.2 million budget was approved (Fitzgerald 2008).

High School Musical's global popularity reveals the advantages that vertically integrated children's television services enjoy in the global market and at the same time the difficulties small independent producers face when competing with such a powerful player. Disney was able to use its sophisticated marketing strategies and new multi-platform distribution capabilities to adroitly maximize the cultural visibility and profitability of *High School Musical* in the US and then throughout its global subscription services. Indeed the sophisticated marketing campaign which launched *High School Musical* in the States was, at Disney's insistence, replicated as closely as possible by all its international channels.

As part of the movie's launch campaign, its American premiere was heavily promoted on the Disney channel, with a countdown 'bug' on screen letting viewers know exactly how long they had to wait for the very first transmission. The second screening on the Disney

Channel was hosted by the movie's cast. Viewers were encouraged to go online at the end of the movie, so that they could print out sheets of the movie's song lyrics in preparation for the next day's transmission of a sing-along, open captioned version. (Party kits for this version had already been distributed via the website, so that viewers could host their own sing-along parties at home.) Over its launch weekend, and four separate transmissions, *High School Musical* attracted audiences totalling 33 million. Pay-TV channels' tendency to play much of their output repeatedly, thus extending its value to the channel, is tolerated and indeed often welcomed by their young audiences (Lury 2002).

Merchandising generated a valuable revenue stream. The movie's soundtrack was the biggest selling CD of 2006 in America, while the DVD sold 7.8 million copies worldwide, making it the fastest selling television movie of all time. A series of books about the characters sold 4.5 million copies and approximately 300 licensed products have been created including live productions such as *High School Musical* On Ice (Bloomberg 2008). Disney's animated movies have always been synergistically merchandised with video and DVD, theme park rides, transmission on Disney channels, TV series spin-offs, books and magazines all ensuring each item of Disney merchandise in a particular range feeds off and leads to another in the range (Bryman 2004: 88).

High School Musical's success demonstrates how very efficiently global media companies are able to market and monetize the programmes they both produce and transmit while they control content and distribution on a global scale. It also shows how children became accustomed to access television via multiple platforms including pay-TV, free-to-air channels, DVDs and online during the digital transition. Disney's astute use of *High School Musical* also conforms to four of the five 'protodigital' institutional practices described by Caldwell which 'prefigure and bridge' television's transition to digital, that is repurposing, branding, stunting and syndication (Caldwell 2004). As with its long-established merchandising practices, Disney excels at these newer institutional practices, unlike many free-to-air commercial networks that are struggling to retain their audiences, and advertising revenues, in a digital world. In digital regimes, new means of distribution allow a relatively small proportion of a channel's overall production and output, such as *High School Musical* to produce very large revenues particularly if that channel is adept at scheduling and marketing this output.

Pan-global children's service such as the Disney Channel can take advantage of digital-era content and carriage arrangements to efficiently distribute and repurpose their children's content in international markets. In the distribution and re-purposing of content, US conglomerates create children's television with an infinite shelf life in various iterations including in merchandise. Thus success in the domestic market is amplified globally through effective marketing and distribution with pay-TV systems facilitating programming's distribution across national borders. In these systems, transmission on broadcast television is just one small step in the process of marketing children's drama on a global scale.

US conglomerates like Disney and Viacom view the children's television programmes they produce in the same way as all their digital-era output, that is as 'quantities to be drawn and quartered, deliverable on cable, shippable internationally, and streamable on the

Net' (Caldwell 2004: 49). Such an approach is the antithesis of the Australian free-to-air commercial networks' treatment of the children's programmes in which they invest.

Disney's skilled distribution and merchandising practices exemplify the advantages that US producers have always enjoyed in a global market place. These include their economies of scale, access to new markets via digital transmission, large market share due to the scale of their operations and long established marketing and audience maximization strategies (Hoskins & McFadyen 1991). So although *High School Musical* is an American production, created by one of the largest companies in the world, its global success with young audiences—it has been seen by more than 295 million people worldwide—means its gargantuan presence in children's television viewing habits cannot be ignored when considering the impact of new global television settlements on Australian children's television production.

Securing access on a leading pan-global channel, as Shiff did with *H2O: Just Add Water* can be enormously beneficial to Australian independent producers. This kind of distribution deal exposes their programmes to international audiences many, many times the size of the domestic market audience in Australia. At the same time, the market dominance that accompanies the control of both content and carriage in children's television by vertically integrated corporations threatens to squeeze out small independent production companies from the market entirely. For independent production companies that do not have formalized or structural connections with international partners, organizations like the ACTF play an important role in supporting the international distribution of their programmes.

Conclusion

It is clear from the analysis of these examples of children's television made during the digital transition that internationalization has a significant impact on the production and distribution of Australian children's television. The advantages of internationalization for Australian producers have been and remain considerable. Jonathan Shiff benefited through his partnership with German public service broadcaster ZDF on all his children's drama productions. ZDF's involvement provided production capital while triggering Australian funding from Screen Australia. The relationship with ZDF provided secure carriage arrangements on global children's networks for Schiff's distinctive quality brand of children's drama. Shiff managed to accumulate these production advantages while crucially maintaining his creative autonomy and absolute authority as producer/director in each of his dramas.

In contrast, without a long-standing international partner such as ZDF Enterprises, Ewan Burnett was obliged to stitch together production funding from a variety of sources for *Animalia*, one of which obtained the US distribution rights also. There were cultural differences between the various production partners which were compounded by the different programming needs of their various channels. Further, Burnett's inexperience in animation production, compounded by a skills shortage in Australia, caused the production budget to spiral. For Ewan Burnett, the erosion of his creative autonomy as producer, and the concomitant diminution in the status of a single author/director, affected the overall production quality, which was not as well received in international markets.

The pay-TV channels like Nickelodeon and Disney that provide dedicated children's services alongside robust public service broadcasters like the BBC and ZDF value and pursue the lucrative child audience in a way that is inconceivable to the Australian commercial free-to-airs. This is largely because while the C drama category has been critical to Australian producers' success in creating quality content which has traditionally sold well in international markets, it is also responsible for ghettoizing children's content on Australian commercial free-to-airs as niche programming.

For advertiser-funded networks in Australia, the niche child audience is either too small or too problematic in providing advertising revenue. Although both *H2O: Just Add Water* and *Animalia* were commissioned and broadcast by Network 10 as part of the C drama quota, they were never perceived as an opportunity for commercial exploitation as, for example, family entertainment because of their role in filling the CTS obligations. Thus under the present system there is no commercial driver for children's content on free-to-air, advertiser-funded networks and Network Ten is unusual in its sustained support for Australian live action drama.

Networks in Australia are forced to invest in C drama but refuse to attempt to monetize the genre and thus remain in the analogue-era model of the child audience as an obligation. They have little interest in, for example, the kind of dedicated advertiser-funded children's channel that digital expansion of the bandwidth permits. Ironically, in Australia, the ABC successfully commercialized branded children's preschool television, such as *The Wiggles* and *Bananas in Pyjamas* from which it has made a great deal of money in international sales, while investing less resources in the production of live action drama for school age children.

The increased internationalization of Australian children's television and the rise of the global children's channel during the digital transition led to several important developments in the Australian children's television production ecology. First, under pressure to secure international investment and distribution in global television markets, Australian children's television has tended to become less culturally specific. Even children's programmes that are shot in iconic Australian locations may not mention a geographical location by name; the majority of Jonathan M Shiff's productions do not. Second, the increasingly complicated co-production arrangements that have come to characterize the production of Australian children's television may lead to a loss of creative autonomy for the producer, as the competing demands of multiple partners in different territories prove difficult to manage. Finally, global subscription services for children must maintain distinctive brand values to distinguish themselves from their competition. Brand Australia and the reputation for quality programming first established in the 1980s can represent significant value in crowded markets. Jonathan Shiff's 2013 deal with Netflix is evidence also of the demand for high-quality stories from specialist suppliers looking to attract subscribers.

The implications for the creation of public value in Australian children's television, a deliberately localized genre which must nonetheless circulate in international markets, of these industrial and economic changes, are profound. Any erosion in cultural specificity and reduction in production values erodes the ability of children's television to situate Australian children within their own culture and hence its public value. Yet at the same time, new means of distribution and access to global markets provide enormous opportunity for Australian producers of children's television. The role of state subsidy is not however to facilitate the creation of private value for investors, even if those investors happen to be state funded agencies such as Screen Australia. Historically, state subsidy was introduced for a genre at risk of market failure in response to the Australian public's concern about the lack of good quality, locally made television available to the child audience.

When the private returns created for investors become, quite rightly, a cause for celebration (and this is by no means a common occurrence in children's television), the importance of public value in justifying state subsidy for the genre can be eclipsed. The Australian child audience then becomes peripheral to economic and industrial arrangements with an outward looking focus, for which the local is merely a means of generating initial demand and investment for programmes aimed squarely at global markets. In such scenarios, state subsidy is reduced to nothing more than a measure of industry protectionism. Internationalization is therefore both a very good and very bad thing for Australian children's television.

Chapter 6

Policing the Settlement: Policy and Public Value in Children's Television

The Australian children's television production industry can, in many ways, be thought of as a policy construct. Much of the demand for programmes is generated by the content quotas enshrined in the CTS, while their creation is underpinned by direct and indirect state subsidy. Taxpayer-funded organizations, such as Screen Australia and the ACTF, support and promote Australian children's television, much of which appears on a dedicated children's channel funded almost entirely by government appropriation. The public value of television that speaks directly to Australian children, helping them to identify with Australian themes, language and society is considered justification for the taxpayer-funded support that spares audiences, broadcasters and producers its full cost.

This chapter examines the effects of media policy on the production, cultural integrity and public value of Australian children's television during the digital transition. The analysis will first consider the ageing policy mechanism the CTS, and the extent of the ABC and pay-TV's formalized obligations to the child audience. During the digital transition, a rethinking and recalibration of various policy instruments and state-funded organizations associated with the production of Australian screen content occurred. The effects of the reworking of these policy settings and the establishment of new screen agencies are described here.

The chapter concludes with analysis of the effects of international policy regimes in key territories the UK and US on Australian producers. Local policy settings affect a production industry whose success depends on the extent to which it can distribute Australian screen content in international markets. As a necessarily global enterprise, Australian children's television circulates within media industries characterized by vertical integration, concentrated ownership and pan-global distribution networks. Its production is therefore highly sensitive to alterations in policy settings in both Australia, and internationally.

While the introduction of new policies and screen bodies during the digital transition acknowledged the changes wrought by convergence and fragmentation, regulators still struggled to accommodate their effects. Key policy objectives appear to have been the further internationalization of the screen production sector and concomitantly the safeguarding of local content and the goals of national cultural representation. The intersection of these incompatible policy objectives in the spaces of local production contributed to a loss of public value in Australian children's television. Indeed much of the children's C drama supported by the increasingly anachronistic CTS was the logical outcome of these non-coincident policy settings.

The Role of the CTS in Australia's Digital Regime

Of the various state supports available to prevent market failure in children's television occurring, the most important is the CTS. In their current form the CTS express the requirements of a regulatory regime for children's television contained in the *Broadcasting Standards Act 1992;* they are administered and enforced by the ACMA. The CTS do not exist merely to ensure that television that is classified as suitable for children is present in the schedules. They are intended to maintain and improve the quality of children's television, redressing in some way the market forces that would minimize programme costs (Simpson 2004). Indeed in 2000, then regulator the ABA acknowledged that the C classification had 'helped to facilitate the development of an Australian children's television production industry with a worldwide reputation' (Aisbett 2000: 7).

In order to qualify as Australian content and be eligible for screen subsidies, local drama including children's drama must be considered to be under Australian creative control, as defined by the Australian Content Standard (2005), which sets minimum levels of Australian content, including children's television, on Australia's commercial networks. The standard is intended to:

> promote the role of commercial television broadcasting services in developing and reflecting a sense of Australian identity, character and cultural diversity by supporting the community's continued access to television programmes produced under Australian creative control.
>
> (ACMA 2005: 4)

The various criteria associated with this test are intended to ensure that the majority of the creative labour on a particular production is drawn from Australia. Creative control is the key to a programme's ability to qualify as Australian content and be eligible for state subsidy, although no explicit requirements for cultural specificity are embedded in the criteria.

The CTS are regularly reviewed, with the most recent review commencing in 2007. According to the ACMA, this review was prompted by the explicit need to position the CTS 'in the future digital and multi-channel broadcasting environment' (2008: 5). Unfortunately the new standards that emerged in 2009 did not directly address the effects of fragmentation on networks' resourcing of children's television or formally recognize the changes in children's viewing habits caused by new means of distribution. The lack of acknowledgement of Australia's digital transition suggests the CTS are vulnerable to 'policy drift'—policy-making that is unable to adapt in the face of political, social, economic or technological change and becomes, in the process, redundant (Parker & Parenta 2008). The ACMA did, however, rule out the possibility of a junk food advertising ban in Australia, suggesting the regulator was all too aware of the danger to local television production posed by a similar ban in the UK (Potter 2007).

While they play a crucial role in creating demand for local children's television, aspects of the CTS are problematic, particularly the lack of clarification that exists around their key terms. For despite the importance placed on children's television needs, the CTS do not contain a detailed definition of children or the state of childhood; they stipulate only that a child can be understood to be less than 14 years. Further details about age groups and classification norms intended to assist the production sector are provided in the ACMA's 2013 *Guide to Children's Television Classification*. The guide states that the C age band can be divided into three categories, Early C (5–7 years), Middle C (7–11 years) and Late C (10–13 years). But this kind of classification assumes a consensus among experts about the experiences and perspectives of these respective age groups that does not exist, rendering any interpretation of the television requirements of each age group highly problematical. Such chronological definitions fail also to acknowledge the diversity of children's lived experiences and backgrounds and the fact that childhood is 'historically, socially and culturally variable' (Buckingham 2000: 6). Neither do the ACMA's definitions provide a safeguard against the inevitable degree of subjectivity inherent in the classification process, which is coloured by the classifier's own understanding of the state of childhood and conception of 'the child' (Simpson 2004).

In its 2013 age-specific classifications the ACMA discloses it is relying on information supplied by child psychologist Kevin Durkin in a report undertaken for the ACMA in 2002. A reliance on a 2002 assessment of children's development assumes also that the state of childhood and children's lived experiences remain constant. Such an unambiguous position sits in stark contrast with the contemporary debates surrounding the changing nature of childhood and children's lives. Childhood, it is claimed, is being rapidly altered and even destroyed by the influence of television and new media technologies in children's lives (Palmer 2006; Postman 1983; Steinberg & Kincheloe 1997; Tapscott 1998). In its advice to producers, the ACMA also states that 'whether or not the program includes child characters, C and P programs must convey a child's perspective and deal with themes that are of interest to the target age group'. The lack of definition of a child and the state of childhood and therefore of a child's perspective renders this instruction vague and open to multiple interpretations (Simpson 2004).

Other criticisms have been levelled at the CTS by the production sector. In stipulating that children's programmes need to be made specifically for the child audience, the CTS have been accused of ghettoizing the child audience, because they exclude family entertainment which parents might want to watch with their children. Family entertainment is not as vulnerable to market failure as children's television, thus it is not considered deserving of regulatory support. A lack of flexibility in the CTS and a tendency to cater to the lower end of their target age group, so older or tween viewers are denied the opportunity to watch more challenging content, have also been identified (AFC 2007). Similarly some producers object to their inability to cater to children's aspirational viewing by including characters who are older than the under-fourteens predicated by the C classification (Screen Australia 2013a). The risk also exists that the CTS stifle innovation, because they fail to acknowledge the realities of contemporary multi-platform distribution and the online access to programme resources that most broadcasters provide (AFC 2007; ACTF 2008).

Further barriers to innovation are created by producers developing a tendency to self-censor, in order to create programmes that will be likely to achieve a C classification easily, thus avoiding any risk taking. The financing arrangements that underpin the production of children's television mean producers rather than networks carry the majority of the financial burden, which helps explain producer caution. Without the C classification, their programming has no value to commercial networks. Innovation and experimentation in the programme production mandated by the CTS are further discouraged by the networks' general lack of interest in the programmes in which they are obliged to invest for the child audience. In its 2007 submission to the CTS Review, the Australian Film Commission suggested that in order to encourage innovation and diversity, the ACMA might send out signals about its readiness to consider risky projects (AFC 2007). This was not a proposal that was pursued in the 2009 CTS Review's final recommendations.

Quality Considerations and the CTS

Concerns about the ways in which the CTS are expressed or enacted are somewhat mitigated in the production sector by the understanding that without this policy mechanism in place, little, if any, local children's television would appear on the commercial networks. But content quotas were never put in place merely as industry protectionist measures. Considerable taxpayer funding is invested in the production of Australian children's television because children require high-quality, culturally specific television made especially for them.

Unfortunately notions of quality in children's television are not interrogated or included in the CTS. As a result, quality in CTS-mandated children's programmes is difficult to define and measure. The public value of Australian children's television is predicated however on it being high-quality, with any reduction in quality standards therefore eroding its public value. Meaningful attempts to evaluate the notion of quality in CTS-mandated Australian children's television must be made if the extent to which contemporary children's television achieves its policy objectives is to be understood.

The closest standard in the CTS corresponding to the production elements that indicate quality for a children's programme is 2(c) the requirement that a children's programme is: 'Well produced using sufficient resources to ensure a high standard of script, cast, direction, editing, shooting, sound and other production elements' (ACMA 2009). In their 2013 guidance notes, the ACMA indicates that the quality objective of this standard is:

> the skilful and professional use of sufficient resources in all areas of production, which include the initial research of the concept, style and target audience, scripting and final on-screen presentation [...] For a C or P programme to be successful, it requires sufficient resources and high production values.
>
> (ACMA 2013: 11)

The guidance notes also specify that not only should C and P programming achieve high standards in 'scripting, casting, direction and post production elements' but they must also maintain a child's perspective and 'meet the viewing needs of a contemporary child audience'. Producers would achieve this 'by understanding the emotional, intellectual, social and other characteristics relevant to specific age groups of children' (ACMA 2013: 11). Once again these specifications rely on a construction of the child that is never clearly defined and a uniformity in child development and needs that does not exist. They also appear to assume a specialized knowledge of child developmental psychology that might reasonably be expected to be beyond the average television producer.

Despite these weaknesses, many producers consider the CTS ensure quality storytelling, which enhances the reputation of Australian children's television in international markets. A number of producers also believe that the CTS ensure that the child audience can be challenged by television in a safe way. This belief seems slightly at odds however with claims made at the same time that the CTS compromise creativity by forcing producers to be overly cautious (Screen Australia 2013a).

In contrast, some independent producers including Ambience Entertainment's Monica O'Brien see the CTS as having value beyond the demand they create for children's content, because they provide criteria by which producers can critique their own work. In doing so, O'Brien believes the CTS support producers' efforts to maintain competitive quality standards in their programmes. Of course producers have a further incentive to maintain quality standards because they are also competing with high-quality, international children's programming in global markets (Ward & Potter 2007).

Others working in the children's television industry dispute that the CTS were ever intended to safeguard programme quality, suggesting they were always focussed on generating demand for specialized children's television in Australia. According to Tim Brooke Hunt, controller of ABC3 in 2013:

> I think the CTS have been effective in assuring the age appropriateness of children's programs, and the fact it was produced by Australians. But quality? All ACMA can do is review scripts and budgets on a broad level. How are they going to assure quality? Once ACMA has given a project a provisional certificate based on reading scripts, it's hard for them to refuse to give a final certificate—that rarely happens. I think that the belief ACMA ensures quality has always been a bit of an illusion.
>
> (Personal communication June 12 2013)

Children's producer Noel Price maintains the lack of specificity in the wording of the CTS is actually an advantage for producers:

> Within themselves they're not terribly important because they basically require producers to make a series of motherhood statements that no producer could really get in a lather about. So providing you're not making shows that are overtly sexual or violent, generally

> you can make programs that will pretty much accord with what they ask. What the CTS do is throw an onus on the producer to say 'we're serious about making this children's program, we're going to have this kind of budget level, these kinds of creative values, we're going to try to meet the audience's needs in this way'. It's a series of statements of intention, which is alright, what else can it be? If it's too detailed and definitive then it's prescriptive, any broader and it's nonsensical.
>
> (Personal communication June 12 2013)

Price also highlights the challenges producers face in maintaining quality standards because:

> It's no secret that the commercials have never been in love with children's TV and only do it because they have to. So clearly the interest for them is how to fill their quota and meet the CTS standards for the cheapest possible price. So producers have to be innovative in how they put together their financing models so that they can meet the networks' needs while still delivering quality. It's no easy task and it's very competitive.
>
> (Personal communication June 12 2013)

Price concedes however that 'the primary determinants of quality are almost always the licence fees the networks are prepared to pay and the imagination and skills of those making the program' (personal communication June 12 2013). He notes, however, that the professional imperative for producers to maintain their reputations helps safeguard quality standards:

> Having your show supported by significant investment from a number of experienced industry players [who can't afford to invest in content they don't believe will work] is as clear an indication to both Screen Australia and ACMA as is possible to get that you're serious about hitting a high level of quality. Apart from anything else, it's pretty obvious that self-interest alone will motivate producers to want to ensure delivery of the very best content they can muster to these investors.
>
> (Personal communication June 12 2013)

Unfortunately Standard 2(c) makes no reference to adequate licence fees in its description of desirable attributes for children's television; this absence allowed commercial networks to reduce their investment in C drama during the digital transition.

Analysis of the ACMA's recent annual reports reveals an extremely high success rate for C drama applications. Of the 78 applications submitted to the ACMA for a C drama classification between 2008 and 2012, only one was refused, in 2012 (ACMA 2010, 2011; 2012; 2013). No information is provided about why this programme was refused classification. But as Kim Dalton, ABC head of television 2006–12 pragmatically observes:

> If the ACMA only gave C drama classifications to series that met the productions standards of a series like *My Place* then producers wouldn't be able to fund it. There just wouldn't be the money in the system; there just wouldn't be the material.
>
> (Personal communication June 11 2013)

Dalton's remark goes to the heart of the threat to quality standards and public value in children's television that developed during the digital transition. As networks reduced the licence fees they were prepared to pay, the rates at which C drama classifications were dispensed by the ACMA barely faltered. The production of high-quality drama with cultural integrity which speaks directly to the Australian child and in doing so achieves the policy objectives of the CTS is impossible without the means of securing its adequate funding.

In June 2014 the ACMA called for comment on proposed amendments to the CTS intended to reduce the 'regulatory burden' on licensees and, importantly, remove the ACMA from its long-standing role as classifier of C and P programmes. Given the rates at which C drama classifications are dispensed by the ACMA, any decision to allow commercial networks to classify children's programmes in-house appears unlikely to remove crucial processes of quality control.

Licence fees may be a key determining factor but notions of quality in television are also subjective. Producers and commissioning editors will have their own, internalized understanding of quality, which includes more than programme resourcing. Conceptions of quality vary and can include the technical expertise, cultural significance, and critical reception of programmes (Albers 1996). Quality standards may also have little or no bearing on the kind of television children prefer to watch. The most popular programme on ABC3 is not high-quality, culturally specific, live action drama but the reality comedy series *Prank Patrol*, which is based on a Canadian format.

In *Prank Patrol*, an invariably young, handsome, male host (Barney, Scotty and Andy in the Canadian, Australian and the UK versions respectively) assisted by two Ninjas helps children devise, set up and execute pranks on their friends and family. Hidden cameras capture the prank as it is played. *Prank Patrol* rates extremely well on ABC3 while generating high levels of multi-platform, fan-based activity.

In contrast, while ABC3's flagship drama *My Place* won awards and critical acclaim for its high production values and cultural significance, it did not resonate with the child audience. The series attracted only 37,000 viewers on Sundays on ABC3, compared with 176,000 watching *Peppa Pig* on ABC2 at the same time (Knox 2011). *My Place*'s cultural specificity also hampered its distribution in international markets. On the other hand, Network Nine's game show *Kitchen Whiz*, not a genre immediately associated with high-quality children's television, generates a transnational format which sells all over the world, as do the Australian episodes.

During Australia's digital transition, *Prank Patrol* and *Kitchen Whiz* enjoyed popular and economic success, in stark contrast with the low ratings and limited distribution of *My Place*, which was commissioned by ABC3 and made with ACTF and Screen Australia funding. So the attributes more commonly associated with quality in children's television, particularly the privileged status of culturally specific live action drama, are demonstrably at odds with the commercial realities of producing children's television for digital regimes. In the case of *My Place*, they are also at odds with children's viewing preferences.

While the ABC is widely recognized for paying Screen Australia minimum licence fees for its live action drama, the requirements for quality in children's programmes contained in the CTS are not attached to any specific levels of investment. Networks may choose to offer Screen Australia minimum licence fees; they may equally choose not to. No provisions exist then to ensure producers have sufficient resources to allocate to particular standards in development, production and post-production in C drama. As a result, while the CTS may guarantee production volume, they do not guarantee production values in children's television. Networks can simply offer producers lower licence fees, in a market characterized by an abundance of production companies competing for a finite number of programme commissions. So while Screen Australia's investment guidelines recognize licence fees as a mean of securing certain quality standards in the production of children's television, the CTS do not.

When commercial networks are free to fill their children's quotas without financial strings attached, the ability of that television to contribute to national cultural expression and achieve its policy objectives is impossible to guarantee. Indeed the separation of policy objectives from the means of their achievement contributed to the erosion in the public value of a significant proportion of the children's television commissioned by Australia's commercial networks during the digital transition. In the production of many CTS-mandated television programmes, the free market is operating efficiently within the very workings of a policy mechanism designed to prevent market failure. Economic expedience can be seen in networks' refusal to pay minimum licence fees and in the skewing of the C drama ratios towards animation. The production of deliberately internationalized children's television while in receipt of state subsidies designed to contribute to the goals of national cultural representation is another contemporary practice underpinned by the CTS.

Any meaningful analysis of quality in children's television must be conducted within the context of the sociocultural objectives that the CTS were originally intended to achieve. These objectives were grounded in the special status of the child audience and children's rights to culturally specific, high-quality age appropriate television. Unfortunately during the digital transition, the ascendancy of co-produced animations destined for international markets led to a significant decline in the cultural specificity of much of the children's television commissioned by Australia's free-to-air commercial networks. The CTS, and the ACMA's application of the Standards, failed to halt that decline.

The ABC and Public Value in Australian Children's Television

The expansion of the bandwidth that led to the establishment of ABC3 simultaneously contributed to the commercial networks' reduced investment in children's television. As the sands shifted under the business model for commercial television during the digital transition, ABC3 represented a significant new player in the production ecology. When considering the public value the CTS are intended to secure and their lack of relevance to the operations of the nation's public service broadcaster, the impact of ABC3 on the production ecology requires careful evaluation.

Although the provision of specialized children's television may a defining principle of public service broadcasting, the ABC has always been divorced from the policy settings intended to safeguard supplies of high-quality Australian children's television. Consequently, since the introduction of the CTS in 1979, the onus to produce minimum levels of drama for Australian children has lain predominantly with the commercial networks, not the public service broadcaster. Somewhat ironically then, prior to the digital transition, public value in Australian children's television lay largely in the programmes produced by Networks Seven, Nine and Ten rather than the nation's public service broadcaster.

The ABC's charter is generally considered an adequate safeguard for its treatment of the child audience, despite its lack of specific provision for children's programmes. The charter is contained in *The Australian Broadcasting Corporation Act 1983* which states that the functions of the corporation include 'broadcasting programmes that contribute to a sense of national identity and inform and entertain, and reflect the cultural diversity of, the Australian community' and 'broadcasting programmes of an educational nature' (ABC 1983).

Even so, while the ABC's charter refers to the broadcaster's need to be innovative and comprehensive, children are only mentioned specifically in the ABC's Code of Practice. There is little concrete detail to be found though in the code's stated principle that children's programmes should be 'enjoyable and enriching'. Further, while instructions are provided about the ABC's responsibility to protect children and young people from potential harm, content quotas are not (ABC 2014). In contrast the BBC's charter, obligations to the child audience are spelt out in its constitutional Agreement to provide two dedicated children's channels for UK children (BBC 2006).

The lack of specificity around the public service broadcaster's obligations to the child audience meant that pre-ABC3, considerable variations occurred in the amount of local children's programmes the ABC commissioned each year. Indeed the absence of quotas permitted an obvious lack of local commissioning during the digital transition, particularly between 2003 and 2008 (see Chapter 5).

Kim Dalton, director of television at the ABC 2006–12, maintains that before the introduction of ABC3, the ABC tended to overlook the child audience in the allocation of its resources:

> The public broadcaster, when times got a bit tough as far as its funding went, just de-prioritised children. Children were not part of the priority at the ABC for a number of years. Content just disappeared off our screens by and large.
>
> (Personal communication June 12 2013)

Low investment in local children's programmes was particularly apparent prior to the introduction of ABC3, despite the suggestion that in 2000 'the youngest of viewers were still the best served' at the ABC (Inglis 2006: 476). The lack of local production led to the broadcaster's reliance on US and UK imports and repeats to fill its children's schedule.

The ABC was able to abrogate its responsibility to the child audience during much of the digital transition, because of the lack of specific quotas in its charter, which meant its resources could be allocated to other areas, including News and Current Affairs. The introduction of $67 million in tied funding for the establishment of ABC3 in 2008 was greeted with derision by Friends of the ABC and the Community and Public Sector (CPSU) trade union, but it safeguarded funds for Australian children's television for the first time. Nonetheless the ABC, with the nation's only free-to-air-air children's channel, remains entirely outside the relationship between content quotas, the CTS and the any formalized regulatory acknowledgement of the special status of the child audience.

The CTS guarantee a certain annual volume of production hours, but these numbers do not change from year to year. There is therefore a permanent regulatory cap on demand for children's television on Australia's commercial networks. As the ratios between animation and live action drama in the filling of C drama quotas became skewed in animation's favour during the digital transition, the launch of ABC3 with $67 million of tied funding generated additional demand for children's drama. Unfortunately no overall increase in drama production levels occurred in the independent sector, because ABC3's commissions coincided with, and masked, declining levels of live action drama on the commercial networks. So while ABC3 has inevitably created extra demand and resources for the production of children's television, overall levels of culturally specific, high-quality Australian drama have not increased since its establishment.

But the introduction of ABC3 had much wider implications for the CTS and the production of children's drama in Australia beyond the creation of additional demand. The CTS do not apply to the ABC, therefore there is no point in the Screen Australia-funded, culturally specific, award-winning live action drama commissioned by the ABC since its inception engaging with the C classification process. No formal engagement exists between the CTS and the series *My Place* (2009), *Dance Academy* (2010), *Nowhere Boys* (2013) and *Worst Year of My Life, Again* (2013), all of which are recognized as examples of excellence in Australian children's television.

These children's dramas epitomize and embody all the qualities that the public demanded, and the CTS were intended to deliver for the child audience. They are well resourced, have high production values, tell Australian stories and situate Australian children within their culture. Some are in receipt of national and international prizes; the majority have sold well in international markets, while remaining identifiably Australian. But none of them has been classified as C drama. Consequently the establishment of ABC3 and its role as the principle source of commissions for live action drama contributed to the erosion of the CTS as a marker of quality and public value in Australian children's television.

Rather than being associated with the production of the best contemporary children's television in Australia, the C drama classification is now more closely related to non-culturally specific animation made deliberately for distribution in global markets. The CTS are no longer then an expression of public value in children's live action drama, although this role was integral to their creation and a key feature of the programmes they supported prior to Australia's digital transition. The erosion in the quality associations of the C drama classification has been exacerbated by the ACTF's involvement with many of ABC3's live action drama commissions since 2008.

The ACTF worked for many years with Australia's commercial networks in the production of acclaimed children's drama such as *Round the Twist, Mortified* and *Lockie Leonard*. This state-funded organization with a sustained commitment to the production of high-quality Australian children's television is now much more likely to be involved in children's television series made for ABC3, rather than for the commercial networks. As the networks increased their use of less expensive animation to fill C drama quotas, projects of the calibre of *Lockie Leonard or Round the Twist* became a distant memory.

The close working relationship between ABC3 and the ACTF is not a deliberate construction, but developed because the projects which the ACTF supports have generally ended up as commissions for the ABC rather than the commercial networks. CEO Jenny Buckland states that it is the reluctance of the commercial networks to pay the Screen Australia minimum licence fees required to produce high-quality live action drama that restricts ACTF involvement with their C drama. She notes too that the ABC has also chosen not to commission projects to which the ACTF has been very committed and strongly supported, so they have not been produced at all (personal communication December 22 2013).

The lack of relevance of the CTS to the ABC, and to the productions with which the ACTF has had most involvement recently, weakens the connections between the C drama rating and notions of public value in children's television. Indeed since the mid-2000s, the involvement of one or all of the government-funded institutions the ABC, ACTF or Screen Australia has become a much more reliable marker of public value in Australian children's television than the policy instrument designed for that very purpose. Yet the CTS and the lack of children's television quotas on the ABC ensure that the commercial networks remain at the heart of the production of Australian children's television.

Despite the effects of fragmentation and the downward pressure they exerted on licence fees during the digital transition, the commercial networks represent the legislated driver of demand for Australian children's drama. The CTS continue to guarantee a certain volume of production in children's television, although they cannot guarantee minimum spending levels on the genre. The erosion of the public value of Australian children's drama made with taxpayer-funded subsidies seems likely to continue, in the absence of any discernible measures to reverse the networks' reduced investment in their quota obligations.

Pay-TV and the NEDE Scheme

Despite the demonstrated importance of free-to-air television to the production of children's television, approximately 32 per cent of Australian homes with children have pay-TV. Since July 1, 1999 pay-TV channels in Australia have been obliged to invest in local content including children's programmes, under the New Eligible Drama Expenditure Scheme (NEDE) scheme. This scheme replaced a voluntary compliance scheme which failed to secure the requisite investment by channel providers.

In order to comply with the NEDE requirements, licensees and channel providers must spend a minimum of ten per cent of their programme expenditure on new Australian drama each year. The compulsory investment in local drama applies to subscription channels which identify as drama channels, a category which the ACMA defines as channels with an output of over 50 per cent drama. The regulatory requirement is not specifically designed to support children's content, but includes children's drama as a subset of drama generally.

In Australia in 2013 eligible pay-TV children's channels were Boomerang, Cartoon Network, Kids Co, Disney Channel, Playhouse Disney (but not Nick Jr), Nickelodeon, and CBeebies. While the new eligible drama supported by the scheme has to be first release Australian drama, it does not have to appear first (or indeed at all) on the investing pay-TV channel. So channels may co-produce or co-fund children's drama for which they will have repeat rights but which is initially broadcast by a free-to-air broadcaster. Channels may also carry forward a deficit and acquit their obligations the following year.

The NEDE scheme brings certain advantages to children's pay-TV channels, including access to locally made live action drama at a fraction of its actual cost. Pan-global channels such as Disney and Nickelodeon can effectively purchase expensive live action drama by contributing a small proportion of the budget for the rights to repeat transmission. Children's live action drama series including *H2O: Just Add Water, Pirate Islands, Mortified, Lockie Leonard, The Sleepover Club, Holly's heroes* and *Blue Water High* have all appeared on pay-TV channels in Australia as a result of these licensing arrangements.

These live action drama series, all of which were produced with direct and indirect state funding, often attract higher audiences on children's pay-TV channels than they do during their free-to-air transmission. Free-to-air commercial networks tend not to promote them or schedule them in popular slots, so they have not previously been seen by many children. As a result, pay-TV providers receive significant benefits from the C drama quotas, not the least of which is the commercial free-to-air networks' contributions of between 20 – 40 per cent of the budget of these popular, high-quality programmes.

Pay-TV's ability to secure the rights to high-quality C live action drama for between $10,000 and $25,000 per half hour rather than the $105,000 per half hour commercial networks pay, without having to go through the process of commissioning its own productions, has been criticized by the ACTF which argued in 2007 that:

> Pay television operators can make minimal investment in Australian children's programs while obtaining the rights to play these expensive productions on their channels. Indeed it has been argued that it is Australia's Pay television channels which are the biggest beneficiaries of the new draft CTS, which maintains these arrangements.
>
> (ACTF 2007)

Whether or not these arrangements represent public value for the Australian taxpayers who subsidized these programmes is debatable. The public value of the rest of the children's television created under the NEDE scheme is similarly difficult to gauge, given the lack of transparency that surrounds the ACMA's reporting of the NEDE scheme, and as a result, pay-TV channels' fulfilment of their obligations.

The commercial, free-to-air networks are required to report their compliance with the CTS annually to the ACMA, on a licensee by licensee basis. Data include broadcast hours, programme titles and annual programme expenditure by genre—all of which is in turn made publically available. In contrast while the ACMA releases lists of programmes that pay-TV channels have nominated towards the new drama quotas, it does not list all programmes, claiming this is commercial-in-confidence information. The ACMA does not reveal either which programme applies to which channel provider or individual expenditure figures per channel. It reports instead on compliance with the scheme on a 'whole of industry' aggregated basis that includes adult and children's drama together.

The lack of transparency in reporting makes it difficult to ascertain actual levels of investment in local children's programmes by the pay-TV industry in Australia. Nonetheless in 2012–13 the amount invested in the NEDE scheme on Australian and New Zealand drama decreased significantly, to $13.7 million, down from $24.38 the year before, leaving an aggregated shortfall requirement of $25.76 million, which the ACMA stated was to be met in 2013–14 (ACMA 2014).

No specific obligations exist for pay-TV children's channels to produce Australian children's television beyond the NEDE scheme. Further, some pay-TV children's channels viewed by Australian children may not be under any obligation to provide Australian content. Cartoon Network and Boomerang, both Turner Entertainment channels, arrive by feed from Asia. They are therefore classified as 'pass through providers'. As a pass through provider they do not have to invest in new eligible drama; the obligation falls instead on Foxtel, as the licensee. But Foxtel does not have to spend the money on content for the Turner channels, or even on children's drama. So the funding obligations of the NEDE are not tied to children's channels or children's content specifically.

The US conglomerates that provide the majority of the pay-TV services available to the Australian child audiences generally control content and carriage, distributing their programming (and associated merchandising) across multiple platforms on a global scale. Although data on the financial performance of US conglomerates' children's television services is hard to obtain, children's television is a very profitable business. Cartoon Network makes more money than CNN (Alexander & Owers 2007).

While an Australian presence allows pay-TV channels to increase their merchandise sales, develop their global branding and market their programmes, the amount of money invested in local content by pan-global conglomerates is generally limited to their regulatory obligations. The low demands of the NEDE ensure that pay-TV makes a minor impact on the production ecology, despite the size and resources of the parent companies distributing these channels worldwide.

Policy Developments during the Digital Transition 2001–13

During the digital transition, in acknowledgement of the effects of convergence and fragmentation, various policy settings around the production of local film and television content underwent review and some alteration. Key regulatory and screen bodies were also restructured during this period. In 2005 Australia's converged media environment was recognized when the ABA and ACA were merged to create the ACMA. Then in 2008 three screen bodies (The AFC, the FFC and FAL) became Screen Australia, with the primary function 'to support and promote the development of a highly creative, innovative and commercially sustainable Australian screen production industry' (Screen Australia 2010: 14).

With the establishment of Screen Australia an increased focus on the internationalization of the screen production sector was developed, without any obvious reduction in the prioritising of the goals of national cultural representation. The pursuit of these incompatible policy objectives for much of the digital transition caused subtle but significant changes in the production sector that contributed to a gradual erosion of public value in Australian children's television.

Screen Australia differs from its predecessors in a key area that has the potential to have a significant effect on the production of Australian children's television. Since its inception, the organization has not participated in the policy arena in the way that its predecessor the AFC did during major cultural policy debates between 1975 and 2008. These policy debates included discussions about the nature of the Australian film industry, the merit of different forms of state subsidy and the role of the commercial networks and pay-TV in the provision of local content. The AFC also voiced stiff resistance to any reduction in local content quotas during Free Trade Agreement negotiations. During these debates the AFC lobbied determinedly for certain policy outcomes intended to safeguard local screen content, including children's content.

Similarly the ACTF describes itself as a 'national children's media production and policy hub' (ACTF 2013) and clearly embraces vigorous participation in policy debates and discussions as a key part of its role in advocating for the child audience. Most recently the organization was a vital catalyst in the establishment of ABC3 and has been a long-time campaigner for maintaining the content quotas for children's television on the commercial networks.

In contrast while Screen Australia conducts extensive research into the screen production sector through its Strategy and Research Unit, no explicit policy emphasis is present in its reports and the organization does not have a dedicated policy unit as the AFC did with its Policy, Research and Information Branch. Screen Australia tends instead to confine its public discussions to the dissemination of research and information, and advocacy for local screen content, rather than active involvement in policy debates and lobbying activities. Less analysis and discussion of the ways in which Screen Australia's activities contribute to the achievement of stated policy objectives, including those around children's television, necessarily occurs than did prior to the AFC's demise. Consequently the levels of discourse around the achievement of local policy objectives, particularly the provision of high-quality local children's television, have been reduced by the nation's leading screen body's apparent reluctance to play a key role in the policy arena.

In 2007 just before the establishment of Screen Australia, a key new production support mechanism, the Australian Screen Production Incentive was introduced. The incentive scheme includes three important supports for local production, the PDV offset, the location offset and the producer offset. Under the producer offset, government funding shifted from tax breaks for private investors to rebate schemes that provided funds directly to the producer. The change was partly intended to ensure that producers retained the intellectual property of their programming, while providing financial support to the production sector. With equity in their own programming and thus a greater share in the profits, it was hoped producers would be working under a more sustainable, self-funding business model. In a critical regulatory development, the rules for the producer offset rebate changed from 65 episodes to 65 hours of programming in November 2011. This change freed Australian producers of half-hour series from the loss of production funding that even very successful examples of drama series suffered halfway through their third series.

Another production support mechanism designed to nurture a sustainable production sector was established by Screen Australia in 2009, the influential Enterprise Program. The scheme can allocate a company a maximum of $350,000 per year, for a three-year period. Since its 2009 launch, a total of $19.5 million has been distributed to 29 companies (Screen Australia 2013b). According to Screen Australia, the Enterprise Program:

> supports a diverse range of screen businesses that have identified opportunities to develop, step up and expand in terms of turnover, scale of production and range of business activities undertaken to enhance the company's sustainability.
>
> (Screen Australia 2013c: 1)

The Enterprise Program brings considerable benefits to the Australian independent production sector. It has increased the resilience, capacity and resources of a number of small independent production companies, allowing them to expand and professionalize their operations. The production companies which received funding in the first round experienced an overall increase in revenue of 59.9 per cent and a 21 per cent increase in profits over their three years of funding (Screen Australian 2012).

Describing the effect of the Enterprise Program on the sector, Kim Dalton, head of ABC Television 2006–12 observes:

> It's consolidated the production sector and meant that a number of medium sized companies have emerged. With that tag comes the ability of those companies to have basic infrastructure around research, financing, business affairs, development processes

> and in turn that's assisted with the sorts of volume of production those companies are dealing with. In turn that brings a certain degree of corporate weight and expertise.
>
> (Personal communication June 11 2013)

The increased resources and professionalism of what were, in some regards, cottage industries for many years has led to a maturing and a consolidation of the industry which has also benefited Australian broadcasters. Again, according to Dalton:

> From a broadcaster's point of view, if someone comes along with a proposal that aligns with what you're looking for, you can make a commitment to that programme knowing that you're dealing with an entity that will be able to pull the rest of the finance together locally and internationally, will be able to attract the right key creatives to deliver on the creative vision of that project and will have the infrastructure, systems, processes and expertise in place to actually follow through and deliver something of the quality that you as a broadcaster want.
>
> (Personal communication June 11 2013)

In 2009 in its first round of funding the Enterprise Program supported companies, such as Goalpost Pictures, providing the resources to make key creative appointments and to develop the globally successful movie *The Sapphires* (2012). Goalpost partner and *Sapphires* producer Kylie Du Fresne appreciates the positive effects the funding mechanism had on the company, saying 'it's been a big part of our business'. She acknowledges particularly the way the company's increased resources freed up producers to allow them to concentrate on the creative process (personal communication June 13 2013).

Another benefit the Enterprise Program brings to the Australian company in question is the way in which their enhanced production capacity and resources render them an attractive takeover target for larger, vertically integrated conglomerates looking to establish operations in Australia. The enhanced international collaborations which Screen Australia lists as a key guiding principle of the Enterprise Program encourage the conditions under which these acquisitions occur. The global trend towards vertical integration in the screen production sector provided further impetus for these new structural formations to develop in the Australian independent production sector during the digital transition.

Despite its considerable benefits, the Enterprise Program can also create certain disadvantages for producers and broadcasters. Once companies increase their staffing and other overheads, they need to maintain a certain volume of production to be able to pay for their expanded operations, or risk finding themselves in financial difficulties. The costs inherent in professionalizing and adequately resourcing companies that had previously operated much more precariously can also create inflationary pressures on their programmes, costs which must eventually be borne by the broadcaster. Nonetheless as Kim Dalton observes 'we could say that's just the reality of having to pay for the real cost of things, rather than somebody doing it from their front room and on the cheap' (personal communication June 2013).

The example of Matchbox Pictures, which was successful in the inaugural round of Enterprise Program applications in 2009, usefully illustrates how competing policy agendas can play out in the spaces of local screen production. Matchbox Pictures has a reputation for producing high-quality television drama for Australian broadcasters including *The Slap* (2010), *The Straits* (2012) and children's live action drama *My Place* (2009) and *Nowhere Boys* (2013) for the ABC. The company has strong connections with the broadcasting industry; producer Penny Chapman was the ABC's head of drama and head of television during the 1990s, while managing director Chris Oliver-Taylor held senior production roles at the ABC between 2000 and 2011 including head of business and operations.

After two years of receiving $350,000 a year in Enterprise funding, the small, independent company renowned for its high-end, diverse drama production slate was purchased by US conglomerate NBC Universal, in 2011. NBC Universal has multiple media interests which include a US television network, a movie studio, television production companies in the US, Canada and the UK, cable television services, the online movie service Hulu, and theme parks. NBC's globally distributed subscription channels have more than 400 million subscribers in 150 territories across Europe, the Middle East, Africa, Latin America and Asia.

At the time of NBC Universal's acquisition of its majority share in Matchbox Pictures, Screen Australia's chief operating officer Fiona Cameron stated that companies with majority foreign ownership could still be eligible for Enterprise Program funding because 'the test is centred on who has creative control' (Swift 2011). In 2009 the draft Enterprise Guidelines stated that Australian producers with 'Australian owned, controlled and registered companies are entitled to apply to the Enterprise Program for funding' (Screen Australia 2009: 2). In contrast the 2013 Enterprise Program Guidelines do not specify Australia ownership of companies as being eligible, but refer instead to 'Australian companies' and 'Australian producers' without specifying exactly what this entails (Screen Australia 2013c: 1).

With the increased resources provided first by the Enterprise Program and then the capital injection from its acquisition by NBC Universal, Matchbox was able to hire senior production executives, some of whom had long-standing connections with Australian broadcasters, to manage its expanding slate. Such appointments have a reputational worth; executives who have worked in senior production roles with local broadcasters are likely to become trusted suppliers. They will have extensive contacts and networks with local broadcasters, which give them a considerable advantage in the pitching and commissioning process.

Becoming part of a vertically integrated conglomerate brings advantages beyond capitalization and increased resources. Access to the parent company's distribution network helps secure sales and distribution advances for the Australian company's productions; the local branch will usually get access to the parent company's transnational formats. In 2013 Matchbox Pictures split its operations into Scripted and Unscripted content and branched into reality television, producing an original format *Formal Wars* (2012) for Network Seven and a local version of the US format *The Real Housewives* for pay-TV service Foxtel in 2013. Thus Matchbox is now involved in the production of original and non-original formats. A production company which is part of a vertically integrated transnational ownership structure may also get the opportunity to distribute their scripted formats in international markets; NBC Universal was reported to be making a US version of *The Slap*, with Matchbox, in 2012 (Idato 2012).

As well as being in receipt of Enterprise Program funding, Matchbox Pictures is a significant beneficiary of additional Screen Australia funding support for its television drama. The company's extra funding included, in 2009, $2,212,587 for the children's series *My Place* and $1,050,000 for *The Straits* and in 2010, $1,620,260 for *The Slap* and $480,000 for *Sex: An Unnatural History*. In 2011 Matchbox received funding that included $410,000 for *Next Stop Hollywood* and $645,000 for the TV movie *Underground*. The company also received $1,750,939 for children's live action drama *Nowhere Boys*. Analysis of Screen Australia annual reports reveals that between 2009 and 2013, during which it was majority owned by a US conglomerate, the company received a total of $9,330,736 in Screen Australia funding for its productions, including interactive and multiplatform resources.

Indeed virtually all of the indubitably high-quality, critically acclaimed drama produced by Matchbox Pictures since the company received Enterprise Program funding in 2009 also benefited from additional Screen Australia investment. As managing director Chris Oliver-Taylor notes:

> We understand the model. We move shows around, to another round, if needed. And we talk at length with Screen Australia and our broadcasters. I can`t recall in the two years I`ve been [at Matchbox] a show not being funded.
>
> (Quoted in Kriston, Oct. 16 2013)

Without the initial Enterprise Program funding, Matchbox Pictures would have struggled to increase its production slate to the extent that made it an attractive acquisition for NBC Universal. Without ongoing Screen Australia investment in its critically acclaimed drama, a large proportion of which is made for the ABC and all of which contributes to the achievement of the goals of national cultural representation, Matchbox would have been unable to secure production funding. Thus the company epitomizes the logical outcome of the competing policy agendas of localism and internationalism in Australian screen production. In January 2014 NBC Universal announced it had fully acquired Matchbox Pictures with Oliver-Taylor declaring:

> We are thrilled to cement our successful relationship with NBC Universal. The fact that NBCU have decided to fully-own the company is testament to both the wonderfully talented staff here at Matchbox and NBCU's confidence in Australia's creative industry, of which we are immensely proud to be a part.
>
> (Knox 2014)

It would appear then that under Screen Australia's funding model, 'creative control' enables a US conglomerate to indirectly access state subvention designed to support the Australian independent production sector. These financial arrangements would seem to represent something of a remaking of the rules and a reshaping of the policy settlement. These new production circumstances also beg the question of whether Australian television including children's television needs to be produced by an Australian production company in order to have public value. If creative control is the key criteria for generous, sustained state subsidy then logic suggests Australian children's drama could be made anywhere in the world (as is already the case with some C drama animation).

Decisions made by Screen Australia in the allocation of its resources are as important as the policy environment in which it operates. Something of a conflict of interest appears to exist for the organization in its dual role as administrator of the Enterprise Program and distributor of funds for the development, production and marketing of local screen content. One of Screen Australia's key performance indicators (KPIs) for State and Industry Partnerships is 'At least a 15 percent increase in the number of projects completed by production companies that have received Enterprise funding' while a second is 'at least a 12 percent increase in these companies' revenues' (Screen Australia 2012: 100).

Screen Australia has a finite amount of money to invest in local production and competition for its production support funding is intense. Despite the introduction of the Enterprise Program, local content quotas for Australian television have not increased or, in the ABC's case, been introduced (although additional funding received by the ABC in 2009 helped fund an increase in local drama production). The finite number of commissions (including children's drama) in the local production sector and its own KPIs could encourage Screen Australia to favour the production funding applications of companies in receipt of Enterprise funding. Screen Australia investment in their productions makes it a great deal easier for Enterprise funded companies to increase their completed projects by 15 per cent.

In addition to the Enterprise Program, which encourages international connections, partnerships and indeed ownership of the production sector, Screen Australia also supports internationalization in the production of children's television through the annual Asian Animation Summit. This Screen Australia initiative (with the ABC, Korean and Malaysian broadcasters) is designed 'to showcase Asia's strongest animated projects looking for investors and partners' and 'to stimulate co-production and co-financing in the region' (Screen Australia 2013d). Screen Australia offers travel grants and other financial supports for Australian producers living in Australia with an animation TV project aimed at children and endorsed by an Asian broadcaster. In the ten years to 2013, more animation co-productions than live action drama co-productions were made in nine of those years.

Although animation lends itself more easily to co-productions than live action drama, the rise in production levels and the state subsidies available in many territories for the genre threaten to produce a global glut of content. As many broadcasters pay reduced fees (or sometimes no fees at all) for their animation, because of its producers' need to have their series on air in order to generate merchandising sales, distribution advances have dropped. Many specialist children's channels also make their own animated series in-house, which further reduces demand for the genre. Again the public value of the animated children's television produced with the support of Screen Australia as part of these internationalizing activities is unclear, given its limited capacity for national cultural expression.

The challenges posed to Australian policy instruments during the digital transition and the continued need for local content supports in a transforming, increasingly internationalized media environment led to the establishment of the Convergence Review in 2012, which was undertaken through the Department of Broadband, Communications and the Digital Economy. One of the issues with which the review grappled was the protection and support of local content when new platforms of delivery threaten to render content quotas meaningless and unworkable. The review recognized that:

> Convergence of media content and communications technologies has outstripped the existing media policy framework. Many elements of the current regulatory regime are outdated or unnecessary and other rules are becoming ineffective with the rapid changes in the communications landscape.
>
> (Convergence Review 2012: 1)

In its final report, which was released in April 2012, the Convergence Review made a number of recommendations, some of which were quite radical. In recognition of the difficulties of administering content quotas in multi-platform media environments they included the establishment of local content obligations for content service enterprises or 'large enterprises providing professional content services to a significant number of Australians' rather than traditional broadcasters. Under the proposed safeguards for local content, these content service enterprises would make contributions to a 'uniform content scheme' designed to support the production of Australian content (Convergence Review 2012: 2).

The review also recommended doubling content sub-quotas, including for children's television on Australia's free-to-air commercial networks but allowing broadcasters more flexibility by letting them put their CTS quotas on their multi-channels. The review also suggested the 55 per cent Australian content quota be extended to the ABC, in acknowledgement of the vulnerability of local content to the current ABC charter. Of these recommendations, only the moving of children's quotas to networks' multi-channels was acted on however, meaning the commercial networks could create dedicated destinations for the child audience from January 2013. The ABC remains free of content quotas for Australian drama, including children's drama.

The UK Context

Despite the influence of Australian cultural policy on Australian children's television, the domestic market is too small to sustain a viable children's television industry and Australian producers are economically bound to distribute their programmes in international markets.

They are therefore sensitive to alterations in policy settings in co-production territories, including the UK where communications industries regulator Ofcom introduced a junk food advertising ban in 2006. The combination of certain structural similarities in both countries' markets, and a shared strong public service ethos means that children in both countries are still considered a special audience. With the C classification serving as a marker of quality during the 1990s, co-production arrangements and pre-sales with UK broadcasters, including the BBC, were also common. The relationship between the Australian production sector and UK broadcasters changed during the digital transition, as increasingly divergent policy settings developed in each country.

New delivery platforms and new children's television services challenged policy settings surrounding children's television in the UK, just as they did in Australia. In 2014 30 dedicated children's channels were on air in the UK and television remained the most popular form of media for UK children (Ofcom 2012). Prior to the *2003 Communications Act*, UK free-to-air advertiser-funded channels had quotas for children's content (but not for drama). With the ratification of the Communications Act, these quantitative quotas for children's television were quietly dropped with few in the industry recognizing the significance of the changes until it was too late (Steemers 2010).

As a result, once the 2006 junk food advertisement ban was brought in, leading free-to-air commercial broadcaster ITV could reduce and eventually more or less abandon its commitment to funding children's drama, leaving the majority of investment in local children's drama to the BBC. Thus in the UK the public service broadcaster is the most significant source of funding for children's drama, as opposed to the commercial networks. The absence of government subsidies (until the animation supports of 2012) and quotas for children's programming and the presence of a well-funded public service broadcaster mean the BBC is likely to remain the most important source of funding for UK children's drama.

In contrast in Australia, advertiser-funded, free-to-air networks are the primary investors in and publishers of Australian drama including children's drama. So despite its key role in commissioning live action drama since 2009, ABC3 still only spends about one third of the commercial networks' enforced investment in children's drama each year. The ABC is also a much smaller organization than the BBC and its commercial arm ABC Commercial lacks the capacity to distribute globally ABC programming, channels and merchandise in the way that BBC Worldwide does for the BBC. So the ABC was never in a position to become the most significant player in children's drama production in the way that the BBC became during the UK's digital transition.

In 2012 after a long campaign by industry groups and children's media advocates, the UK government introduced a taxation subsidy scheme designed to support the production of animation, which had dropped by half in the preceding five years. Long-established companies including Chapman Entertainment, Cosgrove Hall and Chorion were forced to close during this period. The 25 per cent rebate on 80 per cent of the animation budget was heralded as a lifeline by UK producers while its introduction appeared likely to increase supplies of animation globally.

By 2013 the production of UK children's television had recovered slightly. The animation tax subsidy and ITV's decision to exploit the intellectual property of its children's properties including *Thunderbirds* by remaking these shows as original productions led to increased activity in the sector. Nonetheless the BBC remained the primary source of UK children's television funding, sourcing 45 per cent of its children's content from the UK independent sector and spending 100 million pounds each year on British-made children's content (Godwin 2013). The BBC regularly acquires Australian children's television from the ABC, and occasionally enters into co-production arrangements, with levels increasing since the launch of ACB3. Productions in which the BBC has been a significant investor include *Dead Gorgeous* (2009), *Me and My Monsters (2009), Dennis and Gnasher* and *Worst Year of My Life, Again* (2013).

Conclusion

Domestic policy frameworks, particularly local content quotas, have a profound impact on the quantity, quality and public value of Australian children's television. Policy instruments such as the CTS and the Enterprise Program play a central role in regulating the levels of demand and state subsidy associated with Australian children's television. They also exert considerable influence on the children's television that is made with taxpayer funding subsidies, particularly its cultural specificity, production values and ability to speak directly to Australian children. But the creation of public value and indeed the public themselves were noticeably absent from the intramural conversations between policy makers, the production industry and broadcasters that were such a feature of the digital transition.

The CTS remained vital to the Australian children's television production industry during the digital transition. In their current form however, they treat all forms of C-rated drama in the same way, regardless of genre and cost. There is therefore no regulatory incentive to invest in more expensive genres such as live action drama, which is often more difficult to distribute internationally than animation. Quality standards become increasingly difficult to maintain in the absence of minimum licence fees or other budgetary stipulations attached to the CTS. The CTS' lack of relevance to public service broadcaster the ABC is also problematical. When the vast majority of culturally specific, award winning children's live action drama made by government-funded bodies sit entirely outside the C drama classification process, the C drama inevitably loses its quality connotations. The absence of quotas on the ABC is similarly problematical, given the institutional neglect of the child audience that can, and has, occurred in their absence.

Australian governments are inevitably going to tend towards policy settings that support the expression of the goals of national cultural representation. This is because in Australia, prior to the introduction of content quotas, screen content sourced from outside Australia was the norm, to be supplemented by much smaller amounts of local programmes. Australian governments will continue to create media policy that foregrounds the achievement of the goals of national cultural representation in its justifications, because Australia's television system is so much smaller than the UK or US systems. Without these protectionist policy regimes imported content would once more dominate the schedules and the local screen production industry would be decimated.

The internationalization of children's television in Australia can nonetheless be seen to be facilitated at several levels by various Australian national policy frameworks. Firstly, media policy around the establishment and operations of pay-TV services in Australia facilitated market entry for children's subscription services. Second, the limits to Australian content requirements mean that globally distributed children's programming appears on these channels and on other Australian free-to-air channels. Government funding models for the ABC ensure that the nation's public service broadcaster also relies heavily on US and UK children's television to fill its schedules. Finally policy settings around government funding and subsidies for television drama allow transnational companies to produce and distribute subsidized children's television drama in Australia and beyond. It is clear then that national broadcasting policy regimes operate on a number of levels to determine how transnational companies from foreign countries operate in Australia while at the same time ensuring a stable marketplace within which to do so.

Policies surrounding the production of Australian children's television are being worked through in television settlements that were transformed by the introduction of digital technology, global moves towards de-regulation in audio-visual markets and the vertical integration of media conglomerates. Certain Australian media policies supported and administered by Screen Australia developed mutually incompatible aims during the digital transition, although both sets of aims might be important and legitimate. In a particular policy conundrum, the achievement of the goals of national cultural representation through protectionist measures like quotas and subsidies for children's drama, and the encouragement of international ownership and investment in the Australian screen sector contribute to a loss of public value. They do this by subsidizing the operations of US transnational corporations, even as these same policy settings secure the production of high-quality, culturally specific drama, including children's drama.

Chapter 7

Producing Children's Television for Digital Regimes: Case Studies from the Production Sector

The following case studies, of production companies and the children's television they create, illustrate how the myriad elements of Australia's children's television production ecology interact with one another. They are emblematic of the key trends and production norms that gradually developed from 2001 to 2014. They reveal the difficulties Australian producers face in financing children's television and the vital role state subsidy plays in the creation of culturally specific Australian children's drama. They equally reveal the talent, resourcefulness, ingenuity and passion for storytelling of those working in the production sector and the extraordinary capacity of the Australian screen production industry to consistently punch above its weight. These case studies also demonstrate how national cultural expression became more difficult to achieve during the digital transition, due to the effects of the fragmentation that characterizes digital regimes.

Goalpost Pictures and *Lockie Leonard*

Sydney-based independent production company Goalpost Pictures makes a wide variety of screen content including drama, feature films, telemovies and documentaries. It has established a reputation for producing high-end screen content and supplies programmes to Australia's free-to-air networks, including the ABC. In 2012 Goalpost Pictures enjoyed remarkable global success with the musical comedy feature movie *The Sapphires*, the 14th highest-grossing Australian film of all time. The company was in receipt of Screen Australia Enterprise Program funding from 2009 to 2011.

The need to balance creative and commercial considerations in the production of high-quality Australian children's television can be seen in Goalpost Pictures' only foray into children's television production, the live action drama *Lockie Leonard* (2007–09), of which two series were made. *Lockie Leonard* was commissioned by Network Nine, with Screen Australia investment. It was one of the last Network Nine C dramas to access the funding subsidy, which suggests it was also one of the last dramas for which Nine paid minimum licence fees.

Lockie Leonard is based on the award-winning trilogy by Australian author Tim Winton, to which Goalpost Pictures had the rights at the time. The semi-autobiographical books are set in Angelus, a small town in Western Australia where 12-year-old surfing devotee Lockie moves with his family after his father, a policeman, is stationed there. They contain some themes not normally associated with C drama, including mental illness and teenage sexuality.

Goalpost Pictures' reputation for successfully producing ambitious, quality drama projects led to Network Nine approaching them with a proposal to turn the books into C drama as part of the network's CTS obligations. As producer Kylie Du Fresne explains:

> The books were difficult to adapt for the C classification because of some of the content. I think some other production companies over the years had attempted it but it hadn't worked out.
>
> (Personal communication May 2 2013)

While Network Nine agreed to pay minimum licence fees and the series received Screen Australia funding, it was very difficult for the first series to attract the significant international investment it required to complete the production budget.

The international presale market for Australian children's live action drama is a small one and broadcasters tend to work repeatedly with production companies with whom they have established relationships based on trust. Goalpost Pictures did not have an international reputation for making children's television or established relationships with children's broadcasters in other territories. *Lockie Leonard* eventually secured international investment when Series One sold to Jetix TV, a European children's channel skewed to a male audience, which launched in 2005. The new channel wanted a distinctive commission to help forge its identity. A French partner also came on board.

For Du Fresne, an experienced producer (her recent producing credits include *The Sapphires* and *An Accidental Soldier*) who had not previously worked on children's drama, the lack of familiarity with the genre proved to be an advantage. Du Fresne, who admits 'we were quite naive about what the C classification meant', did not have an overly-protective attitude towards the child audience. She was aware that some of the books' themes might be problematic but believed that any screen adaptation of Tim Winton's novels could not avoid the potentially controversial issues. As she observes, '[T]hese are very well loved and successful books. We knew we'd have to be clever about how we approached it, but we had to attempt all of it (personal communication May 2 2013).

Various creative decisions shaped the series that was made; in particular the decision to choose certain crew members who had no previous experience in children's television seemed to contribute to its high production values. Du Fresne deliberately chose drama writers who had not written children's series before and would not anticipate the regulator's possible objections to their scripts. The lack of advertising revenue associated with children's television meant less scrutiny of the series' scripts by Network Nine while Goalpost Picture's reputation for excellence also contributed to the creative autonomy Du Fresne enjoyed. As the network did not act as a gatekeeper on the content, Du Fresne was able to tackle the books' more controversial issues including Lockie's wet dreams and the bouts of depression suffered by Lockie's mother. Du Fresne says of the writing process:

> We wanted writers not to be constrained by what their experiences with the C classification might have been previously. We felt that we had to unburden the series from that. The naiveté would allow the writer to go somewhere that they might not if they'd previously been through the process of 'you can't do this [...] you can't do that' [...] which perhaps some children's TV goes through.
>
> (Personal communication May 2 2013)

Du Fresne also decided to stretch the boundaries for the child audience while protecting children from any explicitly sexual content. The series resolutely tackled teenager sexuality, in a way that had not previously been seen in C live action drama, electing to use humour to subtly construct the narrative. As Du Fresne explains:

> We wanted to do an episode involving Lockie and wet dreams. And we worked very hard to find funny and comedic ways in terms of the sexuality, to deal with that, a bit like the model of *The Simpsons* where it's at different levels. Kids and parents will read it differently.
>
> (Personal communication May 2 2013)

The wet dreams episode, which relies on a garden makeover analogy to illustrate how the arrival of puberty leads to the development of a 'water feature', was approved by the then regulatory the ABA at script level and went to air on Network Nine. According to Du Fresne the regulator's need to protect the child audience led to a focus on certain elements in the script that surprised her:

> We were quite successful with the ABA at script level over things like that (the wet dreams episode), but then they would come back with really unexpected things about kids wearing a helmet while skateboarding.
>
> (Personal communication May 2 2013)

In an interesting example of the classification norms that prevail in different countries and the difficulties inherent in making children's television for multiple broadcasters, when the BBC acquired the series, they refused to air the wet dreams episode in the UK. The public service broadcaster (the home during the 1990s of envelope-stretching dramas *Grange Hill* and *Byker Grove*) argued the wet dreams episode would be too controversial for UK audiences.

Du Fresne also had a clear sense of the child audience for whom the series was being made, which underpinned her decision to include some of the stronger themes from the Tim Winton's novels. She explains that she and the writers thought of children as a sophisticated audience, capable of taking on board a lot of complex and emotional issues: '[W]e didn't want to dumb down. Let's not patronise our audience, we were very clear about that' (personal communication May 2 2013).

The decision to avoid preconceptions about the child audience did not only mean that Du Fresne deliberately chose drama writers who had not written children's series before but even extended to the hiring of the production crew. Du Fresne eschewed the use of directors who had previously worked in children's television, because of the assumptions about a children's television drama they might make. In order to achieve the quality standards she wanted the series to have, Du Fresne also deliberately recruited some members of the crew from a film rather than television background:

> So we used all adult directors or short film directors who'd done TV and film. The Director of Photography came from more of a film background. So it's just those kinds of choices that affect quality, the crew you put on that are going to give a series a certain look. We'd done a fair bit of TV by then, a lot of TV movies [...] we were just trying to bring our philosophy to kids' TV production.
>
> (Personal communication May 2 2013)

Lockie Leonard is identifiably Australian, although during the production several factors including BBC funding did lead to pressure to reduce its cultural specificity. Both series were filmed entirely in Western Australia, where the books were set, which Du Fresne believed was vital to the success of the adaptation:

> With *Lockie Leonard* we didn't have a lot of resources. But we felt it's Tim Winton, his landscape and the feel and look of his landscape [...] he's such a visceral writer, we have to create a series that captures that, as well as the drama.
>
> (Personal communication May 2 2013)

Shooting on location in Albany put a significant strain on resources however, because the entire cast and crew required accommodation in a remote location. The decision to set the series against the visually exciting backdrop of one of Australia's greatest icons, the surf beach, leaves little doubt as to its location. Further Australian signifiers include the character Egg, Lockie's best friend, who is Indigenous; the edgy humour of the series; and the cast's Australian accents. The series therefore speaks directly to the Australian child audience. But with international investment came pressure from the European channel to internationalize the series and to reduce its cultural specificity:

> We had that international voice of people that we trusted saying 'we love it because it's unique but don't make it so Australian because it's not accessible'. So we did have a little bit of that pressure, they had script approval and other normal approvals.
>
> (Personal communication May 2 2013)

The pressure increased when a second series of *Lockie Leonard* was commissioned by Network Nine. Series Two secured a presale to the BBC, a prestigious connection but one that involved more attempts at creative control and more concern about the need to protect the child audience. The production of Series Two was also affected by changes in personnel at the UK broadcaster. As Du Fresne observes:

> In Series Two, when we had the BBC on board, it was very different experience. They had many more script comments about its appropriateness for children. At the BBC the original commissioning editor left just as we started production. Then we worked with their replacement, who was very good. We had a great relationship with her. But it was probably much more of a conservative voice than we had on Series One.
>
> (Personal communiation May 2 2013)

A more conservative gatekeeping role at the BBC helps explain the BBC's decision not to play the wet dreams episode, which might, in fact, have proved perfectly acceptable to UK audiences. Its perceived unsuitability is indicative of the felt need to protect the child audience that can contribute to the overly-cautious attitude to the production of children's television that Du Fresne was so keen to avoid.

Despite *Lockie Leonard*'s evident quality and potential audience appeal as family viewing, Network Nine initially scheduled it at 4pm on a week day. Unfortunately the series went on to suffer from erratic and disrupted scheduling, which saw it suddenly taken off air and subsequently transmitted at different times in different markets. Having premiered with over 100,000 viewers, the audience dropped as low as 50,000 for later episodes (Screen Australia 2013a). *Lockie Leonard* did, however, receive critical acclaim and won numerous awards in Australia, including the Australian Film Institute Award for Best Children's Drama, the Australian Teachers of Media Award for Best Children's Television series in 2007 and the 2008 TV Week Logie Award for Best Children's Television series. Both series of *Lockie Leonard* aired on the BBC in the UK while Series Two went on to sell to the Disney Channel HD in the US.

Although *Lockie Leonard* was made with state subsidy, to help fill Network Nine's children's content quotas, the audience for whom it was intended, Australian children, struggled to find it in the schedule. Network Nine may have commissioned this high-quality, identifiably Australian children's drama for which it agreed to pay Screen Australia minimum licence fees. But the way in which *Lockie Leonard* was scheduled suggests Network Nine was more interested in filling quotas than bringing Australian live action drama to Australian children. Clearly the series aligned with Australian cultural policy objectives, but Network Nine's poor scheduling practices undermined its public value by limiting its cultural visibility.

Since the production of *Lockie Leonard*, Goalpost Pictures has concentrated on the production of feature films and television movies for adult audiences. The series remains the only children's production the company has made to date. As Du Fresne explains:

> I suppose we felt we'd been quite spoilt by having the chance to do *Lockie* and were incredibly proud of what we'd achieved on that. So we didn't want to do just anything.

> We didn't see it suddenly being a huge part of our business. It had to be the right kind of project.
>
> (Personal communication May 2 2013)

Du Fresne also concedes that the downward pressure on licence fees and the general reluctance of commercial networks to pay Screen Australia minimum licence fees would have led to a compromise in quality standards that Goalpost Pictures was not prepared to accommodate:

> We pitched something but it was at the point where the commercials were only wanting to do cheaper live action and we thought that's not really our business, our business is quality drama, whether for the small or large screen.
>
> (Personal communication May 2 2013)

Goalpost Pictures' broad production slate provided the creative and financial freedom to withdraw from the production spaces of Australian children's television. Smaller production companies for which children's television is a larger part of their portfolio might struggle with the consequences of a similar decision.

The production of *Lockie Leonard* underscores the importance of direct state subsidy as well as international investment in the production of high-quality Australian children's drama. While the need to accommodate different broadcasters' perspectives during the production process created some complications, *Lockie Leonard* is nonetheless a culturally specific Australian drama and thus speaks directly to the Australian child audience. In 2006 Network Nine was sold to the private equity company CVC. The network's last children's live action drama commissions were *Lockie Leonard* and *A GurlsWurld*, in 2009. Since then Network Nine has largely relied on animation to fill its C drama quotas.

Ambience Entertainment, *Figaro Pho* and *Kitchen Whiz*

Sydney-based Ambience Entertainment was established in 1991 and acquired by Australian entertainment company Omnilab Entertainment in 2004. It is part of a vertically integrated ownership structure, but operates as a separate business. Ambience Entertainment has a broad production slate across a range of genres of children's screen content including feature films and game shows. The company specializes in 3D-animation.

Ambience's children's productions include animations such as *Erky Perky* (2006–07) and *The Adventures of Figaro Pho* (2012–), the 2012 feature film *Tomorrow When the War Began* (which took $13.5 million at the Australian box office); live action entertainment such as the preschool series *Magical Tales* (2010); and game shows *Pyramid* (2009–10) and *Kitchen Whiz* (2011–). The company supplies children's programmes to both the commercial networks and the ABC, regularly accessing Screen Australia funding for its children's drama. Ambience's creative director David Webster confirms the importance of the CTS to the children's production sector, describing them as 'critical' to the success of the business (personal communication April 29 2013).

One of Ambience's recent animated productions, Series One of *The Adventures of Figaro Pho* (2012) was made in Australia as an ABC3 commission, with funding subsidies from state agencies including Screen Australia, the South Australian Film Corporation, Screen New South Wales and Film Victoria. As a small production company, Ambience occasionally works cooperatively with other independent producers, and *The Adventures of Figaro Pho* was made in partnership with Melbourne-based production company Chocolate Liberation Front (a recipient of Screen Australia's Enterprise Funding Scheme in 2011).

The series is based on creator Luke Jurevicius' original one-minute animated shorts, with each transformed into seven-minute episodes detailing a particular phobia afflicting the main character, Figaro. Its distribution in international markets was split between ABC Commercial, Germany's ZDF Enterprises in Europe, and a third distributor in Canada, all of whom put up a distribution advance.

The production of high-quality CGI animation such as *The Adventures of Figaro Pho* is expensive. Nonetheless ABC3's willingness to pay Screen Australia minimum licence fees, the availability of state subsidies from various screen bodies and the partners' established reputation for producing high-quality animation secured production funding. The absence of significant international co-production partnerships meant the entire production process occurred in Australia, which is very unusual for animation. Once an animated series has secured an international co-production partner, its production will tend to be shared among the contributing territories.

A recurring theme across the children's production sector is the difficulties in securing production budgets when local broadcasters refuse to pay the minimum licence fees that trigger Screen Australia funding. While producers can still claim the 20 per cent producer offset, the gap left by the loss of Screen Australia funding has to be filled from other sources. Although the ABC did pay minimum licence fees for *The Adventures of Figaro Pho,* which meant the series was able to attract Screen Australia funding, Ambience's executive producer international Patrick Egerton confirms this is by no means a common occurrence for the productions in which he is involved:

> Our challenge and the challenge for all kids' producers is the $115,000 half hour level to trigger Screen Australia funding. Broadcasters can be unwilling to commit licence fees at that level, especially on animated content.
>
> (Personal communication April 29 2013)

The further challenge for all producers working in the current production environment is how to maintain quality standards in high-end animation or live action drama when minimum licence fees have not been paid. The need to work with multiple investors to fill the financial shortfall also increases the complexity of projects, making them more difficult and increasingly time-consuming to get off the ground. The longer the lead time and the more work involved in getting new productions green lit 'the harder it becomes to sustain yourself as a business in the feast and famine gap when you're trying to put it together' (Patrick Egerton personal communication April 29 2013).

Describing the creative partnership that led to the production of *The Adventures of Figaro Pho*, Ambience's creative director David Webster says:

> The series came from Luke Jurevicius the creator, so a lot of the tone was already cast before we got involved. It appealed to me as soon as I saw the shorts that Luke had done. I thought they were extremely high-quality, a level of animation that we like to make. And Luke had seen *Erky Perky* which he was impressed with. So there was a meeting of the minds there.
>
> (Personal communication April 29 2013)

The Adventures of Figaro Pho is identifiably high-quality animation and received international recognition including two Kidscreen awards in 2013. Despite considerable success including sales to Canal+, HBO Czech, BBC Kids Canada, Cartoon Network South and Latin America, *The Adventures of Figaro Pho* has not been picked up in US and UK markets in the way that award-winning animation might be expected to. As the series was commissioned by ABC3 it was aimed at 8 to 12 year olds, which meant the production team were able to push the boundaries a little. As Webster points out, this was consistent with the original shorts that were broadcast on the UK's ITV, but ITV did not pick up the series (personal communication April 29 2013).

The series' failure to sell in certain territories, given its obvious quality, is symptomatic of some of the difficulties that can accompany the commissioning process, particularly when a series is being made for a carefully branded niche channel operating in fiercely competitive markets. For example, Nickelodeon has purposely designed its brand identity as an alternative to the wholesome, often pedagogic quality of The Disney Channel, adopting a humorous irreverent tone of address that constructs a brand identity around children's empowerment and rebellion (Banet-Weiser 2007). It therefore has an interest in edgier content, which complements its brand values.

Producers are also accustomed to working with commissioning editors who represent corporate positions that may themselves change during the course of a production. A network's position may alter if the network starts to receive a large number of subscriber complaints about a particular type of programme. Alternatively a channel may decide to realign its content against its competitors if it feels there is too much similarity in its programming, to ensure brand distinctiveness and to retain market share. If there is a change of personnel in the commissioning editor's role at the channel, the new appointment will bring personal preferences and priorities to the commissioning process. Given the long lead time involved in television production, producers can find themselves dealing with several different broadcasters' representatives during the lifespan of a single production.

Despite the complicated processes of raising production finance and accommodating the programming requirements of multiple investors, producers refuse to allow their creativity to be stifled by the economics of production and distribution. As David Webster explains:

> We try and free up the creative process and not be burdened by financial considerations. Then once we're all really passionate about a concept it's a question of then placing commercial limitations on it. We push it as far as we can creatively and then say how are we going to make this show? We don't start the other way round and try and make a cheap show; it's just not the way we work.
>
> (Personal communication April 29 2013)

Both Egerton and Webster acknowledge the special status of the child audience and the gatekeeping role assumed by all children's television producers during the creative process, with Egerton stating 'I think there's a duty of care for anyone who makes kids' content of any kind to make sure that it's not leading them astray, that it's not a bad influence, and that it's constructive and entertaining' (personal communication April 29 2013).

Webster agrees with the need to protect the child audience:

> I like stuff that challenges, the idea of a series based on fears I thought was great and would challenge kids. And the feedback I've got from kids is that the fear is really tantalising to them. But we've got to be extremely careful about what storylines we are putting out there. The creative team involved produces out of Melbourne, the Chocolate Liberation Front, our partners. So there are two guys there, Luke, myself and a story editor as well, plus the ABC. There were quite a few heads coming together on each storyline and challenging those storylines if we thought they were too controversial.
>
> (Personal communication April 29 2013)

Despite its award-winning status as high-quality Australian drama for which minimum licence fees were paid, *The Adventures of Figaro Pho* is not culturally specific. Given the animated series is set in somewhat surreal environments and is dialogue free, there were limited opportunities to include overtly Australian markers.

While Egerton acknowledges the importance of the ABC in supporting local content, he is also pragmatic about the need for programmes to circulate in the international market place:

> I think the ABC want to, and should, and do, champion Australian content. But the reality of the international market place is that if you make something which is chock full of Australian accents with lots of kangaroos hopping about—well there's probably only room for one or two of those series. Generally you're trying to make a product that will sell to an international audience because you can't finance it unless you do. *Figaro Pho* is peculiar because there was some private investment that enabled that show to be made entirely in Australia.
>
> (Personal communication April 29 2013)

Both Egerton and Webster[1] remain enthusiastic about their work in animation and proud of the series they have made, despite some of the travails associated with producing high-quality animation in a fragmented market. Their ultimate goal (which they share with most children's animation producers) appears to be the creation of a series that will create ancillary rights and enjoy global distribution. As Egerton observes:

> The holy grail is a brand that goes for 10 or 20 years and there's lots of track records around the world—shows like *Dora the Explorer* and *Thomas the Tank Engine*—that have worked. That's the holy grail for us; to create a brand that has longevity and can spin out a whole lot of brand loyalty from kids.
>
> (Personal communication April 29 2013)

Ambience Entertainment also produces live action entertainment for children including cooking quiz show *Kitchen Whiz* (2011–) for Network Nine, a genre that does not qualify for Screen Australia funding. The series is filmed at Fox Studios in Sydney, with participants drawn largely from local schools. While quiz shows do not enjoy the status of live action drama or high-end animation, both the series, and the format of *Kitchen Whiz* are distributed in international markets. It therefore represents a highly sustainable model for culturally specific, locally produced Australian children's television.

Kitchen Whiz producer Monica O'Brien maintains that unlike animation, the cultural specificity of *Kitchen Whiz*, which features Australian children answering questions from the Australian school curriculum, is no impediment to its distribution in Asia, because parents want their children to learn English. She is careful to cultivate and maintain relationships with programme buyers in Asia and makes regular trips each year to these territories. The format for *Kitchen Whiz* also exports to English-speaking territories such as Ireland, with Ambience providing a production bible and the quiz programme software to producers who then produce local versions for their domestic markets.

As a producer of Australian content, O'Brien believes working in a small production company can be an advantage:

> Being attached to a larger organisation can lead to larger costs and overheads, so smaller companies can often do better, because they're more nimble and don't have to sustain high overheads. Children's TV can be made in a very cost efficient way if you're organized.
>
> (Personal communication June 13 2013)

She also acknowledges that the co-production model for Australian children's television is challenging. However O'Brien remains convinced that it is possible to reconcile local regulatory and international market requirements: 'If you understand the CTS and understand your audience, you can make content that will comply and work internationally' (Personal communication June 13 2013).

As a small production company specializing in children's television, Ambience Entertainment benefits from demand for its shows such as *Kitchen Whiz* and *Erky Perky* generated by the quota obligations in the CTS. The state supports provided by organizations such as Screen Australia also underpin the production of the company's high-quality animation for ABC3. Nonetheless *The Adventures of Figaro Pho,* despite its obvious merits and presence on Australia's public service children's channel, does not speak directly to the Australian child audience in a way that the inexpensive format *Kitchen Whiz* does. Made with significant state support, this award-winning animation was always intended for international distribution, on global children's channels. As such, the public value of the series is less clear, despite the contributions its production undoubtedly made to the sustainability of the production sector and Australia's reputation for expertise in the production of CGI animation.

Werner Film Productions and *Dance Academy*

Joanna Werner established Werner Film Productions in 2008 in Melbourne. Prior to setting up her own production company, Werner spent seven years as a producer with Jonathan M Shiff Productions, working on children's series such as *Wicked Science, The Elephant Princess* and *H2O: Just Add Water.* Werner Film Production's first children's series, *Dance Academy* (2010–12), on which Bernadette O'Mahoney from the ACTF was an executive producer, was one of the earliest children's series commissioned for ABC3. Three series of the live action drama were eventually made, although the final series consisted of 13 rather than 26 episodes because of Screen Australia funding restrictions.

The creation of *Dance Academy* first began in 2005 after Joanna Werner and casting assistant Samantha Strauss, both of whom were working on *H2O: Just Add Water* at the time, went for a pre-shoot drink. Strauss asked Werner what show she would make if she could make any show in the world. Werner replied that she would make a show about a girl from the country struggling to make it at Australia's top ballet school. The next day Strauss gave her a script that she had been working on for five years, based on an almost identical concept. Over the next three years, as they worked together on live action drama for Jonathan M Shiff productions, Werner and Strauss continued to develop the series together. With a pilot script and bible, Werner was able to pitch the series to the ABC.

The support of government-funded organizations in Australia and an existing relationship with German public service broadcaster ZDF helped Werner to secure production funding. As ABC3 agreed to pay minimum licence fees when *Dance Academy* was commissioned, the series was able to access Screen Australia funding. With the ACTF as an executive producer and Australian distributor, Werner was able to draw on her relationship with German public service broadcaster ZDF (established during her time as a producer for Jonathan M Shiff Productions with whom ZDF has an output deal) to secure the remaining production funding and rest of world distribution. The ACTF was the Australian and

New Zealand distributor, while ZDF's commercial arm ZDF Enterprises had the rest-of-world distribution rights.

ZDF's involvement was particularly important as the series was deemed 'too old' for the child audience by the BBC while Nickelodeon UK felt it was both too old and too edgy for its target demographic. After *Dance Academy's* popularity in the US with audiences on Teen Nick, Nickelodeon in the UK purchased the series however and it rated very well for them. Werner, like all children's producers, is well aware of the need for Australian children's television to circulate in international markets:

> To make a successful children's drama series which will hopefully go for multiple seasons, you can't just make a show that Australian audiences and ABC3 are going to love. In order to get it financed in the first place, in the vast majority of circumstances an international pre-sale is needed as well. And there are very few international broadcasters who will come in at this stage. For a particularly Australian show it can be very difficult to find international broadcasters who are willing to pre-buy. You don't want the creative to be led by the financing model but it's hard for this not to be the case sometimes.
>
> (Personal communication September 12 2013)

Filmed entirely in Sydney, *Dance Academy* is set in a fictitious elite ballet school, The National Academy of Dance, which students enter in the equivalent of year 10. In the first series, country girl Tara arrives at the Academy with ambitions to become principal ballerina, only to find herself in fierce competition for the role with fellow student Abigail. Filmed against a backdrop of the Opera House and Sydney Harbour and featuring carefully choreographed, specialist dance sequences, *Dance Academy* is visually spectacular. Its sun-drenched harbour-side settings appeal particularly to European audiences.

After launching on ABC3 in 2010 with a second series in 2012, *Dance Academy* quickly became an extremely successful children's drama, to the extent that Carla De Jong, ABC children's head of commissioning and development referred to it as a 'channel defining brand for us' (ACTF 2010: 1). The second series of *Dance Academy* was scheduled on ABC3, from Monday to Thursday at 6.30pm, a time when children could also view the series with their families. Here it attracted an audience that averaged 177,000, while the first episode of Series Two also attracted 1.8 million programme plays on iView and the ABC3 Watch Now website (Screen Australia 2013a).

The series attracted critical acclaim and significant audiences, won multiple awards including a Logie, was nominated for an International Emmy and sold in over 138 countries. The involvement of ZDF was creatively significant as it led to the series being filmed in Sydney, rather than Melbourne as Werner had originally planned. As she explains:

> ZDF said they'd come on board if it was shot in Sydney. And I decided to really embrace that. And we didn't really feel that any shows had thoroughly embraced Sydney and used

> Sydney as a character. New York is so celebrated in shows like *Gossip girls* and *Sex in the City*. We decided to take that approach and have the Harbor Bridge and Opera House in shot as much as possible. We centred the show in the most picturesque parts of Sydney. We didn't do it just for the international market. I think Australian audiences want to see that too.
>
> (Personal communication September 12 2013)

The series also benefited from policies introduced in New South Wales to encourage screen production in the state, which came into effect just prior to the shooting of Series One. These significantly reduced location fees, allowing filming to occur around iconic locations such as the Opera House, which the budget would not have been able to accommodate previously. Nonetheless ensuring setting the series in Sydney and maintaining high production values strained the budget:

> On the first series money was very tight. Shooting in Sydney is not cheap. All the dance sequences [...] locations. Comparatively we had a good budget. We didn't have to compromise on production values. We put every single cent on the screen!
>
> (Personal communication September 12 2013)

The production of Series One also benefited from a downturn in long form television production activity at the time in Sydney. The reduced competition for creative labour enabled Werner, who had previously worked largely in Melbourne, to recruit—and retain for all three series—a highly skilled crew. While their creative pedigrees contributed to the series' high production values, the use of a largely Sydney-based crew also reduced production costs:

> We got the best people. Our head of makeup was Academy Award nominated, our Director of photography was Martin McGrath who's an icon and shot so many wonderful features and series. I didn't have established relationships because I hadn't worked in Sydney before, but because Series One was such a collaborative success and everyone enjoyed it, I was able to secure them for the second series which was an incredibly busy time in Sydney. If I had been crewing up for the second series for the first time I would not have got that quality crew. The majority of the crew stayed for all three series, it was a very collaborative experience.
>
> (Personal communication September 12 2013)

Dance Academy is aimed at a young teen audience, rather than very young children. The series' themes—the pursuit of excellence, family, peer friendship, romance and rivalry—form part of storylines that include stronger elements, such as homosexuality and death. (Unlike *Lockie Leonard*, the series did not need to obtain a C drama classification as it was commissioned by the ABC rather than a commercial network with C drama quotas to fill). Without any need to conform to the C classification, Werner had a greater degree of creative freedom:

> We were keen to have older characters and to be able to show the reality of being 15 and sometimes the C classification can mean that it's very hard to show those realities. We wanted to be as true to the teen experience as possible but in a responsible way.
>
> (Personal communication September 12 2013)

Werner used writers who had not worked in children's television before and pitched the scripts at different levels of understanding, as Du Fresne did on *Lockie Leonard*:

> We thought of it as teen TV rather than children's. We just let the writers go for it. Swearing, sex and drugs were the things that were moderated. I am conscious of the show being a good role model without being goody goody, because a teen audience won't see that as cool and that was definitely something we wanted the show to be. Writers who had to write episodes where there's drinking or sexual references just had to work a bit harder so it could be read on different levels. We didn't think there was anything we couldn't do; we just had to be clever about how we did it.
>
> (Personal communication September 12 2013)

With much of the filming taking place around the Opera House, an Australian cast and a highly skilled Australian production crew, *Dance Academy* is a culturally specific Australian drama with high production values. It has also enjoyed critical and commercial success around the world. *Dance Academy* delivers public value in return for the direct and indirect state supports it received. The ABC's scheduling of the series and its availability on online catch-up services also ensure that, unlike *Lockie Leonard,* children can access it easily. The sophisticated online resources also provided by ABC3 increase *Dance Academy's* cultural visibility while facilitating the audience's deeper engagement with the series.

Despite its considerable successes, *Dance Academy* fell victim to Screen Australia's funding policy of not funding more than two series of Australian drama unless there are exceptional circumstances. Strong support from the ABC, ZDF and the ACTF and an Emmy nomination helped established the series' exceptional circumstances. Nonetheless Screen Australia were only prepared to fund a 13 rather than a 26-episode run. Werner's efforts to fill the financial gap were unsuccessful, although she remains grateful that she was able to produce the third series at all:

> In the end I was very relieved just to be able to get to those 13 episodes. Creatively the series was always designed to be three seasons. The students enter in the equivalent of year 10 and it's all aimed at trying to get a company contract at the end of the third year.

> Series Two ends with a character's death, it was all very up in the air. It would have been unfinished and unsatisfying for the fans. I would have felt we'd really failed the audience if we hadn't managed to produce the third series.
>
> (Personal communication September 12 2013)

Having established her own small production company, Werner is content to remain as an independent player, rather than become part of the increasing trend towards vertical integration in the production sector. For Werner, the creative autonomy engendered by independence outweighs any reduction in production capacity:

> So far I've actively made the choice to remain independent and that's impacted a lot of decisions. I just felt with *Dance Academy* I made the show I wanted to make and remained completely creatively within the company. And to be able to do that on the next show would be ideal.
>
> (Personal communication September 12 2013)

Partly because of the small scale of Werner's company and her desire for creative autonomy, the ACTF's involvement, in resourcing, mentoring and distribution, was a key factor in the success of *Dance Academy* and contributed to its public value:

> Having the ACTF's support has been vital, I couldn't have done it on my own, especially organising the finance for the first series. You can feel very alone as the producer; it was great to have their back up.
>
> (Personal communication September 12 2013)

The production of *Dance Academy* marked a turning point in the production of high-quality, Australian live action drama, which is now commissioned more often by ABC3 than the commercial networks. The series is unusual in being culturally specific, although clearly intended for distribution in international markets. It also benefitted from being spared the rigours of the C classification process, meaning it could quite deliberately be pitched at a teen audience with content, such as a homosexual kiss, which would struggle to qualify for a C rating.

Werner's experience producing live action drama with Jonathan M Shiff meant she had an understanding of the market for teen-centred live action drama and a professional rapport and trust-based relationship with ZDF and its commercial branch ZDF Enterprises, whose involvement proved both important and influential. The role of the ACTF in supporting and distributing high-quality Australian children's television is exemplified in the organisation's professional partnership with Werner Film Productions. It is also indicative of the ACTF's gradual and reluctant withdrawal from involvement with the children's television produced by commercial networks, due to the lack of suitable projects commissioned by the networks since the mid-2000s. The networks' lack of enthusiasm for paying Screen

Australia minimum licence fees limits their ability to commission high-quality, live action drama such as *Dance Academy.*

Fremantle Media Australia, *As the Bell Rings* and *Bindi's Bootcamp*

Fremantle Media Australia has offices in Melbourne and Sydney and is part of the transnational super-indie UK-based Fremantle Media. The Australian company is the product of a merger between Grundy and Crackerjack Productions, which were both acquired by Fremantle Media in 2006. Parent company Fremantle Media has production operations in over 22 countries that produce almost 10,000 hours a year of original programming (Fremantle Media 2013).

Fremantle Media Australia has a broad production slate for Australian broadcasters, which includes drama, factual and entertainment. The company also produces children's television, including *As the Bell Rings* (2006–11) for Disney Channel Australia and, in partnership with Sydney-based Sticky Pictures, *Bindi's Boot Camp* (2012–) for ABC3. Fremantle Australia does not have its own children's department, preferring to either hire freelance production crew members or to partner with a small independent production company to produce its children's content.

The Disney Channel format *As the Bell Rings* is a one set, six-minute, live action drama/ comedy individually made and broadcast in various territories including the UK, Israel, Russia, France, Germany, Spain, Singapore and China. Its production represents a deliberate corporate strategy of glocalization adopted by The Disney Corporation in the mid-2000s. The series is set in the universal setting of a high school, in this case in the five minutes between classes, the start and finish of which are signalled by the eponymous bell. The series localizes The Disney Channel while adhering to notions of globalization and efficiencies of practice.

The Australian version was first produced for the Disney Channel Australia and New Zealand in 2006. Series One was made with an entirely US script but by Series Four Australian writers were writing each episode, as the format became truly localized. When announcing production of the initial series by drawing attention to its local relevance, Michael Cairns, managing director of Walt Disney Television International (Australia/New Zealand), said:

> I'm thrilled we've discovered 13 exciting young actors who will not only bring the show's Australian characters and stories to life, but will connect with our viewers as they see kids just like themselves on their Disney Channel. This is our first locally-produced comedy series made especially for and starring, Australian kids.
>
> (girl.com.au n.d)

Each series was filmed in Docklands Studios, Melbourne, in a four-week production schedule, with a week of rehearsals before three weeks of filming. The Disney Channel

Australia has an average daily reach of 361,000 viewers (Screen Australia 2011: 81). *As the Bell Rings* rates well in its Friday PM time slot with 5–15 year old children, winning the time slot on Australian subscription television.

While the local production of *As the Bell Rings* generated sector revenue and employment for Australian television production personnel, local versions of the format generally have limited shelf lives and distribution. Indeed *As the Bell Rings* represents a significant anomaly in the production of Australian children's drama in that it is an Australian production where the first and final market is Australasia. The value for Disney is derived from the distribution and replication in multiple territories of the characteristics of the formats to which they are made, and their effectiveness in localizing a channel.

Although children's pay-TV channels in Australia are not subject to the quota obligations of the CTS, The Disney Channel Australia submitted the first series of *As the Bell Rings* to the ACMA for a C classification. The submission to the ACMA could have been a form of quality control or perhaps The Disney Channel was investigating the possibility of selling the series to the commercial networks. The ACMA duly classified the six-minute, one set format as C drama. This short format, made with a US script, appears unlikely to contribute significantly to the creation of a sense of cultural identity in young Australian viewers. Neither does it appear to be 'a fully scripted screenplay or teleplay in which the dramatic elements of character, theme and plot are introduced and developed so as to form a narrative structure' (ACMA 2009: 9). In awarding the series a C drama classification the ACMA's interpretation of the CTS criteria did little to uphold the public value of C drama rated Australian children's television.

Having moved into the spaces of children's television production with *As the Bell Rings*, in 2012 Fremantle Australia partnered with Sydney-based independent production company Sticky Pictures to make the reality adventure show *Bindi's Bootcamp* for ABC3. The series was shot entirely at Australia Zoo on Queensland's Sunshine Coast, which is also the home of the Irwin family. According to Tim Brooke Hunt, ABC3's controller of children's television, the production of *Bindi's Bootcamp* represented a deliberate corporate strategy by the parent company's distribution and licensing arm Fremantle Media Entertainment to begin to franchise the Bindi Irwin brand globally. It therefore emerges from very different set of institutional circumstances from the majority of Australian children's television.

The ABC was enthusiastic about its own role in the establishment of this franchise and agreed to commission *Bindi's Boot Camp* to prepare audiences for the launch of a second comedy series also starring Bindi Irwin. According to ABC3's Tim Brooke Hunt:

> Fremantle was a key part of the project. The Irwin family have a relationship with Fremantle Family Entertainment and the ABC had previously featured Bindi in another show, when she was younger, and we wanted to develop her as a personality on ABC3. Fremantle and their Australian partner Sticky Pictures also wanted to make a show called *Safari in the City* starring Bindi, and *Bindi's Boot Camp* was a way of establishing Bindi and giving her a platform from which we could launch her sitcom.
>
> (Personal communication May 2 2013)

Producer Donna Andrews of Sticky Pictures, which devised the concept for *Bindi's Boot Camp*, welcomed the production partnership with Fremantle Australia because at the time Sticky Pictures was relatively inexperienced with producing reality television and game shows. As Andrews explains, '[I]t's very different shooting a reality/challenge/game show to your studio shoot or location shoot for a narrative story' (personal communication May 3 2013). The genre also allowed a greater degree of cultural specificity than some of Sticky Pictures' animation series, with Andrews agreeing, 'I guess of all of our projects, that's one that had a very big focus on Australia, because of the nature of what it is' (personal communication May 3 2013).

As each child was only involved in filming for one day, there was only very limited time available to explain the process, in contrast to a live action drama shoot where producers have several months to work closely with the same small number of children. Like many producers of reality television for children, Andrews sees her role as protecting the participating children from any negative experiences:

> There were no hidden agendas, this is a game show and a chance for children to have a competition, to have fun with that competition, maybe learn a little something along the way and have the chance to interact with some form of animal or physically do an obstacle course. We wanted kids to look at it and think 'I want to do that, I want to have a go at it'. If a child had done something we felt they might be embarrassed about then there's no way we would have included that.
>
> (Personal communication May 3 2013)

The crew filmed the entire series of Bindi's *Boot Camp* in a month, at Australia Zoo and its surrounds, with generous access to the zoo's inhabitants. In order to be able to maintain the pace they needed, there were three separate camera crews and three separate film producers who had to move freely around the zoo in order to be able to film the competing children. There was little opportunity to reshoot, given the time constraints and pressure to produce large amounts of television in a short time.

The partnership with Fremantle Australia allowed Sticky Pictures, a long-time supplier of animation and live action drama to Australian broadcasters, to expand its production slate while benefiting from Fremantle Media's distribution capability. Although Andrews welcomed the opportunity to partner with a vertically integrated transnational on the production of *Bindi's Bootcamp*, she values the creative autonomy that accompanies her company's status as a small, independent production company:

> I quite like being the master of our own domain; it comes with its own challenges of course. But I appreciate the flexibility that comes with being a smaller company. I appreciate that if we do a deal for something then it's up to us to deliver it and we're not relying on others.
>
> (Personal communication May 3 2013)

Fremantle Australia also benefitted from the partnership. With the production of *Bindi's Bootcamp*, the company became supplier and distributor of a children's programme for ABC3, the most widely viewed dedicated children's channel in Australia.

With its sale to Discovery Kids Asia in 2012, *Bindi's Bootcamp* became another example of culturally specific, ordinary Australian children's television made with state support that succeeds in international markets while speaking directly to Australian children. As such, this example of ordinary television has public value, due to its ability to situate Australian children within their own culture. It nonetheless remains children's television produced and distributed by a transnational super-indie as the basis of a corporate campaign to franchise a child, Bindi Irwin, as the face of globally branded and distributed children's television.

Southern Star Entertainment, *A Gurlswurld* and *In Your Dreams*

Australian production company Endemol Australia (formerly Southern Star Entertainment) provides another example of the advantages and efficiencies enjoyed in the Australian production ecology by local branches of transnational super-indies. Parent company Endemol, the largest producer of programme formats in the world, has production companies and joint venture operations in multiple territories. Southern Star Entertainment the company was originally established in Australia in the early 1980s and eventually became the largest and most profitable television packager in Australia, apart from Grundy (Moran 2009). In 2000 the company was acquired by Endemol, and, like Fremantle Media Australia, produces local versions of programme formats supplied by its parent company, including ordinary television such as *Deal or No Deal* and *Big Brother*.

Endemol Australia is also a prolific supplier of home-grown Australian drama for domestic broadcasters and, as Southern Star Entertainment, produced successful Australian drama series including *Rush* (2007–11), *Offspring* (2010–), *Spirited* (2010–11), *Paper Giants: The Birth of Cleo* (2010) and *Puberty Blues* (2012). The company also produces children's programmes; its most well-known production is probably the preschool series *Bananas in Pyjamas* for the ABC. Its live action slate includes *Blue Water High* (2005–08) also for the ABC, the C drama *A Gurlswurld* (2008) for Network Nine and *In Your Dreams* (2012) for Network Seven. All these series received Screen Australia funding, suggesting minimum licence fees were paid.

Producer Noel Price is in charge of the production of children's television for Endemol Australia and based at the company's Sydney headquarters. He confirms the difficulties all children's television producers face, even those that are part of vertically integrated super-indie production companies, in putting together production budgets:

> Financing children's shows is hard. It has always been so and it gets harder every year as licence fees get tighter and the number of potential co-production partners that can bring significant funds to the table decreases.
>
> (Personal communication June 12 2013)

Nonetheless as the producer of *In Your Dreams*, Price succeeded in creating Screen Australia-funded live action drama for Network Seven, an unusual commission for a network that is known in the industry for its reluctance to pay Screen Australia minimum licence fees. The decision to commission *In Your Dreams* (2012) represented a break with Network Seven's recent patterns of children's C drama commissions, which have tended to be animation. Indeed the live action drama was the first Screen Australia-funded drama Network Seven has made since the telemovies *Gumnutz* and *The Adventures of Charlotte and Henry* in 2007 and 2008 respectively. According to Price:

> You have to be as ingenious in financing shows as you are in creating and making them. Getting the finance together requires finding and maintaining strong partner relationships but even then, producers still need a lot of ingenuity and fleet footedness.
>
> (Personal communication June 12 2013)

Price also concedes that the networks' refusal to pay minimum licence fees for the majority of their C drama quota requirements renders high-quality live action drama an increasingly difficult genre to produce when he states:

> It's no secret that the commercials have never been in love with children's TV and only do it because they have to. So clearly the interest for them is how to fill their quota and meet the CTS standards for the cheapest possible price. So producers have to be innovative in how they put together their financing models so that they can meet the networks' needs while still delivering quality. It's no easy task.
>
> (Personal communication June 12 2013)

Price believes that the special status of the child audience in Australia is a key factor in Australia's considerable success in producing and exporting high-quality children's television, noting that

> Australian children's TV is one of the biggest cultural exports of Australia and has been for 20 years. Given the size of the population, Australian children's TV has flourished beyond a level that one would expect. One of the reasons is childhood is also generally highly valued by society and children are by and large well provided for in this country—and that includes ensuring that appropriate TV content is available to them.
>
> (Personal communication June 12 2012)

But he emphasizes that the production of Australian children relies equally on state subsidy, the ABC's commitment to the child audience and the CTS quotas and quality requirements. Price believes the CTS provide a level of quality control because:

> I think they try to implicitly say to producers, 'these are the issues that are important to consider and you need to demonstrate that you've thought about them and that you'll

back them up with the hard evidence of a decent budget, expertise and backing from broadcasters and distributors'.

(Personal communication June 12 2013)

Price maintains that despite the need for internationalization, Australian children's drama has certain immutable, culturally specific characteristics. He describes these qualities as

> [e]ncouraging kids to have a go. Encouraging creative problem solving, within a cohesive set of social relationships. [The programs] are also aspirational and optimistic and comedy plays quite a part in them as well. These values are not necessarily unique to Australia but the way they're combined and the tone with which they're told marks them out as Australian.
>
> (Personal communication June 12 2012)

He believes the presence of these qualities outweighs the internationalization pressures faced by Australian producers, to the extent that their programmes may not even be made in Australia:

> Everything we do has to be made for the international market because that's the way things are financed. However the stories are always told from an Australian perspective—they have to be because that's who we are. Australian values therefore implicitly inform the content of our shows—even though in some cases they mightn't even be entirely filmed in Australia. So even though we make shows for international markets with international partners, they are very distinctly Australian shows.
>
> (Personal communication June 12 2012)

Endemol Australia's recent children's drama is deliberately internationalized and designed to circulate in Asian and European co-production markets. The company has a production office in Singapore and co-production arrangements with Germany's public service broadcaster NDR. The tween-focussed storyline of *In Your Dreams*—featuring twins Samantha and Ben who are sent from their suburban home in Australia to live with ancient, aristocratic relatives in a decaying castle in a remote part of Germany—lends itself to transnational production and distribution practices.

Similarly the narrative of *A Gurlswurld* centres around three teenage girls, Jacky, Emma and Ally, who became close friends at school in Singapore but are now living in Singapore, Germany and Australia respectively. When they are given new software for their computers, the girls discover they can be transported through cyberspace into each other's homes. The series was shot in Australia, Singapore and Germany, a cooperative endeavour that is indicative of the 'strong partner relationships' to which Price alludes.

These recent examples of live action drama made by Endemol Australia succeeded in maintaining high production values. Nonetheless, they avoided Australian cultural specificity by being deliberately shot across the various territories of their contributing investors, with cast members similarly drawn from a variety of transnational investor regions.

Price maintains however that these series and their stories are identifiably Australian, despite their transnational pedigree, arguing that:

> You can see with shows that have come from the UK or Europe and even the US that there's a strong tonal difference. We tend to be a bit more innocent, optimistic, and aspirational in our storytelling than Europe and UK where there seems to be a far greater stress on 'social realism'. At the same time we're less sentimental than the US.
>
> (Personal communication June 12 2013)

That these productions still managed to secure Screen Australia direct funding subsidy despite their transnational production arrangements makes them even more attractive to international investors, for their high production values and transnational relevance.

Both Networks Seven and Nine commissioned their Screen Australia-funded dramas, *In Your Dreams* and *A Gurlswurld*, from Endemol Australia (then Southern Star Entertainment). Price confirms the reputational capital possessed by established production companies gives them a significant competitive advantage in the commissioning process. Networks will have their trusted suppliers to whom they will turn to for their children's quota programming needs, which can also make it difficult for less experienced producers to get a foothold in the market. According to Price:

> It helps if the networks know you have a strong track record. A key tenet of our business—and it's been set in stone for many years now—is that we always deliver on time and on budget. And the networks know that we have a long history of making good shows that work well for the target audiences. So if you can deliver good shows, do it on time and on budget and do it as cost effectively as possible, then broadcasters know they can trust you and that counts for a lot.
>
> (Personal communication June 12 2013)

Australia's policy settings, particularly its local content quotas for drama on the commercial networks are vital to the Australian independent production sector in driving demand for local commissions. Endemol Australia's brand value as a trusted supplier of live action drama and unscripted formats for both adult and children's audiences ensures a regular supply of commissions from the commercial networks in the filling of these quota obligations.

The company frequently accesses Screen Australia funding for its drama slate and makes culturally specific television with high production values, much of which resonates with local audiences. Yet Endemol Australia remains the local branch of a European transnational, which benefits from the policy settings designed to nurture Australia's independent production sector, including Screen Australia investment and the producer offset tax rebate.

Price faces similar difficulties in raising finance for his children's productions to those faced by smaller, independent production companies. He concedes however that there are advantages in being part of a transnational, vertically integrated production company. It is important to be able to focus creative energy on the production of a steady supply of children's television, rather than the constant struggle to raise production finance:

> The thing about being part of a larger company is that your overheads are guaranteed and you can call on the company's resources at various stages of the production process. You don't have to mortgage your house to generate cash flow or provide your personal savings as the basis for a bank loan to fund production. That takes away an awful lot of pressure. It also means that you can stay in play. And staying in play is the key platform that enables you to develop projects, obtain partners and find finance.
>
> (Personal communication June 12 2013)

Price is familiar with the vicissitudes associated with raising production finance encountered by other independent companies. Nonetheless Endemol Australia's children's television appears to travel well, presumably due to the involvement of its co-production partners. As shared projects with the Singapore Media Authority and Germany's NDR, live action dramas such as *In Your Dreams* and *A Gurlswurld* have production partners with a vested interest and the ability to secure their cultural visibility in territories beyond Australia.

These live action drama series, produced by the local branch of a transnational super-indie with international co-production partners, are, unequivocally, internationalized productions. Shot in three territories with a mixture of Australian and non-Australian actors, they seem carefully designed to speak to all children, rather than the Australian child audience specifically. Whether such deliberately multinational children's drama represents the best return on Screen Australia's taxpayer-funded investment is unclear. The public value of children's television made under these industrial arrangements is also unclear, given state subsidies were always intended to support small, independent production companies that would be at much greater risk of market failure than transnational super-indies.

Children's live action drama series such as *A Gurlswurld* and *In Your Dreams* are emblematic of Screen Australia's mutually exclusive policy objectives around national cultural representation in children's television and an agenda of internationalization in Australian screen production. The availability of public funding to companies that are majority owned by US corporations or transnational super-indies provides further encouragement for these creative and commercial circumstances to develop.

For Screen Australia the status of 'under creative control' appears to alleviate any concerns about the ways in which incompatible policy objectives are secured, which include the commitment of significant state subsidy to productions which are largely shot outside Australia. Questions surround the public value returned to the taxpayer by the children's live action drama produced for Australia's commercial networks and, its public service broadcaster by companies such as Endemol Australia and Matchbox Pictures, given their status as the local branches of much larger international production operations.

Conclusion

This chapter has examined the operations and creative works of a number of production companies involved in the production and distribution of Australian children's television, including small, independent companies and the local branches of vertically integrated super-indies. The interaction and tension between creative, cultural, commercial and regulatory imperatives can be seen in the examples included here of Australian children's television produced during Australia's digital transition. Despite the challenges involved in financing and distributing Australian children's television, most producers remain passionate about their creative endeavours. The creative autonomy that comes with working in a small production company is particularly appreciated.

The first-hand experiences of some of Australia's leading producers of children's television reveal how fragmentation shaped creative practices and production norms during the digital transition. The business model for Australian children's drama remains problematical for all producers, including those that are part of vertically integrated ownership structures. Even the exceptionally successful drama series *Dance Academy* could not raise the finance needed to produce an entire 26-episode third series but had to settle for 13 episodes instead.

The case studies illustrate the pressures producers face to internationalize their programmes, given the majority of the finance may well come from investment sourced outside Australia by channels with their own sets of demands and expectations. Under these circumstances, national cultural expression and the creation of programmes that speak directly to the Australian child audience look increasingly unattainable; the cultural specificity of the historical drama *My Place*, which made it an effective educational resource for Australian children, severely limited its international distribution.

The case studies also illustrate how cultural specificity in Australian children's television can be a considerable asset. *Dance Academy's* use of Sydney as a stunning visual backdrop and *Lockie Leonard's* Western Australian beach locations were attractive to landlocked European audiences as well as being central to the series' storylines and contributing to their very high production values. Quiz show *Kitchen Whiz* is culturally specific but circulates easily in Asian markets.

Other production paradoxes see high-quality, Screen Australia-funded animation *The Adventures of Figaro Pho* largely devoid of Australian signifiers, while examples of ordinary television such as *Bindi's Bootcamp* or *Prank Patrol* are extremely culturally specific. Ordinary television with high production values, which resonates with Australian children while situating them within their own culture, has public value. It also provides a less expensive contribution to national cultural expression than live action drama. Drama remains the only genre eligible for Screen Australia investment, due to its higher production costs and much greater risk of market failure. Nonetheless drama, as it is interpreted in the CTS quotas, includes inexpensive animation that may not even include Australian accents or stories.

Children's television producers universally acknowledge the importance of the CTS in creating demand for their productions; they see the quotas as the single most important driver of demand and are accustomed to accommodating the regulatory requirements for age specific, children's television. They seem at times somewhat less mindful of the obligation for C drama to be suitable for Australian children particularly, rather than children the world over. ACMA's classification of the Disney format *As the Bell Rings* suggests however that creative control carries far more weight than cultural specificity in the classification of Australian children's television.

In these market conditions, the increased presence of transnational super-indies and US conglomerates in the spaces of local production assumes a certain market logic. Vertical integration and diverse production slates provide economies of scale and risk-spreading opportunities. The ability to access Australian state subsidies originally designed to support an immature local production industry provides a further benefit to the parent company, which would not collapse without the CTS quotas. The public value of the internationalized children's programmes made under these industrial arrangements is less clear, particularly when taxpayer-funded subsidies designed to nurture an independent production sector producing television that speaks directly to Australian children are paid to US corporations and European super-indies.

The case studies here confirm how important ABC3 and the ACTF are to the production of high-quality, live action Australian drama, despite their budgetary restraints, which limit the amount of drama they can commission. The influence of Kim Dalton and Tim Brooke Hunt, both of whom no longer work for the ABC, in their championing of local content commissioned by the ABC for Australian children must be acknowledged here. The provision of tied funding for a children's channel and ABC3's practice of commissioning most of its original productions from the independent sector are also important to the production of live action drama.

During the digital transition, Australian children's television was popular with Australian audiences and continues to attract critical acclaim and commercial success in international markets. Aside from these certainties, the public value of much of the children's television produced during the digital transition is less obvious, particularly some of the children's programs made with Screen Australia funding for Australia's free-to-air broadcasters.

Note

1 In October 2013, Egerton and Webster left Ambience Entertainment to establish their own production company, Cheeky Little Media.

Chapter 8

New Settlements in Children's Television: Key Trends and Future Outlook

In this chapter the key trends and pressure points that characterize the new settlements in Australian children's television will be examined more closely, in order to evaluate their effects on its production, distribution and public value. These key trends and pressure points include a skewing of the ratios between animation and live action drama in the filling of C drama quotas with a concomitant loss of quality in the C drama classification, the shift towards ACTF and Screen Australia involvement as markers of quality and cultural specificity in children's television and the increased internationalization of not only Australian children's television but also of the independent production sector responsible for its creation.

The chapter considers also the means by which supplies of culturally specific, high-quality Australian children's television, particularly live action drama, might be safeguarded. The creation of public value remains central to any steps taken to preserve supplies, as public value justifies the state subvention required to produce high-quality television for the child audience in Australia. After the introduction of television, it took several decades for Australian broadcasting, policy settings and a local screen production industry to mature sufficiently to create children's television, including drama, with high production values that spoke directly to the Australian child audience. The speed with which new settlements were created in children's television during the digital transition suggests swifter responses to the challenges of producing live action drama will be needed now.

The various digital transitions that occurred in the Australian, UK and US broadcasting systems brought abundant supply, multi-platform delivery, the ability to cater to niche audiences and a remarkable change in status for the child audience. Digital regimes therefore offer enormous opportunity for new ways of producing and distributing children's television, including dedicated destinations for children on Australia's commercial networks for the first time. Nonetheless Australia's small domestic market means that without appropriate state support, particularly content quotas and a well-funded public service broadcasting service, local children's drama is unlikely to be made available to the child audience. The recalibration of these supports and a renewed emphasis on the creation of public value became increasingly important during Australia's digital transition.

The CTS, the C Drama Classification and Public Value in Children's Television

Unlike the Australian Content Standard, which supported a level of Australian content for adults that was gradually emerging anyway, demand for children's drama in Australia is artificially created. Thus supplies of C programming have historically filled a demand shaped by legislated quotas rather than the workings of the market. As the second most expensive form of television after drama made for adults, children's live action drama is a genre that has always been at risk of market failure. Australia's commercial networks have a vested interest in reducing programme costs and extra incentive to do so in fragmented digital markets. They will therefore only commission children's drama under regulatory duress and will often gravitate to animation rather than more expensive live action drama. Content quotas, combined with direct and indirect funding subsidies, ensure supply of Australian children's television on Australia's free-to-air commercial networks. State subvention also supported the establishment of a children's television production industry to supply these programmes, as Chapter 2 described.

Australia's transition from an analogue to a digital television regime brought considerable benefits to the child audience, for whom television supplies multiplied, along with the means of their distribution. Further state support for children's television enabled the ABC to take advantage of the end of spectrum scarcity to launch a dedicated free-to-air children's channel, ABC3. The launch of ABC's children's channel was part of a global trend towards television services for niche audiences, including children, engendered by multi-channelling. Public service broadcasters (including the UK's BBC) used these channels as an opportunity to re-establish the centrality of their offerings in digital regimes that initially threatened to undermine long-standing justifications for their existence.

As Chapter 3 revealed, children embraced the new means of distribution that became available during the digital transition, while ABC3 quickly became the most popular children's channel in Australia. New digital platforms often supplemented and enriched television viewing rather than replacing it, with second-screen activities accompanying the viewing of programmes on a linear schedule. The dedicated children's channels provided by pay-TV services and the ABC used their online offerings to build brand loyalty among the child audience and keep them within the channel's orbit.

On the other hand, despite the evident opportunities for the production and distribution of Australian children's television provided by digital regimes, one key effect of the fragmentation that characterized the digital transition was a downwards pressure on the licence fees that commercial networks would pay for children's television, as Chapter 4 explained. Thus fragmentation presents significant challenges for the funding of Australian children's television. As the networks reduced the investment they were prepared to make in Australian children's television, producers were forced to look for increased international investment to fill the funding gap in their programme budgets. The networks' reluctance to pay Screen Australia minimum licence fees for children's drama skewed the ratios between the use of live action drama and animation in the filling of C drama quotas. The effects of this skewing of the ratios were evaluated in Chapter 4.

The use of internationally co-produced animation in the filling of C drama quotas undermined the status of the CTS as a quality control mechanism during the digital transition. So too did the ease with which these series were granted a C drama classification, when the primary purpose of this policy instrument is to secure supplies of high-quality, culturally specific children's television in the commercial networks' schedules. The increased internationalization of Australian children's television was born out of economic necessity but often eroded its cultural integrity. For producers, internationalization could, in certain circumstances, lead to the global embrace of their Brand Australia live action drama. For others, the need to accommodate multiple production partners proved to be fraught with difficulty and reduced the capacity of their programmes to speak directly to the Australian child audience, as Chapters 5 made clear.

The public value of C drama produced with taxpayer-funded subsidy lies in its status as age-specific, high-quality programmes with a capacity to speak directly to the Australian child audience. During the digital transition, the CTS gradually lost their status as a signifier of quality in local and international markets; of the 78 applications submitted to the ACMA for a C drama classification between 2008 and 2012 as the use of animation exponentially increased, only one was refused. Such a success rate suggests producers are either extraordinarily good at responding to the CTS criteria or that the ACMA is at risk of becoming something of a rubber stamp on C drama rather than a gatekeeper of public value. Chapter 6 showed how during the digital transition the C drama classification became more redolent of quantity than quality, a trend that intensified from the mid-2000s. The launch of ABC3 and the new channel's commissioning of live action drama series, which were made with ACTF and Screen Australia investment, further delineated the C drama classification from more recent Brand Australia children's drama.

Under these economic, regulatory and technological conditions, the public value of Australian children's television, particularly the television used to fill C drama quotas gradually declined. This reduction in public value of the television made with generous state subsidy for Australian children during the digital transition could be seen as symptomatic of a policy regime that began to serve producers and broadcasters rather than children. The intramural conversations that took place at this time among the production sector, broadcasters and regulators ignored the public, and notions of public value. In doing so they risked rendering important policy instruments and long-standing financial support for the independent production sector in Australia nothing more than tools of industry protectionism.

Of course, significant economic pressures shaped the classification norms that developed during the digital transition, due to the difficulty in funding children's television and the networks' widespread reluctance to pay minimum licence fees that are required for the production of live action drama. The case studies in Chapter 7 confirmed the challenges that Australian children's producers face in globalized media markets dominated by the US conglomerates that control the means of production and, crucially, the means of distribution of the majority of the world's supply of children's television. Nonetheless the CTS remain an expression of public value, not a means of generating commissions for production companies or allowing networks to minimize their obligations to the Australian child audience.

Prior to the digital transition, the quality demands that accompanied the C classification meant it was also a signifier of quality in international markets for children's drama. New means of distribution that developed during the 2000s, particularly Internet-based television services, confirmed the global market for quality children's television filmed against Australia's stunning natural landscapes. The creation of this sort of Brand Australia children's drama was not just associated with the aesthetics of television programming filmed in attractive and exotic locations. It also included high production values, prosocial messages and a narrative designed carefully to appeal to a child audience. These characteristics are particularly true of the C drama produced with ACTF involvement (Rutherford 2001) but also apply to Jonathan Shiff's children's production slate. Local licence fees from Australia's commercial networks were supplemented by international sales and co-production arrangements that supplied the production funding that contributed further to the high production values of children's drama. Any dilution in cultural specificity in these dramas was felt to be balanced by the cultural visibility and larger budgets provided by the circulation of Brand Australia children's drama in international markets. As demands for the highest standards in production values were diluted and the new interpretations of the criteria worked through, the C drama classification's role as a marker of quality in the international marketplace was also gradually eroded.

The reduction in status of the C drama classification will probably continue to occur without attracting a great deal of industry comment from domestic and international broadcasters. Australian free-to-air advertiser-funded networks and the US pay-TV channels in Australia (which often have secondary rights to these series) are unlikely to object to more animation with less identifiably Australian content in their schedules. This kind of drama can generally be made without the need to pay minimum licence fees while cultural specificity in children's programmes has never been particularly important to the commercial networks, which have always resented their C drama obligations. Certainly Networks Seven and Nine very rarely paid the minimum licence fees required for high-quality live action drama during the latter stages of the digital transition and were content to rely on animation for the C drama quota obligations, as Chapter 4 described.

Notable exceptions to the production and classification norms that developed during the digital transition were Network Ten's willingness to pay minimum licence fees for high-quality, identifiably Australian live action drama. Network Ten tended to commission the majority of its live action drama from Jonathan M Shiff Productions during the digital transition. As we have seen, Germany's ZDF Enterprises, another key European partner in the production of Australian children's drama, purchases and distributes virtually all the drama that Jonathan Shiff produces. Thus Shiff's children's slate maintains its quality production values and visual spectacle in order to circulate widely in international markets, as Chapter 5 demonstrated. The sale of Shiff's *Mako Mermaids* to Netflix in 2013 is further evidence of international demand for his live action drama. The distribution model also suggests the impending redundancy of Australia's commercial networks and the C drama classification to Shiff's business model for his children's productions.

Concerns about the erosion of Brand Australia are unlikely to come from the European channels that have had long-standing sales and distribution arrangements with Australian children's drama producers. The main UK free-to-air channels for which Australian producers provided programming pre-2006 were ITV and its dedicated children's channel CITV, and the BBC. Both these channels changed their commissioning and acquisition practices after 2006, the junk food advertisement ban and the contraction in the UK children's drama market. So ITV, which had in pre-2006 co-produced or pre-bought quite significant amounts of Australian drama including *The Saddle Club, Eugenie Sandler PI* and *Pirate Islands*, now relies heavily on brand-funded entertainment for much of its new children's programming. Any erosion in Brand Australia is unlikely to affect ITV.

Similarly the BBC, the public service broadcaster, prefers to acquire and co-produce rather than fully fund children's drama and is under domestic pressure to source original productions from within the struggling UK children's production industry. The BBC's most recent pre-purchase investment *Worst Year of My Life, Again* (2013) was produced by ABC3 and was therefore not submitted for a C classification. The BBC has gradually moved away from the close commissioning relationship it had with Australian C drama during the 1980s and 1990s.Thus the broader interpretation of the C classification has not had a notable impact on European broadcasters, because C drama is a less important part of the schedule than it was pre-2006 and because these broadcasters are also facing the same pressures caused by fragmentation, particularly lower licence fees. Further, the drama acquired by European broadcasters more recently was made with ABC3 and ACTF involvement, and not as part of the CTS quotas.

As the public value of the drama commissioned by the commercial networks to fill their C drama quotas declined, notions of quality in children's television formerly associated with the CTS began to be associated instead with the ACTF and Screen Australia. It appears then that ABC3 and the ACTF will increasingly be seen as quality brands in local and international markets, because the C classification and quality are no longer coterminous. The C drama's separation from Australia's public service broadcaster, the broadcaster that emerged during the digital regime as a key force in the commissioning of children's live action drama, further erodes its status as a signifier of quality in the market. Perhaps then it is time to remove the ACMA from the classification process (an amendment to the CTS on which the ACMA sought public comment in June 2014). Its aversion to refusing a C drama classification appears to have rendered the application process something of a formality. As regulator, the ACMA could still ensure networks comply with their quota obligations, without administering the classification scheme.

The CTS and the C classification remain an extremely important presence in the production ecology nonetheless, because of the demand for children's drama they artificially create. Australia's commercial free-to-air networks remain the most significant investors in Australian children's drama. However given the pressures on programme budgets caused by audience fragmentation, it is likely C drama will continue to be downgraded as the practices noted above continue and even accelerate. As long as policy objectives remain divorced from the means of securing those objectives, the public value of Australian children's television is likely to continue to be undermined by contemporary production practices.

The various ways in which state-funded institutions support Australian children's television merit some reconsideration in this context. The ACTF, which enjoys the status of an independent company rather than a government agency, consistently contributed to the creation of public value in children's television during the digital transition. The ACTF has done this through its support and nurturing of new talent and creativity as well as its campaign to establish ABC3, its work with the independent production sector and with institutions such as Screen Australia and the ABC. The organization has become synonymous with quality and cultural specificity and plays a key role as a quality control mechanism for Australian children's television. Yet the ACTF has been unable to work with the commercial networks for a number of years, due to their reluctance to commit funding to children's television. Further, many of the projects it has supported and helped develop have been passed up by the ABC as well. Increased funding for the organization would support the production of the kind of television the CTS were originally intended to encourage. Indeed the ACTF is well positioned to act as a quality control mechanism for all C drama, given its involvement in much of Australia's most successful—in terms of the creation of both public and private value—television.

The networks' reluctance to pay minimum licence fees and invest in the production of Australian children's television clearly contributed to the decline in public value that occurred during the digital transition. Despite the various ways in which the networks have had to adapt to the changes in their traditional business models, particularly the downturn in advertising revenue caused by fragmentation and compounded by the GFC, their businesses remain viable. The permanent 50 per cent licence fee reduction in 2012 increased their viability without any concomitant increase in their public service obligations. Thus in order to reverse the decline in public value that has been exacerbated by the trend towards lower licence fees, a minimum licence fee for all children's drama on Australia's commercial networks could be considered, regardless of whether or not children's drama is made with Screen Australia involvement. Without a specified minimum financial commitment, the policy objectives enshrined in the CTS will remain entirely divorced from the means of achieving those objectives, as Chapter 6 made clear.

Internationalization of the Production Sector

Chapter 4 explained how the challenges inherent in financing and distributing Australian children's television during the digital transition led to an increasing reliance on international funding sources. It revealed too how the requirement for Australian children's television to circulate in highly competitive international markets contributed to the erosion of the public value of the children's television commissioned by Australia's commercial networks. By 2014 however these processes of internationalization had extended to the very screen production sector itself as previously independent Australian production companies were acquired by, and became in the process local branches of, transnational super-indies and US conglomerates. Ostensibly Australian, under Australian 'creative control', these production companies access funding intended to support a sustainable independent production sector, a sector more often imagined as a diverse group of small and struggling operators, rather than multinational media behemoths. The presence of transnational super-indies such as Endemol, Fremantle Media, All3Media, Shine and US conglomerate NBC Universal in the spaces of Australian screen production became a very significant trend from 2001–14.

While super-indies may be better known for making local versions of internationally distributed programme formats in Australia, their local branches in Australia also produce children's programmes, including Screen Australia-funded drama. Examples of their children's drama include *My Place, Sam Fox: Extreme Adventures, In Your Dreams* and *Nowhere Boys,* all made for Australian broadcasters. Much of the screen content these production companies create in Australia is high-quality and entirely compatible with the goals of national cultural representation, particularly their drama slate. Most, but not all, of their output, including live action drama and transnational formats such as *MasterChef, The Voice* and *The Biggest Loser,* is also extremely popular with Australian audiences.

The local branches compete for resources in the field of cultural production from a position of strength because of the parent company's financial might and the sophisticated international distribution networks to which they have access. As small, independent Australian production companies, including Matchbox Pictures and Screen Time, were bought out by US and European transnational companies, they remained eligible for Australian funding subsidies designed partly to support a local production industry. The resources and distribution networks these companies provided in turn supported Australian producers in international markets. These structural shifts in ownership of the independent screen production sector also contributed to the loss of public value in Australian children's television between 2001 and 2014.

While the sorts of industrial and economic developments that occurred in Australia from 2001 to 2014 have been seen in various iterations in other markets, the systematic nature of these changes in Australia means very different use is being made of the long-standing institutional supports and content quotas for Australian children's television. The vertical integration of production companies that occurred during the digital transition, the pace of which accelerated from the mid-2000s, meant that these institutional supports were often accessed by transnational corporations rather than small, independent production companies. Ownership of local companies also allows the company to collect production fees in addition to local licence fees for their formats and creates supply lines for content including scripted and unscripted Australian drama. These can then be put into their distribution networks and sold internationally. The increased presence of super-indies in the spaces of local production during the digital transition undermined historical justifications for the state support required to nurture a robust independent production sector.

Analysis of the production practices of the Australian companies that are owned by transnational super-indies reveals the advantages that these companies enjoy. They are backed by the resources of the super-indie parent company, guaranteed access to the production of local versions of highly successful programme formats and benefit from diverse production slates that spread the risk and minimize the damage if a series or genre does not work. They are also structurally connected to international distribution networks for any of their productions destined for world markets. As such they are in a much stronger position in the market than the small independent production companies that have been a key feature of Australia's children's production ecology since the early 1980s. The vertical ownership that intensified during the digital transition means that the carriage of the expression of certain goals of Australian national cultural representation now lies with transnational super-indies and US corporations.

Without highly capitalized parent companies or in the absence of long-term strategic international partnerships, Australian production companies must chase international presales and distribution arrangements before being able to begin production. Completion of these time-consuming and complex deals can delay production schedules, leading to longer periods of production inactivity. In these industrial circumstances, the ACTF becomes an important support mechanism for small, independent producers relying on its support during the financing process and its distribution capacities, as with Werner Film Productions and *Dance Academy*.

While these production companies with transnational parent companies still need local commissions from free-to-air or pay-TV channels, they are in a better position than the small, truly independent producers because they can access resources and cash flow from the parent company and bear market risks. Further they very rarely specialize in children's television, which is generally just one part of a broad production slate albeit a part which also happens to attract generous state subsidies. The fact that local branches of the transnational super-indies and the Australian production companies that are majority owned by US corporations are also eligible for subsidies, tax breaks and business support suggests the playing field is less than level. These state subsidies were designed to encourage and underpin the existence of an independent production sector that would otherwise cease to exist, because of Australia's small domestic market. During the digital transition, they were frequently used instead to support the production practices of well-resourced transnational corporations.

A company like NBC Universal, which owns Matchbox Pictures, can access these state supports because the local branch remains under Australian creative control. These corporations are not at risk of collapse without Australian state subsidy; they would not disappear from the production ecology in their absence of children's content quotas on commercial networks. Thus the role of state subsidy of the sector was radically altered during the digital transition in a development that also undermined the capacity of these new arrangements to deliver value to the Australian taxpayer.

When Australian policy settings supporting the production of Australian film and television production were first implemented in the late 1960s, there was an implicit understanding that the telling of Australian stories, and the creation of a sense of cultural identity must necessarily be carried out by Australian production companies. These production companies aspired to quasi-independence and creative control of their work in relation to the Australian television networks and Hollywood majors (O'Regan 1993). This book has shown how Australian children's television quotas and the associated funding subsidies are being exercised now in ways that are advantaging transnational super-indies and US multinationals in the Australian context.

Policy instruments intended to support national cultural expression no longer imply an Australian independent production sector as US conglomerates and European super-indies access Australian subsidy schemes to produce children's programming in the space intended to be a space of local expression. The new production norms raise questions about the public value of the Australian children's television created for digital regimes by the local branches of transnational corporations operating in the spaces of local expression.

It is not clear, as the examples of Matchbox Pictures' *My Place* underscores, that the goals of national cultural expression are diminished purely on the basis of children's drama being made for local and often international audiences by a branch of a transnational production company. If national cultural expression can be achieved without national ownership of the means of production and distribution of children's drama, then the fact that international production practices and flows in programming reduce the relevance of some local cultural policy settings is not in itself a bad thing. Transnational investment helps to support local production personnel and costly production facilities, the existence of which contributes to the achievement of the goals of national cultural representation.

A similar industrial pattern involving the acquisition of local branches of international production companies which then accessed local subsidies ostensibly designed to nurture indigenous production was seen in the US film productions in post-war Europe. The combination of large markets, excellent production and location faculties and generous government subsidies encouraged US production companies to buy British subsidiaries in order to produce movies that could be designated British. The local branch might have had British staff, and produced programming with British production personnel, but its shareholders and corporate policies were entirely US-based (Guback 1969). By the mid-1960s US companies were receiving up to $10 million each year in funding from European funding subsidies. Despite some fears about loss of editorial independence to US backers, the attraction of international distribution and financing arrangements and the profitability of the vast majority of the movies produced under these schemes meant UK production companies were happy to be bought up (Guback 1969).

From his analysis of the circumstances of post-war European film production, Guback drew the conclusion that not only was the UK government aware that local branches of US corporations were accessing subsidies designed to support the British production industry, but that the government actually welcomed these industrial developments. The stimulus provided by US investment created jobs for British production personnel while injecting much-needed revenue into the domestic economy. He concluded that not only was the UK government not concerned about the extent to which its policies were leading to its subsidy of the US film production industry, it was untroubled by the colonization of its own film production industry that occurred in the process. The benefits that accrued from US investment in terms of employment and the international circulation of UK produced films were felt to be worth any cost in subsidies or cultural identity.

Sixty years later a similar situation is occurring in Australia. US and European companies are buying up local production companies that form part of a production industry whose existence has been characterized by struggle, subsidy, claim to the carriage of national cultural expression, and resentment of US and UK programming in Australian schedules. The superior resources to which such ownership structures ensure access present compelling reasons for an independent producer to enter into such an arrangement. Producers also gain access to a guaranteed global distribution network for their programming.

In a fragmented media environment the transnational distributor provides a safer, smoother support mechanism for producers who are otherwise vulnerable to the same kind of unfavourable financial arrangements that led the producers of *Skippy* to abandon independent production. Unlike Australia's free-to-air commercial networks, these distributors also have a vested interest in seeing children's drama do well in international markets. So for many small, independent production companies the goal now is not to maintain independence, but creative control, while ownership falls under a transnational super-indie with all its associated advantages. Indeed such an ownership structure has been an aspiration of Australian independent production companies ever since Grundy's 1995 sale to Pearsons.

In another parallel to the European situation, it appears that federal funding agencies like Screen Australia and hence the Australian government are similarly aware of the ease with which US and European transnationals are accessing funding subsidies and similarly enthusiastic about this turn of events. Their reasons are the same as the British government's in the 1950s—the stimulus to local production and hence employment provided by international investment and the international distribution and profile accorded to Australian drama including children's drama with high production values. Indeed one consequence of Screen Australia's Enterprise Program has been to provide substantial financial support for small independent companies that make the companies a better prospect for purchase, while encouraging international connections between that company and its likely buyers.

The Australian government and its screen bodies are clearly aware of the increased presence of transnational super-indies in the spaces of Australian cultural production, despite a stated emphasis on the goals of national cultural representation. As Screen Australia pursued an agenda of internationalization through funding mechanisms such as the Enterprise Program, the 2011 Report of the review of the Australian Screen industry undertaken by the Office for the Arts stated:

> The Australian Government funds Australian screen content principally because it is considered culturally beneficial to the nation. Given the small size of our market and

> the sheer quantities of screen content produced in larger English-language markets such as the United States, United Kingdom and Canada, Australia would not produce the quantity, quality and variety of Australian content required to achieve cultural benefits without significant funding incentives and regulation by governments.
>
> (DPCA 2011: 1)

The report justified government supports for Australian screen production in terms that are reminiscent of the cultural nationalism discourse of the 1980s, including

> [t]he principal reason the Government funds the screen sector is because of the cultural benefits to the nation. A viable domestic sector is essential if audiences are to have access to quality Australian content.
>
> (DPCA 2011: 11)

The importance and merit of increased international investment, international distribution and international co-productions are nonetheless emphasized in the rest of the report, including the desirability of the co-production of children's animation with Asian countries. The report reiterates also the importance of internationalizing domestic production practices and attracting foreign investment.

In its 2013 discussion paper about the Enterprise Program, Screen Australia also emphasizes the importance of international collaboration on screen production, stating

> ***Collaboration should be encouraged:*** Options should focus on encouraging collaboration with local and/or international partners, as a key plank in establishing and supporting business viability.
>
> (Screen Australia 2013b: 26)

Despite the development of incompatible policy agendas, of national cultural representation and internationalization, the stimulus to the economy and to production industry employment, combined with the international cultural visibility of high-quality Australian programming is clearly considered a reasonable exchange.

Where the Australian experience differs from the post-war European experience is in the loss of quality and cultural specificity that has accompanied much (but by no means all) of the animation that is increasingly used to fill C classified children's drama quotas, reducing its public value. If substantial investment in children's programming, including drama from US and European companies, leads to quality programming with high production values circulating in international markets, then the achievement of the goals of policy grounded in national cultural representation is not necessarily diminished. But the creation of Australian jobs and a more sustainable model of children's drama production may not be a reasonable trade-off for the loss of public value that occurs when Australian children's television loses its capacity to speak directly to the Australian child.

In an increasingly globalized world television system, a small number of pan-global companies such as Disney and Nickelodeon retain enormous influence over content and carriage. These companies also have a presence in Australia as distributors of programmes and of channels. Despite long-standing supports for local screen production, there is simply no scope for an Australian company to produce and distribute children's programming in the same sort of capacity. Even those Australian free-to-air networks like Network Seven that produce some adult drama in-house and Network Ten that produces original children's content have limited capability for distribution. Thus the circumstances of emulation are very different in Australia from the UK and the US. The transnational conglomerates with local branches in Australia can drastically change the new settlements in children's television in their favour, with very little resistance offered by any local media companies.

The lack of political attention paid to these subtle policy and industrial changes is compounded by the muted response from within the production industry. With business booming for those who have been fortunate enough to be bought out while retaining creative control, at this stage there is little to object to in the current regime. The possible diminishment of the national cultural expression for which the first members of the production community campaigned so fiercely appears not to be troubling contemporary producers. When concern for the child audience is replaced entirely by concern for global distribution and profits however, the public value of Australian children's television is diminished, along with the justifications for its quotas and subsidies.

With the industrial internationalization of the independent production sector, television's creative labour became much more mobile. Its movement across the globe is often facilitated by the vertical integration of transnational production and distribution companies. A young mobile workforce is much less likely to have a sense of the historical debates and justifications for the supports that exists for Australian children's television, particularly content quotas. Further, digital technology made the division of animation production across multiple territories an easier and less expensive process. This collective amnesia of the importance of national cultural expression also contributed to the loss of public value in children's television during the digital transition.

Between 2001 and 2014 many of Australia's resourceful and talented children's television producers rode the digital wave, with extraordinary success that confirmed just how good the sector is at punching above its weight in international media systems. For some, however, the struggle to survive in newly fragmented markets competing alongside transnational production companies for fewer commissions and reduced funding became too much. For others, content quotas and funding schemes became a means of generating demand for their creative labour and revenues for their businesses, rather than a means of achieving policy objectives grounded in the special status of the Australian child audience. But the CTS were always intended to be an expression of public value, not a means to secure venture capital for internationalized children's television. Their original purpose appears to have been overlooked by both the ACMA and the production sector at times during Australia's digital transition.

Conclusion

The production practices of transnational super-indies in Australia and a trend towards internationalization in Australia screen policy settings suggest Australian children's drama production has a more sustainable future than at any other time since television was introduced to Australia. The super-indie production companies and US corporations with broad production and distribution slates in multiple territories are far less vulnerable to the vagaries of the market than small, truly independent production companies for whom the loss of a single series commission can threaten to destroy their business. Unfortunately in the creation of these new business models for children's television, the public value of Australian children's television is rarely considered by an industry with a growing sense of entitlement.

From 2001 to 2014 new settlements developed in Australian children's television that gradually eroded its capacity to situate Australian children within their own culture and hence its public value. Nonetheless many Australian producers continued to harness their creativity, imagination and resilience in the production and distribution of children's television that sells all over the world, even as, paradoxically, greater variety and distances developed between digital television systems in Australia, the US and the UK. Australia remains a safe, stable and aesthetically rich country, with a highly skilled creative labour force available to work on screen production. Governments at both federal and state level continue to offer incentives for screen production and strive to attract international producers to Australian locations.

New means of distribution, particularly Internet-based services such as Netflix, confirm that global demand exists for high-quality children's live action drama. New digital-era distribution deals can have a stability and longevity entirely at odds with the commercial networks' commissioning patterns. They also suggest that broadcasters may become redundant in the commissioning and distribution process, as producers begin to distribute their programmes directly to subscribers. As new frontiers for content delivery open up, Australian producers are well placed to take advantage of these opportunities. They have an international reputation for excellence in children's television and a keen awareness of the requirements of the child audience's preferences and broadcasters' requirements in multiple territories.

While a policy commitment to national cultural representation remains evident in the children's content quotas mandated by the CTS, no such guarantees exist for minimum levels of local children's television, including drama, on the ABC. If the ABC's funding were to be cut, few if any safeguards exist to protect minimum spending levels on locally produced children's television. In the past the broadcaster's news and current affairs departments have been prioritized in funding distribution, which led to the almost total absence of local drama commissions for either children or adults during the mid-2000s. Without local content quotas for the ABC (a safeguard also recommended by the 2012 Convergence Review Report), nothing could prevent drama levels falling again.

If Australia's commercial networks are allowed to continue to reduce their investment in local children's content or if they were to be freed from their obligations to the child audience, the risks would be even greater. The creation of one provider for Australian children's television, the ABC, would eradicate competition among commissioning channels, leaving the ABC as a producer's only outlet. Further, without local content quotas on the ABC, children's drama production levels could plummet, meaning the child audience would not be adequately served by either Australia's public service broadcaster or its free-to-air commercial networks.

This book has charted how Australian broadcasting's transition from an analogue to a digital regime led to the creation of new settlements in children's television. It has evaluated the impact of the end of spectrum scarcity on long-standing policy frameworks and the production norms and means of distribution for children's television. It has explained how, as its capacity to situate Australian children within their own culture was reduced, the public value of the children's television made with public subsidy gradually eroded.

The transformations that occurred in Australian broadcasting during the digital transition did not and could not alter societal beliefs about children or the importance of culturally specific, high-quality television to Australian children. The long-standing need to protect the vulnerable child from television's corrupting influence similarly extended to the new forms of its delivery, including the Internet. The democratic will to fund Australian children's television also survived the digital transition, with $67 million in tied funding provided to establish a new children's channel ABC3 in 2009. Indeed the introduction of the producer offset and direct funding from screen bodies combined with Australian content quotas on all Australia's commercial networks ensured that Australia's screen production sector remained one of the most supported sectors in the economy.

Nonetheless under the economic, technological and regulatory conditions that developed during the digital transition, and with policy objectives relating to children's television removed from the means of achieving those objectives, retaining public value in Australian children's television became more and more difficult. At this time fears about childhood obesity led to calls for junk food advertising bans, but generally the public's attention was focussed on other digital platforms. This diversion of public activism to issues divorced from the cultural integrity of children's television exacerbated the challenges inherent in retaining its public value.

To all those interested in ensuring Australian children can easily access television made especially for them, this book serves as a reminder of the need for the public to be involved in discussions around locally produced children's television. It has been argued here also that the creation of public value in Australian children's television is vital to any justifications for its ongoing taxpayer-funded subsidies. State funding entails some reciprocal obligation to Australia's key stakeholder in children's television—the public—and is not merely a means of supporting content deliberately designed for international markets.

Given the new settlements that developed from 2001 to 2014 and their effects on production, distribution and consumption, we have entered a critical phase for Australian children's television. The digital transition might have entailed significant challenges for the production sector but it also provided the means to reinvigorate this vital form of cultural production. The rethinking and recalibration of the means of supporting the production of Australian children's television must therefore occur as a matter of urgency, with the creation of public value at its centre. It is time for the Australian public to re-engage with the children's television they indirectly support, and to question the value that is being created on their behalf. For only when the programmes made with taxpayer-funded subsidy make some contribution to situating Australian children within their own cultural context is their public value secured.

References

ABC 1983, Charter of the Corporation, available at http://www.comlaw.gov.au/Details/C2013C00422/Html/Text#_Toc364342756. Accessed July 13 2014.

ABC 2012, Annual Report 2012, available at http://about.abc.net.au/reports-publications/annual-report-2012-2013-part-2-audience-experiences/. Accessed January 1 2014.

ABC 2013, Annual Report 2013, available at http://about.abc.net.au/wp-content/uploads/2013/10/ ABC-Annual-Report-2013-lo-res.pdf. Accessed January 1 2014.

ABC 2014, Code of Practice, available at http://about.abc.net.au/reports-publications/code-of-practice-2013/. Accessed July 13 2014.

ABS 2009, *Household Use of Information Technology, Australia, 2008–09*, ABS, Canberra. Available at http://www.abs.gov.au/ausstats/abs@.nsf/mf/8146.0. Accessed January 1 2014.

ABS 2013a, *Film, Television and Digital Games,* available at http://www.ausstats.abs.gov.au/ausstats/subscriber.nsf/0/2C444B1A56CDEA58CA257B8D001D80A6/$File/86790_2011-12.pdf. Accessed July 15 2014.

ABS 2013b, *Internet Activity, Australia,* 2013, available at http://www.abs.gov.au/ausstats/abs@.nsf/Lookup/8153.0Chapter3December%202013. Accessed July 17 2014.

ACMA 2007a, *Media and Communications in Australian Families 2007: Report of the media and society research project,* ACMA, Canberra.

ACMA 2007b, *Children's Viewing Patterns on Commercial, Free-to-air and Subscription Television.* ACMA, Canberra.

ACMA 2009, *Children's Television Standards,* ACMA, Canberra.

ACMA 2011, *C and P Programs 2004–11*, ACMA, Canberra.

ACMA 2014, New eligible drama expenditure scheme results, available at http://acma.gov.au/Industry/Broadcast/Television/Australian-content/new-eligible-drama-expenditure-scheme-results-i-acma. Accessed February 27 2014.

ACTF 2007, Submission to the Children's Television Standards Review, available at *http://www.acma.gov.au/webwr/_assets/main/lib310132/49_aust_childrens_tv_foundation.pdf.* Accessed December 30 2013.

ACTF 2008, *Submission in Relation to the Draft Children's Television Standards 2008,* ACTF, Melbourne.

ACTF 2010, *Care for Kids: The newsletter of the Australian Children's Television Foundation,* Iss. no. 118, November 2010.

ACTF 2013, http://actf.com.au/about. Accessed December 30 2013.

AFC 2007, Submission to the review of the CTS, available at http://www.acma.gov.au/webwr/_assets/main/lib310132/76_aust_film_commission.pdf. Accessed December 30 2013.

Aisbett, K. 2000, *Twenty Years of C: Children's programs and regulation 1979–1999,* ABA, Sydney.

Aisbett, K., Sheldon, L. & Gibbs, M. 1993, *Living with Television,* ABA, Sydney.

Albers, R. 1996, 'Quality in television from the perspective of the professional program maker', in S. Ishikawa (ed.), *Quality Assessment of Television*, John Libbey Media, Bolton, UK, pp. 101–44.

Alexander A. & Owers J. 2007, 'The economics of children's television', in J. Alison Bryant (ed.), *The Children's Television Community,* Lawrence Erlbaum, New Jersey, pp. 57–74.

Andrejevic, M. 2004, *Reality TV: The work of being watched*, Rowman and Littlefield, Maryland.

Aries, P. 1962, *Centuries of Childhood,* Penguin, Middlesex.

ASC 2007, Submission to the review of the CTS, available at http://acma.gov.au/webwr/_assets/main/lib310132/48_aust_screen_cncl.pdf. Accessed December 30 2013.

Australian Broadcasting Tribunal 1991, *Kidz Tv: An inquiry into children's and preschool children's television standards,* Australian Broadcasting Tribunal, Sydney.

Australian Government Publishing Service 1977, *Self Regulation for Broadcasters? A report on the public enquiry into the concept of self regulation for broadcasters* Australian Government Publishing Service, Canberra.

Banet-Weiser, S. 2007, 'The Nickelodeon Brand', in S. Banet-Weiser, C. Chris & A. Freitas (eds), *Cable Visions: Television beyond Broadcasting,* New York Press, New York, pp. 235–52.

BBC 2006, *Broadcasting: An agreement between Her Majesty's secretary of state for culture media and sport and the British broadcasting corporation*, available at http://downloads.bbc.co.uk/bbctrust/assets/files/pdf/about/how_we_govern/agreement.pdf. Accessed December 30 2013.

Becker, H. S. 1982, *Art Worlds,* University of California Press, Berkeley.

Bertrand, I. & Collins, C. 1981, *Government and Film in Australia,* Currency Press, Sydney.

Boddy, M. 1997, 'Senator Dodd goes to Hollywood: investigating video violence', in L. Spigel & M. Boddy (eds) *The Revolution Wasn't Televised,* Routledge, New York, pp. 161–85.

Bonner, F. 2003, *Ordinary Television: Analysing Popular TV,* Sage, London.

Bourdieu, P. 1993, *The Field of Cultural Production,* Polity Press, Oxford.

Bryant, J. A. (ed.) 2007, 'Understanding the children's television community from an organizational network perspective', in J. A. Bryant (ed.), *The Children's Television Community,* Lawrence Erlbaum, New Jersey, pp. 35–57.

Bryman, A. 2004, *The Disneyization of Society*, Sage, London.

Buckingham, D. 2000, *After the Death of Childhood: Growing up in the age of electronic media,* Polity Press, Cambridge.

Buckingham, D., Davies, H., Jones, K. & Kelley, P. 1999, 'Public service goes to market: British children's television in transition', *Media International Australia,* vol. 93, November 1999, pp. 65–76.

Caldwell, J. 2004, 'Convergence television: aggregating form and repurposing content in the culture of conglomeration', in L. Spigel & J. Olsson (eds) 2004, *Television after TV: Essays on a medium in transition,* Duke University Press, Durham and London, pp. 41–74.

Caldwell, J. 2008, *Production Culture: Industrial reflexivity and critical practice in film and television,* Duke University Press, Durham.

Child, B. 2008, 'Full marks for *High School Musical* at US box office', *The Guardian,* October 27. Available at http://www.theguardian.com/film/2008/oct/27/high-school-musical-3. Accessed December 30 2013.

Convergence Review 2012, *Convergence Review: Final report*, Department of Broadband, Communications and the Digital Economy, Canberra. Available at http://www.archive.dbcde.gov.au/__data/assets/pdf_file/0016/38023/publication_convreview_100500.pdf. Accessed December 30 2013.

Cordaiy, H. 2007, 'H2O: Just Add Water: A fairytale in a real world', *Metro: Media and Education Magazine*, no. 152, pp. 146–53.

Cunningham, S. 1992, *Framing Culture: Criticism and policy in Australia,* Allen & Unwin, Sydney.

Cunningham, S. 2000, 'History, contexts, politics, policy', in S. Cunningham & G. Turner (eds), *The Australian TV Book,* Allen & Unwin, Sydney, pp. 13–32.

Cunningham, S. & Jacka, E. 1996, *Australian Television and International Mediascapes,* Cambridge University Press, Cambridge.

Cunningham, S. & Turner, G. (eds) 2000, *The Australian TV Book,* Allen & Unwin, Sydney, pp. 13–32.

Cupitt, M. & Stockbridge, S. 1996, *Families and Electronic Entertainment Monograph 6,* ABA, Sydney.

Curthoys, A. 1991, 'Television before television', *Continuum,* vol. 4 issue 2, pp. 152–70.

Department of Communications 2014, http://www.communications.gov.au/television/abc_and_sbs_television/abc_and_sbs_efficiency_study_terms_of_reference. Accessed April 2 2014.

Department of the Prime Minister and Cabinet, Office for the Arts (DPCA) 2011, *Review of the Independent Production Sector,* DPCA, Canberra.

Dyer, R. 1993, 'Entertainment and utopia', in S. During (ed.), *The Cultural Studies Reader,* Routledge, New York, pp. 271–84.

Edgar, P. 2006, *Bloodbath: A memoir of Australian television,* Melbourne University Press, Melbourne.

Fitzgerald, T. 2008, 'Ad-free kid-friendly network beats out the big boys', *Medialife,* Jan 9 2008, available at http://www.medialifemagazine.com/the-top-cable-network-in-2007-disney/. Accessed December 30 2013.

Flew, T. 1995, 'Images of nation: economic and cultural aspects of Australian content regulations for commercial television', in J. Craik, J. Bailey & A. Moran (eds), *Public Voices, Private Interests: Australia's media policy*, Allen & Unwin, Sydney.

Flew, T. & Spurgeon, C. 2000, 'Television after broadcasting', in S. Cunningham & G. Turner (eds), *The Australian TV Book*, Allen & Unwin, Sydney.

Fremantle Media 2013, http://www.fremantlemedia.com.au/shows. Accessed December 30 2013.

FreeTV 2014, http://www.freetv.com.au/media/submissions/2013_0051_LTR_The_Hon_Malcolm_Turnbull_MP.pdf. Accessed April 2 2014.

Girl.com.au n.d., http://www.girl.com.au/as-the-bell-rings.htm. Accessed July 15 2014.

Given, J. 2003, *Turning off the Television: Broadcasting's uncertain future,* UNSW Press, Sydney.

Godwin, J. 2013, 'BBC Children's' in L. Whitaker (ed.), *The Children's Media Yearbook,* The Children's Media Foundation, London, UK.

Guback, T. H. 1969, *The International Film Industry: Western Europe and American since 1945,* Indiana University Press, Bloomington.

Herr Stephenson, R. & Banet-Weiser, S. 2007, 'Super-sized kids: obesity, children, moral panic and the media'. in J. Alison Bryant (ed.), *The Children's Television Community,* Lawrence Erlbaum, New Jersey, pp. 277–91.

Hesmondhalgh, D. 2012, *The Cultural Industries,* Sage, London.

Hesmondhalgh, D. & Baker, S. 2011, *Creative Labour: Media work in three cultural industries,* Routledge, New York.

Heywood, C. 2002, *A History of Childhood: Children and childhood in the west from medieval to modern times,* Polity Press, Cambridge.

Hodge, B. 1989, 'Children and Television' in J. Tulloch & G. Turner (eds), *Australian Television, Programs, Pleasures and Politics,* Allen & Unwin, Sydney.

Hodge, B. & Tripp, D. 1986, *Children and Television, A semiotic approach,* Polity Press, Cambridge.

Horgan, B. 2006, *Radio with Pictures: 50 years of Australian television,* Lothian, Sydney.

Hoskins, C. and McFadyen, S. 1991, 'The U.S. competitive advantage in the global television market: is it sustainable in the new broadcasting environment?', *Canadian Journal of Communication,* 16(2), pp. 207–24.

Hoskins, C. & Mirus, R. 1988, 'Reasons for the US dominance of the international trade in television programs', *Media, Culture and Society,* vol. 10, pp. 499–515.

Idato, M. 2012, http://www.smh.com.au/entertainment/tv-and-radio/slap-set-to-ring-around-world-as-us-networks-come-looking-for-drama-20121007-27784.html. Accessed December 30 2013.

Inglis, K. 2006, *Whose ABC?The Australian Broadcasting Corporation 1983–2006,* Black Inc, Melbourne.

Keys, W. 1999, 'Children's television: a barometer of the Australian media policy climate', *Media International Australia,* vol. 93, November 1999, pp. 9–25.

Kizilos, K. 2007, '*Animalia* animated', *The Age,* July 19. Available at http://www.theage.com.au/news/tv--radio/animalia-animated/2007/07/18/1184559859851.html. Accessed December 30 2013.

Knox, D. 2011, 'Dear ABC it's time to act on my place', http://www.tvtonight.com.au/2011/07/dear-abc-its-time-to-act-on-my-place.html. Accessed January 1 2014.

Knox, D. 2014, 'NBC Universal acquires Matchbox Pictures' http://www.tvtonight.com.au/2014/01/nbcuniversal-acquires-matchbox-pictures.html. Accessed February 27 2014.

Kriston, L. 2013, 'MIPCOM 2013: Matchbox in a nutshell through international eyes', *Screen Hub,* October 16.

Kunkel, D. 2007, 'Kids' media policy goes digital: current developments in children's television regulation', in J. A. Bryant (ed.), *The Children's Television Community,* Lawrence Erlbaum Associates, New Jersey.

Lemish, D. 2007, *Children and Television: A global perspective,* Blackwell, Oxford, UK.

Lisosky, J. 2001, 'For all kids' sakes: comparing children's television policy-making in Australia, Canada and the United States', *Media, Culture & Society,* vol. 23, pp. 821–42.

Lury, K. 2002, 'A time and place for everything—children's channels', in D. Buckingham (ed.), *Small Screens: Television for children*, Leicester University Press, Leicester, pp.15–37.

McMurria, J. 2004, 'Global channels', in J. Sinclair & G. Turner (eds), *Contemporary World Television,* British Film Institute, London, pp. 38, 42.

MCN 2008, MCN'S top performers for week 47 2008, available at www.mcn.com.au/Upload/FileStore/Master/media/971-document.ppt. Accessed December 30 2013.

The Media Report 2007, 'The state of children's television', ABC Radio National, December 6. Available at http://www.abc.net.au/rn/mediareport/stories/2007/2108989.htm. Accessed January 21 2011.

Melody, W. 1973, *Children's Television: The economics of exploitation,* John Wiley, New York.

Mencinsky, N. & Mullen, B. 1999, 'Regulation of children's television in Australia: past and present', *Media International Australia,* vol. 93, pp. 27–42.

Messenger Davies, M. 2010, *Children, Media and Culture,* Open University Press, Berkshire.

Mitroff, D. & Herr Stephenson, R. 2007, 'The television tug-of-war: a brief history of children's television programming in the United States', in J. A. Bryant (ed.), *The Children's Television Community,* Lawrence Erlbaum, New Jersey, pp. 3–32.

Moore, M.H. 1995, *Creating Public Value: Strategic Management in Government,* Harvard University Press, Massachusetts.

Moore, M.H. 2013, *Recognizing Public Value,* Harvard University Press, Massachusetts.

Moran, A. 1985, *Images and Industry: Television drama production in Australia,* Currency Press, Sydney.

Moran, A. 1989, 'Three stages of Australian television', in J. Tulloch & G. Turner (eds), *Australian Television: programs, pleasures and politics,* Allen & Unwin, Sydney.

Moran, A. 2009, *New Flows in Global TV,* Intellect, Bristol.

Murphy, J. 2010, 'Path dependence and the stagnation of Australian social policy between the wars', *Journal of Policy History,* vol. 22, issue 4, pp. 450–73.

Ofcom 2012, *Children and Parents: Media use and attitudes report,* Ofcom, London, available at http://stakeholders.ofcom.org.uk/binaries/research/media-literacy/oct2012/main.pdf. Accessed January 1 2014.

Olsen, S. R. 2004, 'Hollywood planet: global media and the competitive advantage of narrative transparency', in R. C. Allen & A. Hill, *The Television Studies Reader,* Routledge, London & New York, pp. 111–29.

O'Regan, T. 1993, *Australian Television Culture,* Allen & Unwin, Sydney.

Palmer, P. 1986, *The Lively Audience: A study of children around the tv set*, Allen & Unwin, Sydney.

Palmer, S. 2006, *Toxic Childhood: How the modern world is damaging our children and what we can do about it,* Orion, London.

Parker, R. & Parenta, O. 2008, 'Explaining contradictions in film and television industry policy: ideas and incremental policy change through layering and drift', *Media, Culture and Society,* vol. 30, no. 5, pp. 609–22.

Pascari, J. 2009, 'Cakes are the least of poor Bindi's worries', July 14, available at http://www.thepunch.com.au/articles/cakes-are-the-least-of-poor-bindis-worries/. Accessed December 30 2013.

Pecora, N. 1998, *The Business of Children's Entertainment,* Guilford Press, New York.

Postman, N. 1994, *The Disappearance of Childhood,* Vintage Books, New York.

Potter, A. 2007, 'Junk food or junk TV: how will the UK ban on junk food advertising affect children's programs?', *Media International Australia,* vol. 125, pp. 5–14.

PriceWaterhouseCoopers 2011, *How do local content requirements impact australian productions? review and analysis of broadcast sector minimum content requirements,* available at http://www.archive.dbcde.gov.au/__data/assets/pdf_file/0010/148825/PwC-How_do_content_requirements_impact_Australian_productions.pdf. Accessed January 1 2014.

Rankin, B. 1990, *Australian Council for Children's Film and Television: A history (1957–1959),* Australian Council for Children's Film and Television, Victoria.

Royal Commission into Television 1954, *Report of the Enquiry into Television,* AGPS, Canberra.

Rutherford, L. 2001, 'The ACTF (Australian Children's Television) genre', in *Papers: Explorations into children's literature,* vol. 11, issue 1, pp. 5–13.

Schiavone, A. 2009, 'Ten books to read before turning ten', *Sydney Morning Herald,* January 21, available at http://www.smh.com.au/news/lifeandstyle/back-to-school/top-10-kids-books/2009/01/21/1232471367575.html?page=fullpage. Accessed December 30 2013.

Schulz, J. 2007, 'Seven, KKR in 3.2 billion deal' *The Australian,* November 21, available at http://www.theaustralian.com.au/business/media/seven-kkr-in-32bn-deal/story-e6frg996-1111112556686. Accessed July 13 2014.

Screen Australia 2009, *Enterprise Program Revised Guidelines: Draft for comment,* available at http://www.screenaustralia.gov.au/getmedia/7687002d-fabf-4534-9dca-767a532e5253/Draft_Ent_glines_091217.pdf. Accessed January 1 2013.

Screen Australia 2010, Charter *of Operations 2010/11,* Screen Australia, Canberra. Available at http://www.screenaustralia.gov.au/getmedia/0ffc93eb-df24-471b-8360-668f2166cd61/CharterofOperations.pdf. Accessed January 1 2013.

Screen Australia 2011, *Convergence 2011: Australian content state of play informing debate,* Screen Australia, Canberra, available at http://www.screenaustralia.gov.au/research/convergence_stateofplay.aspx. Accessed December 30 2013.

Screen Australia 2012, *Annual Report,* available at http://www.screenaustralia.gov.au/getmedia/f9656485-3088-479d-ae8a-aa09358bae19/AR_1112.pdf. Accessed January 1 2014.

Screen Australia 2013a, *Child's Play: Australian children's television 2013,* Screen Australia, Sydney.

Screen Australia 2013b, 'Enterprise funding: program review & future options', available at http://www.screenaustralia.gov.au/getmedia/3bb4897f-4c33-4b8a-9907-05329ac4d705/EnterprisePaper.pdf. Accessed December 30 2013.

Screen Australia 2013c, *Program Guidelines Enterprise Program 2013, https://www.screenaustralia.gov.au/getmedia/865bd386-9017-4f77-8a2a-50c0b3954210/Gline_Enterprise.pdf.* Accessed December 30 2013.

Screen Australia 2013d, *Travel Grants Asian Animation Summit 2013,* available at http://www.screenaustralia.gov.au/funding/International_Marketing/Travel_AAS.aspx. Accessed January 1 2014.

Simpson, B. 2004, *Children and Television,* Continuum, London.
Steemers, J. 2010, *Creating Pre-School Television: A story of commerce, creativity and curriculum,* Palgrave Macmillan, Basingstoke.
Steinberg, S. & Kincheloe, J. 1997, *Kinderculture: The corporate construction of childhood,* Westview Press, Colorado.
Swift, B. 2011, 'NBC Universal international acquires majority stake in Matchbox Picture', *Inside Film Online,* May 2011, available at http://if.com.au/2011/05/23/article/KZAGXSTXUZ.html. Accessed December 30 2013.
Tapscott, D. 1998, *Growing Up Digital: The rise of the net generation*, McGraw-Hill, New York.
Thussu, Kishan D. 2006, *International Communication: Continuity and change,* 2nd edn, Arnold, London.
Turner, G. 2010, *Ordinary People and the Media: The demotic turn* Sage, London.
TV Eye 1999, *Interview with Gary Gray,* number 15, January 1999, available at http://www.classicaustraliantv.com/INTVWGaryGray.htm. Accessed January 1 2014.
UNESCO 1989, The UN Convention on the Rights of the Child, available at http://www.un.org/documents/ga/res/44/a44r025.htm. Accessed July 13 2014.
Ward S. & Potter A. 2008, 'H2O: Just Add Branding: Producing High Quality Children's TV Drama for Multi-channel Environments', *Media International Australia,* Vol. 133, pp. 31–42.

Index